Virginia's Blues,
Country, & Gospel
Records, 1902-1943

Virginia's Blues, Country, & Gospel Records, 1902-1943

An Annotated Discography

KIP LORNELL

THE UNIVERSITY PRESS OF KENTUCKY

Research for this book was supported by funds granted to the Blue Ridge Institute of Ferrum College by the Virginia Foundation for the Humanities and Public Policy and an Appalachian Heritage Fellowship (Mellon Foundation) awarded to Kip Lornell.

Copyright © 1989 by The University Press of Kentucky

Scholarly publisher for the Commonwealth,
serving Bellarmine College, Berea College, Centre
College of Kentucky, Eastern Kentucky University,
The Filson Club, Georgetown College, Kentucky
Historical Society, Kentucky State University,
Morehead State University, Murray State University,
Northern Kentucky University, Transylvania University,
University of Kentucky, University of Louisville,
and Western Kentucky University.

Editorial and Sales Offices: Lexington, Kentucky 40506-0336

Library of Congress Cataloging-in-Publication Data
Lornell, Kip, 1953-
    Virginia's blues, country & gospel records, 1902-1943: an
  annotated discography / Kip Lornell.
    p. cm.
  Bibliography: p.
  Includes index.
  ISBN 0-8131-1658-9 (alk. paper)
    1. Blues (Music)—Virginia—Discography. 2. Country music—
Virginia—Discography. 3. Gospel music—Virginia—Discography.
I. Title. II. Title: Virginia's blues, country, and gospel records,
1902-1943.
ML156.4.B6L87   1989
016.7899' 1217755—dc19   89-5613
                                                                                                       CIP
                                                                                                       MN

This book is printed on acid-free paper meeting the requirements of the American National Standard for Permanence of Paper for Printed Library Materials. ∞

Contents

Preface   vii
Acknowledgments   ix
Introduction   1
Note on the Discography   17
Key to Record Label Abbreviations   19
Virginia Recording Artists   21
Appendixes   219
   1 Possible Virginia Groups   221
   2 Border Groups   223
   3 Geographical Listing   226
   4 Reissues of Virginia Folk Music   228
General Bibliography   233
Interviews   235
Index of Artists   237

Preface

Virginia is a state of contrasts. Within its political and geographical boundaries, Virginia's diverse cultural landscape contains a rich treasure of traditional music that has been recorded by commercial companies since the turn of the century. Never a wellspring of jazz or "ethnic" music, the Old Dominion is best known for Anglo-American and Afro-American folk music. The Carter Family, Charlie Poole, and the Golden Gate Quartet are three Virginia-associated groups that have had a national, even international impact and reputation. This book consists of entries for all known commercially recorded folk musicians from Virginia and folk musicians closely associated with Virginia up to July 1943.

In most instances it is very clear who should be included in this volume. Performers such as the Norfolk Jazz/Jubilee Quartet, Ernest Stoneman, Luke Jordan, and Bela Lam and his Greene County Singers unquestionably belong here. Several groups or performers are suspected to be from the Old Dominion, but the passage of time has obscured their origins. Label credits such as "L.V. Jones and His Virginia Singing Class" or "Virginia Male Quartet," lend weight for their inclusion in this volume. Appendix 1 covers groups and individuals from this category.

Other musicians—for example, Charlie Poole, who was born in North Carolina and lived there for many years—deserve entry because of the years they spent playing in the Old Dominion, thereby directly influencing other Virginia musicians. Poole's brand of string band music was also common to both sides of the central North Carolina and Virginia border, and he often performed and recorded with Virginia-born musicians such as Franklin County's Posey Rorer. For Poole and a handful of other musicians, including Roy Harvey of Monroe County, West Virginia, and the E.R. Nance Family of Yadkin County, North Carolina, the political boundaries have been ignored in order to accommodate the important cultural and musical aspects of these traditions that transcend state borders.

Other "border" groups, musicians whose careers touched upon Virginia folk music because of their proximity to the state, are also included in this book. For instance, the Red Fox Chasers from Surry County, North Carolina, sometimes played in southern Carroll County and Patrick County, Virginia, during the late 1920s and 1930s. Their style of playing, however, is closely tied to other string bands from north central North Carolina. Groups and individuals from this category are briefly covered in Appendix 2.

The time frame for this volume (1902 to 1943) is not as arbitrary as it might seem at first glance. The earliest entry, the Dinwiddie Colored Quartet, includes some of the first American folk musicians to record for a commercial company. Their Victor recordings are also among the pioneering recordings of Afro-American music.

This book's coverage stops in July 1943 for three important reasons. First, the very nature of the record industry changed radically toward the close of World War II. Prior to 1943 a handful of major companies had dominated the industry. But beginning late in 1943, many small, independent companies issuing folk and popular music went into business. Moreover, technology intruded with the introduction of multitrack recording, the re-editing of multiple takes into a single release, and other such manipulations. Second, the "Petrillo ban," a musicians' union boycott against recording, lasted from July 1942 to November 1943. This ban and its settlement helped to reshape the entire recording industry into its modern form. Finally, and perhaps most importantly, the early 1940s was a period of rapid stylistic change in popular blues, gospel, and country music. New sounds were heard in person and over the airwaves, and by 1943 they began to be more broadly documented by record companies.

Thus 1943 marks a natural breaking point for this work. The years 1942 and 1943 also mark the termination for other major, related discographies of American vernacular music—for example, Robert Godrich and John Dixon's *Blues and Gospel Records 1902-1943*, Brian Rust's *Jazz Records 1897-1942*, and Tony Russell's forthcoming discography of early hillbilly recordings.

Beyond the scope of this volume are noncommercial recordings made for a limited or specialized audience, such as the V-Disc recordings made for the armed services during World War II. Scholarly, private research recordings are also excluded—for instance, discs by the Folksong Archive of the Library of Congress and the cylinders of Afro-American folk music recorded by the Hampton Institute, about 1898. These two broad categories are not listed because such recordings were not intended to be commercially marketed to a broad audience.

In each entry derived from earlier reference sources, biographical and discographical information has been updated to reflect the most recently published research. All of the long-play reissues through June 1988 have been included in the discographies. Appendix 4 is a more detailed guide to the reissue of Virginia's early blues, country, and gospel music.

The field research for this project has also generated and uncovered new primary information. Errors in details of personnel, for example, have been rectified and heretofore unknown personnel are included. The same is true for historical and biographical matters, such as the specifics of Byrd Moore's life. Finally, many of the photographs published in this book are new to print.

Acknowledgments

Most important, I must acknowledge the financial support of the Virginia Foundation for the Humanities and Public Policy, which awarded a grant to the Blue Ridge Institute of Ferrum College to obtain copies of all of Virginia's early folk music recordings, to compile a discography of these recordings, and to conduct oral history interviews with the surviving recording artists. I was employed to coordinate this project by the director of the Blue Ridge Institute, Roddy Moore, who then encouraged me to prepare an annotated discography. The Blue Ridge Institute, therefore, deserves equal credit for the research that produced this book. Finally, a grant from Berea College's Appalachian Heritage Fellowship Program enabled me to interview additional musicians. The generosity of these two funding organizations and the Blue Ridge Institute's support and belief in the importance of the project helped to make this book a reality.

The author is also deeply indebted to the following reference sources. John Atkins, *The Carter Family*, supplied all of the basic data for the Carter Family entry. The discographies for each of the blues and black gospel music, or "race," entries is derived from Robert Dixon and John Godrich, *Blues and Gospel Records 1902–1943*, with some new revisions from Ray Funk, Roger Misiewicz, and Vaughan Webb. Kinney Rorrer, *Rambling Blues: The Life and Songs of Charlie Poole*, served as the biographical and discographical basis for the Harvey, Poole, and Rorer sections. The most comprehensive guide to album reissues is Willie Smyth, *Country Music Recorded Prior to 1943: A Discography of LP Reissues*, which is current to 1983. Complete citations for these books are found in the General Bibliography.

My thanks to the following for their advice or help in supplying discographical and historical information, photographs or graphic material, and tapes of original 78 discs for the Blue Ridge Heritage Archives: Lynn Abbott, Richard Blaustein, Joe Bussard, Helen Nance Church, George Edens, Clarence H. Greene, Rufus Hall, Clivis Harris, Bertha Hewlett, Bill Hill, Grace Hill, Frank Mare, Eula Marshall, Paul Meadows, Dr. Daniel Patterson, Bob Pinson, Gary Reid, Mike Seeger, Doug Seroff, Ed Ward, and Lynn Wolz.

I would especially like to note the vital assistance of Dave Freeman, Ray Funk, Gus Meade, Roger Misiewicz, Kinney Rorrer, and Charles Wolfe. They carefully read parts of this book, helped with minor and major discographical details, copied photographs and tapes, and supplied biographical information. And I am most particularly indebted to Tony Russell, the proprietor and energetic editor of *Old Time Music*. Some of the information appearing here was originally published in his magazine. Even more important, Tony supplied the previously unpublished discographical entries for L.V. Jones, Bela Lam, Byrd Moore, Buck Mountain Band, E.R. Nance, Phelps' Virginia Rounders, and Holland Puckett, from his forthcoming prewar hillbilly discography. Chuck Perdue provided the biographical information on the Bela Lam Family. Without their help this project could not have been completed.

I thank the staff of the Blue Ridge Institute, particularly its director, Roddy Moore, for understanding my eccentric but productive work habits, and Vaughan Webb for his innumerable suggestions. Joe Carter, Dean of Ferrum College, also helped by proofreading and editing the preface and introduction. The two anonymous scholars who read an earlier draft of this book for the Press provided many explicit comments that strengthened the final product, which the editor-in-chief of the University Press of Kentucky, Jerry Crouch, patiently guided from its inception.

Introduction

In the cold February of 1927, Wise County banjo player and singer Dock Boggs learned that a representative from the Brunswick Record Company was auditioning talent in a Norton, Virginia, hotel. Boggs had long wanted to make records, so he traveled to Norton to see whether he could impress the scout. Less than a month later he was on a train to New York City to record.

Accompanying Boggs on this odyssey was Dykes Magic City Trio, a community string band based in Gate City, Virginia (Scott County), and neighboring Kingsport, Tennessee. The members of this string band, Fiddlin' John Dykes, guitarist Hub Mahaffey, and autoharp player Myrtle Vermillion, had not traveled much, if at all, outside of the mountains of southwestern Virginia and northeastern Tennessee. Any doubt that the trip to New York City, by way of Ashland, Kentucky, was a major event is erased by Mrs. Vermillion's account of the trip. A portion of the second letter to her husband underscores Mrs. Vermillion's understandable excitement:

March 9, 1927

Dearest Schuyler:

I thought I would write you again, as they decided that they couldn't get through with us till Friday night. We made 2 and 1/2 records today—besides Mr. "Doc" Boggs [sic] work. We didn't quite get finished. Oh, you just ought to hear the autoharp on the records. They let us hear one that wasn't quite perfect. They sure did brag on it. They told us we didn't have no idea what fine records we made, said they would out-sell any of this scientific stuff.

Well I went walking down Broadway tonight and seen the sights. Oh my I seen a lifetime in one night. Dykes went with me and we went to the Paramount Theater and saw some of the greatest dancing and acting in the world before they opened up the movie.

Gertrude "Trudy" Ederle was there, the only woman in the world that swam across the English [Channel]. They had a big glass basin of water and she done her famous channel swim with the same suit she wore when she swam the channel. Oh I just wish you and all the rest could have seen it. The Brunswick people are floating the bills.[1]

Later that year the Victor Talking Machine Company summoned Luke Jordan, an itinerant black guitar picker from Lynchburg, to Charlotte, North Carolina, to record in its temporary, makeshift studio. Jordan was a roustabout, a hard-drinking man known for his ability to catch fish, play the guitar, and sing. Two years later Victor bought Jordan a train ticket to New York City in order to record him in their main studio. Exactly how Victor came to know about Jordan in the first place remains a mystery.

In sharp contrast to the experiences of Mrs. Vermillion and Luke Jordan, who came from rural backgrounds and had limited recording experience, was the urbane Norfolk Jubilee and Jazz Quartet. Even before their initial recording session in 1921, this quartet had worked along the East Coast as an act on the vaudeville circuit. There is no doubt that they were sophisticated, professional singers by the time that OKeh recorded them. Moreover, the Norfolk Jazz/Jubilee Quartet went on to record, albeit sporadically during the 1930s, for nearly twenty years.

The varied experiences of these Virginians are emblematic of the relationship between the early commercial record companies and folk musicians through the 1930s. The commercial record industry was still in its infancy, and few precedents had been established. The technology involved was still relatively crude, and the ways that talent was recruited were not at all systematized.

Dykes Magic City Trio, Luke Jordan, and the Norfolk Jazz/Jubilee Quartet were not the earliest folk musicians from Virginia to record; that honor goes to the Dinwiddie Colored Quartet (Dinwiddie County), recorded in 1902 by Victor. But Dykes Trio, Jordan, and Boggs were documented in 1927 during one of the peak sales years for the pre-World War II recording industry.

It is ironic that these commercial record companies inadvertently documented even a fraction of the wealth of Virginia's traditional music in their attempt to establish market dominance. Today this music would not interest major record companies because it almost certainly would not strengthen their profit margin. Before World War II, however, the record industry was far different from what it is today.

The industry itself began before the turn of the century, after Thomas Edison's initial commercial production of three-minute cylinder recordings. These early cylinders contained a wide range of material, from recitations to opera singers. Because the very concept of reproducing sound was so novel, no one really knew what the general public would purchase. Traditional music, though, was not a high priority in the minds of commercial record company executives.[2]

As early as 1895, however, Columbia appears to have experimented with the concept of recording traditional music on its cylinder recordings of the Standard Quartette. These early cylinders have never been recovered, but contemporary Columbia listings suggest that this was an Afro-American group, possibly a vaudeville troupe. This contention is reinforced by their repertoire of popular, religious, and "coon" songs typically found on the minstrel stage.

The first documentable folk music group to record for a commercial company, the Dinwiddie Colored Quartet, happened to be from Virginia. At the turn of the century black quartets enjoyed a wide base of community and popular support. They could be heard singing at local churches and on the stages of touring variety shows. The Dinwiddie Colored Quartet toured at the turn of the century, performing to raise money for the Dix Industrial School in Dinwiddie

County.[3] Such widespread public exposure certainly attracted the attention of the neophyte record companies. Touring and public appearances are probably the main reasons why other groups, such as the Fisk Jubilee Quartet of Fisk University, were recorded so early in the century.

The continued popularity of such groups is underscored by the fact that the next Virginia folk group to record, Richmond's Old South Quartette, was similar in style to the Dinwiddie Colored Quartet. The first Old South Quartette session did not occur until about 1912, indicating the uncertainty of the companies in discerning the purchasing patterns of record buyers.

A strong commercial interest in American vernacular music did not begin until the General Phonograph Company brought the itinerant black vaudeville blues singer Mamie Smith into their studios in February 1920. Her release, "That Thing Called Love" and "You Can't Keep a Good Man Down" (OKeh 4113), set a precedent but did not cause an immediate flood of interest in this underserved market. Nonetheless, Smith's recordings did suggest that blacks would purchase discs by their contemporaries.

This fact had special significance in Hampton Roads, a region encompassing Chesapeake, Newport News, Norfolk, and Virginia Beach. Some of the earliest popular black quartet recordings, or "jazz" recordings, as they were labeled, were done by groups associated with Norfolk. For example, about March 1921, the Norfolk Jazz Quartet recorded six selections for OKeh, including the salacious "Jelly Roll Blues" and the anticlerical "Preacher Man Blues." This group followed with many secular and sacred selections and was America's most recorded Afro-American quartet during the 1920s.

Two other groups associated with Hampton Roads, the Excelsior and Palmetto Quartets, were recording for OKeh within a year after the Norfolk Jazz Quartet's debut. These groups were also apparently part of an extensive vaudeville touring network that covered the East Coast. Although Hampton Roads spawned other groups similar to the Excelsior and Palmetto Quartets, OKeh, Gennett, and other companies recorded only a few of them because none of their early offerings sold very well. The record industry itself was in a general slump between 1921 and 1923, which added to the uncertainty about exploiting the large black market.

White folk music was all but ignored until the summer of 1922, when Texas fiddlers Eck Robertson and Henry Gilliland recorded for Victor. In fact, their records remained unissued until the spring of 1923. Robertson's solo fiddling on "Sallie Goodin" turned out to be a classic performance and should be credited as the first country recording to be released to the general public. Significantly, Victor was still not quite certain how to market this music and advertised it as a "vocal and instrumental" selection.

The man who really opened the record executives' eyes to the potential sales of country music was Atlanta-based fiddler John Carson. Born in 1868, Fiddlin' John Carson had developed a wide audience in middle Georgia by the time commercial record companies began to show an interest in country music. Politicians courted him to play at rallies, and Carson was one of the first musicians to perform over Atlanta radio station WSB in 1922.

In June 1923, Atlanta furniture store operator Polk Brockman suggested to Ralph Peer of OKeh Records that recordings by Carson would certainly sell in Atlanta. Peer was cautious but interested enough to invite Carson to New York City, where he recorded "The Little Old Log Cabin in the Lane" backed by "The Old Hen Cackled and the Rooster's Going to Crow." Peer was thoroughly unimpressed by Carson, but Brockman was certain that he could sell this type of music. Brockman personally ordered five hundred copies, and they sold out within a few days. Impressed by this success, Peer invited Carson back to New York City for another session. These records sold well throughout the South, and Fiddlin' John went on to be one of the major country record talents of the 1920s.[4]

It was actually the success of Fiddlin' John Carson's OKeh discs that cleared the way for early Virginia country recording artists such as Henry Whitter of Fries and Coeburn's Fiddlin' Powers and his family. Both traveled to New York City at their own expense for the express purpose of making commercial recordings and were given trial recording dates. It was not until Carson's records began to sell, however, that these Virginia artists were seriously considered by the companies.

By 1925, record companies were slowly becoming more sophisticated in marketing folk music recordings. They created separate "hillbilly" and "race" series in order to appeal to what they inaccurately judged to be musically segregated white and black audiences. About this time they also began to advertise their recordings in unique ads, which appear naive in an era of conglomerate record companies run by executives with MBAs and founded upon large-scale corporate marketing. Sixty years ago, however, the record industry was so new that it did not know how to sell its product to the rural market targeted for the hillbilly and race series.

At that time, records were sold primarily through the mail and by furniture stores. Mail order was important, since many people living in rural areas found it convenient and often necessary to shop by way of the postal system. Furniture stores were a natural outlet for records because they sold the wind-up victrola upon which the discs were played.

By the mid-1920s, the stage was set for the widespread recording and sales of American folk music. The distribution of records was slowly becoming more prevalent, and increased advertising helped the companies to reach a greater audience. But one major problem remained: how could northern-based record companies locate and recruit southern talent?

It is fair to say that until 1925 there was no systematic manner in which record companies looked for folk music talent. This changed, however, when the few black or white traditional musicians on record began to demonstrate their power to sell discs. As it became clear that there was a market to sustain the recording of this music, a scouting system slowly emerged. Virginia was rich in folk music talent, and the interaction between record companies and the musicians themselves serves as a microcosm for the rest of the South.

Most of Virginia's earliest recordings by folk musicians resulted from the musicians' own initiative. Henry Whitter hoboed his way to New York City several times before gaining his OKeh audition. The Fiddlin' Powers Family took the train to New York City and walked unannounced into the offices of OKeh and then Victor. Despite the slow development of a system of searching for talent, such bold, brazen behavior continued for many years. In March 1931, Elder Golden Harris of Floyd County arrived unexpectedly at the New York office of Brunswick Records and ended up making a single record for them.

Musicians such as Harris were convinced that they were as good as the artists they heard on commercial records. Powers, for example, was motivated by the success of his contemporary, Fiddlin' John Carson, who bested him at a Johnson City, Tennessee, fiddlers' contest in the spring of 1924. Carson was clearly the crowd's favorite, in part because of the novelty and appeal of seeing a "recording artist" in person. Ernest Stoneman approached OKeh in 1924 because he was so unimpressed by the recordings of fellow Virginian Henry Whitter that he knew he could do better.

There is no doubt that persistence sometimes pays off, as is illustrated by the attempts of the Four Virginians to record. In 1927 they left Pittsylvania County determined to go north to make records. Their first stop was Camden, New Jersey, home of Victor Records. The Victor officials were not interested in them, so they continued to New York City, where they hoped to audition for one of the other companies. They managed to get in to see OKeh's representatives, who liked their string band music but sent them back to Winston-Salem, North Carolina, to record at a field session held in September 1927.[5]

Record companies slowly began to send their own representatives into the field to search for talent. This was an occupation totally dominated by males, who came to be called "A & R" (artist and repertoire) men. At first it was difficult for these northern-based record executives to decide who could fit the particular demands of this job. Eventually it dawned on them that perhaps their southern distributors could find local talent, which is how Polk Brockman gained his early affiliation with OKeh. Ralph Peer was impressed that Brockman was so adamant and correct about Fiddlin' John Carson and quickly pressed Brockman into scouting "southern talent" of all sorts.

Because in the 1920s America was still explicitly segregated, southern folk talent was quickly allotted a separate series. Columbia designated its "14000" series of releases, which began in December 1923 and ended in April 1933 with 14680, for black artists. In mid-1927 Paramount began a "3000" series dedicated to white country artists. This series consisted of about 323 discs and finally staggered to a close in the summer of 1932. The black series were usually referred to as "race" recordings, probably in reference to the term "the colored race." But what to call the series featuring white country artists?

A 1925 encounter between a musical group from southwest Virginia led by Al Hopkins and A & R man Ralph Peer of OKeh Records placed the "hillbilly" moniker on early country music. Al Hopkins and his band were from Carroll and Grayson counties and were inspired to record by John Rector, a local banjo player who had traveled to New York City to record with Henry Whitter. Rector helped to arrange the session with OKeh and, after a three-day journey to New York, the group arrived at the OKeh studios. A few technical problems delayed the session, but it was finally completed on January 15.

When Peer asked for the name under which they wanted the records issued, the band realized they did not have one. Al Hopkins replied, "We're nothing but a bunch of hillbillies from North Carolina and Virginia. Call us anything." Peer took them literally and their initial recordings were issued with the name "The Hill Billies."[6]

A & R men used a variety of techniques to locate musicians. The Carter Family, for example, was lured to Bristol, Tennessee, to audition for Victor by an announcement printed in the Bristol newspaper in July 1927. The same newspaper article attracted the attention of black blues singers Steven Tarter and Harry Gay, who were then living in Johnson City, Tennessee. The novelty of field recording sessions, which began in 1923, was certainly front-page news and no doubt attracted the attention of many Virginia musicians.

Record companies also kept their eye on folk artists who performed on the vaudeville circuit. This is almost certainly how black quartets such as the Palmetto Quartet, the Excelsior Quartet, and the Norfolk Jubilee and Jazz Quartet came to record for OKeh in the early 1920s. In later years, after A & R men came on the scene, the H.M. Barnes' Blue Ridge Entertainers were fixtures on the Loews Vaudeville Circuit when they were recorded by Brunswick.

A & R men also worked closely with the store owners who sold the records. These store owners knew the local musical talent, and A & R men did not hesitate to ask their opinions. Bela Lam and His Greene County Singers were recommended to OKeh by John Evans, a record store owner in Elkin, Virginia. Similarly, Danville music shop operator Luther B. Clarke recommended a local band led by fiddler Charley La Prade to a Columbia Record salesman early in 1926; within a few months the Blue Ridge Highballers were in New York City for their first recording session.

Radio broadcasts were another obvious source of folk music talent. During the 1920s and 1930s, most radio was conducted live and the stations featured local performers. One example of this networking involves OKeh and at least two Virginia radio stations, WDBJ in Roanoke and Richmond's WRVA. In an attempt to recruit talent for a session set for Richmond, Virginia, in October 1929, OKeh's Middle Atlantic distributor, Charles Rey, turned to radio performers.

Based in Richmond, Rey first contacted performers featured on WRVA and recorded the Hall Family (Orange County), the Virginia Ramblers, Patrick County-born Babe Spangler and Dave Pearson, and other popular local radio entertainers. Rey apparently also scouted WDBJ, since he brought in WDBJ's Herndon Slicer, the Roanoke Jug Band, and the Salem Highballers from the Roanoke Valley.

Many other traditional musicians were recorded by OKeh at this 1929 Richmond session. These include such enigmas as the Mote Brothers, Cotton Butterfield, and the Imperial Quartet. Although almost nothing is known of them, it is possible that they were also radio performers who were scouted in the same fashion. Perhaps Rey also contacted radio station WTAR in Norfolk, as at least three of the black acts—the Monarch Quartet of Norfolk, Blues Birdhead, and the Golden Crown Quartet—were from the Hampton Roads region.

Among the other recording artists in Richmond were Bela Lam and His Greene County Singers, who had previously recorded for OKeh in New York City. They were apparently invited to Richmond to reprise their earlier success. The Richmond Starlight Quartette also participated in this session, though none of their sides was released. This quartet had previously recorded for QRS Records in Long Island City, New York.

The appearance of the Richmond Starlight Quartette points out another way that Virginia's folk talent interacted with the record companies—veteran recording artists trying their hand with a new company. Henry Whitter enjoyed a four-year career with OKeh before he approached Victor about a new contract. He and fiddler G.B. Grayson also recorded for the Gennett Company at nearly the same time; thus, Whitter moved to two companies almost simultaneously.

Another persistent veteran artist was singing-school teacher E.R. Nance, who was living in Booneville, North Carolina. He first approached Art Satherley about recording his family at the American Record Corporation in 1930. Few of the records from their lengthy stay in New York City were ever released, and Nance was very interested in having more of his music available on record. Now familiar with the system and having established a modest track record, Nance approached Brunswick and Gennett. Both companies decided to take a gamble, and in quick succession the Nance Family had recordings out on Brunswick and on Gennett's subsidiaries, Champion and Superior. Unfortunately, the year was 1931 and no records were selling well.

Two other musicians from south central Virginia, Charley La Prade and Kelly Harrell, also moved on to other companies after being dropped by Columbia and OKeh, respectively. La Prade's Columbia recordings sold well, and it is unclear why the Blue Ridge Highballers were not called back for another session. Convinced that he could still sell records, La Prade literally regrouped and went to New York City where the band made four selections for Paramount. Disappointed by Paramount's poor-quality pressings and equally poor sales, the Blue Ridge Highballers never recorded again.

In 1924 Kelly Harrell went to New York City to record for Victor, where he was saddled with some uncomfortable-sounding studio musicians; his initial records did not sell well. Harrell went to Asheville, North Carolina, the next year, and was there introduced to the OKeh scouts by Henry Whitter, who had been invited to make more records and who accompanied Harrell on the guitar and harmonica. This session also proved disappointing, but Harrell did not give up. In 1927, after moving to Henry County, he assembled a new band of local musicians. Once more he approached Victor, which approved of his new sound and brought Harrell and the Virginia Stringband into the studios for several sessions before the Depression almost extinguished the industry. Throughout the 1930s Harrell planned a comeback on the record scene, but he died in 1941 without recording again.

Harrell's experience with Henry Whitter illustrates perhaps the most common way that Virginia folk musicians came to record during the prewar days. A & R men tended to invite their best-selling musicians back to the studios, and they often asked these musicians about their peers. In the same vein, sidemen were often asked to perform as bandleaders later. Certainly many musicians were recorded on the strength of their friends' recommendations or their prowess in the recording studios.

Such an entree resulted in committing the music of Bluefield's Roy Harvey to disc. Harvey served first as a sideman to Charlie Poole and within two years moved into the spotlight as a leader. Galax musician, photographer, and raconteur Eck Dunford came to the attention of Victor Records after he served as Ernest Stoneman's fiddler on several sessions. Holland Puckett, a Patrick County guitarist, harmonica player, and vocalist, was introduced to Gennett Record officials when he traveled to Richmond, Indiana, with his friends Da Costa Woltz, Frank Jenkins, and Ben Jarrell. There is no evidence that any Virginia musicians served as official, paid talent scouts, which contrasts with the practice in Memphis, Tennessee, where blues performer Will Shade carefully scouted his fellow musicians for Victor.

The only Virginia musician to fulfill a role remotely like Shade's was Ernest Stoneman. Unlike Shade, who arranged sessions for a variety of black musicians, Stoneman scouted talent specifically for his own sessions. Between 1927 and 1929 Stoneman regularly arranged sessions for Victor, Edison, and Gennett using a wide assortment of musicians from Carroll and Grayson counties. These recordings are of high quality, emphasizing Stoneman's ability to pick fine musicians and find strong material to record.

From a geographical perspective these early recordings reveal several important trends. Appendix 4 lists each performer's home city, county, or region, and it highlights the areas of dominance for recordings by the commercial record companies: Carroll and Grayson counties, Hampton Roads (particularly Norfolk), south central Virginia, and southwestern Virginia. Approximately eighty percent of Virginia's recorded prewar performers come from these sections of the state.

The work habits of the A & R men clearly account for the spatial patterns created by the recording artists. Since they frequently located talent through established artists, the A & R men kept going back to these four general areas and tended not to look for talent elsewhere. If they continued to find salable talent in Henry and Pittsylvania counties, why look to some relatively remote section such as Bath County in the Allegheny highlands? Virginia is not unique in this regard, as one preliminary study makes clear.[7]

The work of talent scouts held implications that are only now becoming clear. For young northern enthusiasts who became interested in string band music during the 1960s, 1970s, and 1980s, the "Galax sound" became the strongest influence. Many made the pilgrimage to the annual Galax fiddlers' convention, where they learned directly from master folk musicians. This also meant that the vintage recordings by the Sweet Brothers, Emmett Lundy, Ernest Stoneman, and others were held in awe and copied by revivalist bands such as the New Lost City Ramblers and the Highwoods Stringband. In turn, the "revival" versions of Galax string band tunes became better known and more influential than the recordings of their mentors. If Henry Whitter had come from Franklin County rather than Fries, would today's string bands be playing the tunes of Ferrum artists like Dr. Lloyd and Howard Maxey with equal vigor and reverence?

Such a geographical bias further meant that many sections of Virginia are underrepresented or unrepresented. For example, no recordings were done by musicians from the upper Shenandoah Valley. Central Virginia is poorly represented, even though it is clear that folk music talent was there in the 1920s and 1930s.[8] Commercial record companies did a fine job of documenting Virginia's traditional music, but they missed some extraordinary talent.

On at least two occasions in Virginia, frustrated individuals took matters in hand by starting their own record companies. Small, regional, independent record companies became commonplace after World War II, but were unusual during the 1920s and 1930s. In Richlands (Tazewell County), Virginia, William

Myer operated the Lonesome Ace label between 1928 and 1930. Myer was a lawyer and entrepreneur who didn't like the playing and singing of Jimmie Rodgers. Lonesome Ace record labels clearly state that their product does not contain yodeling ("Without A Yodel"), which Myer despised.

Myer began Lonesome Ace by writing to Paramount Records in Port Washington, Wisconsin, asking for the addresses for such artists as Blind Joe Taggart. He also contacted OKeh Records inquiring about one of their artists, Mississippi John Hurt. Myer corresponded with Hurt in Avalon, Mississippi, and sent him several of his own compositions that Myer wished Hurt to record. The proposed session with John Hurt never materialized, but Hurt recorded several of these songs after his "rediscovery" in 1963.

Myer did manage to record two regional artists—Dock Boggs of Norton, Virginia, and Emry Arthur, a native of eastern Kentucky. Unfortunately, Myer's record company failed, largely because of poor distribution and the onset of the Depression. Lonesome Ace issued only three records, each of which sold in small numbers.[9]

In Floyd County several years later, Primitive Baptist Elder Golden Harris had a similar plan. He went back to New York City, where he had recorded for Melotone in 1931, and later had a single disc custom pressed. Harris sold this record locally and through the mail from his Indian Valley home. The initial shipment of perhaps five hundred records sold out, and he ordered more, this time with a slightly modified label. In addition to marketing his record, Harris and a partner, Monroe Simpkins, went into the retail phonograph business, selling handmade Blue Ridge Phonograph Company machines. Harris was in business in 1932 and 1933, which meant that his ventures were almost sure to fall victim to the Depression.[10]

Despite the recording activity, commercial discs did not accurately reflect all of Virginia's contemporary folk music styles. The aforementioned geographical bias favored the recording of black gospel quartets and Anglo-American string band music. Important traditions such as black string band music and unaccompanied ballad singing were almost entirely overlooked by record company talent scouts during the prewar era. Nor were blues singers well represented on commercial discs.

The intent of Columbia, Gennett, and other companies was primarily and understandably commercial rather than artistic or scholarly. They were in business to sell records, not document the wealth and variety of Virginia's folk music. We are fortunate that these companies found so much talent within the state and that some of these groups were recorded in great depth.

With so many Virginia folk artists recording, it was inevitable that a few of them would enjoy significant commercial success. Certainly the Carter Family was by far the most prolific and best selling folk group from the Old Dominion.

Introduction

The trio recorded scores of selections for three major companies over the course of fourteen years, and their gentle sound is one of the important roots of early recorded American country music.

Carter Family records were also released to an international audience. During the 1930s some of their Decca recordings were issued by Decca's South Africa and Australasia affiliates. More than a score of their Victor recordings were widely disseminated in the British Isles and Australia on Regal Zonophone, and were available into the 1940s. Although a few other groups had a handful of records issued to an international audience, no other Virginia folk group enjoyed the same worldwide popularity.

Within the southeastern United States two other Virginia groups (Charlie Poole and the North Carolina Ramblers, and Ernest V. Stoneman) proved to be very popular. Poole's Columbia recordings had the fifth largest combined sales of Columbia's entire "Old-Time" 15000 series, which lasted from 1925 until 1932. Stoneman, on the other hand, recorded extensively for several companies and is the second most prolific Virginia recording artist from this period.

The black community bought more recordings by the Norfolk Jazz/Jubilee Quartet than by any other Virginia race artist or group. This quartet recorded over a span of nearly twenty years, and their records sold tens of thousands of copies. Their Paramount disc "Father Prepare Me" and "My Lord's Gonna Move This Wicked Race" (Pm 12035) was one of the most popular prewar black gospel recordings and remained in catalog for almost nine years. Because Paramount Records were advertised in newspapers and so widely sold through the mail, the Norfolk Jazz/Jubilee recordings influenced black singers throughout the country.

It is clear that the recordings by Virginia folk musicians during the prewar era were of major musical importance. Virginia musicians such as the Carter Family and Ernest Stoneman are synonymous with old-time music, and their recordings sold across the country, influencing a whole generation of musicians. The smooth, intricate harmonies of the Norfolk Jubilee group and other Hampton Roads quartets helped to set the stage for the later popular groups, such as the Mills Brothers.

Such individual innovators as Jack Reedy (Smyth County) with his unique finger-picked banjo style documented on records as early as 1928, are important to acknowledge. Reedy's playing is a direct forerunner of the bluegrass banjo style that developed ten to fifteen years later. Another innovative group associated with Virginia, The Hillbillies, included many creative musicians, such as Jack Reedy, Al Hopkins, and Tony Alderman, who provide some of the early links between old-time string band music and the popular swing music of the 1930s.

Byrd Moore is another important, underappreciated influence in the history of hillbilly music in America. Though he was a drifter and a rounder, Moore was one of the first folk musicians to actively recruit other musicians for recording sessions. He was always working on a new angle to get his group back into the recording studio. Moore himself led half a dozen sessions between 1928 and 1932, but he was a regular sideman in the Gennett and OKeh studios during this period.

An innovator, Moore saw the potential of the recording industry and what it could do to promote his type of music. He single-mindedly set out to achieve his goal with a variety of musicians not only from Virginia but also from Georgia, the only state to rival Virginia in hillbilly recordings during the 1920s and 1930s.

Just how well did these folk-oriented recordings sell? This is problematic, since the sales figures, especially for smaller, long-defunct companies like Gennett, are difficult to obtain. Million-selling records were almost nonexistent until after World War II, when the record market was expanded by pent-up demand and more aggressive sales tactics. Certainly the records by the Carter Family sold in the greatest number because of their immense following and the sheer number of releases. However, exact sales figures for their Decca and ARC releases are not available.

Some of the sales figures for Columbia old-time artists have been unearthed, and even the best-selling records by an artist such as Charlie Poole appear modest by today's standards. Poole's initial recording, "Don't Let Your Deal Go Down Blues" and "Can I Sleep in Your Barn Tonight, Mister?" (Co 15038), released in the summer of 1925 near the beginning of Columbia's old-time series, sold just over 100,000 copies. Breaking the 100,000 sales mark was a milestone that no doubt pleased Columbia's A & R man Frank Walker, and he stuck by Poole until the banjo player's death in 1931. By then the Depression had devastated the market to such an extent that Poole's final release, "Write a Letter to My Mother" and "The Only Girl I Ever Loved" (Co 15711), sold a paltry 857 copies.[11]

This dramatic pattern, in which the strong sales of the mid-to-late 1920s plummeted after 1930, held true for other artists as well. For example, Roy Harvey's most popular record, "Steamboat Man" and "When the Roses Bloom Again for the Bootlegger" (Co 15326), sold 72,545 copies. Contrast this figure with his final Columbia recording, "Willie, Poor Boy" and "Dark Eyes" (Co 15714), which was released in November 1931. Sales of this disc reached only 625 copies.[12]

With the exception of the Norfolk Jubilee Quartet recordings, none of the Old Dominion's black folk musicians sold large numbers of records prior to World War II. In addition, white musicians outrecorded Virginia's black artists by better than three to one. The targeted audience for race records was, of course, much smaller. Artists such as Tappahannock's William Moore also had the misfortune to record for Paramount, a company without a strong distribution network. Precise sales figures are unavailable, but none of Moore's records sold very well. Even a Victor artist like Luke Jordan, whose initial records were released during the boom year of 1927, probably did not sell as well as a contemporary hillbilly artist like Charlie Poole. In fact, not a single copy of Jordan's circa 1932 release "If I Call You Mama" and "Tom Brown Sits in a Prison Cell" (Vi 23400) has been found.

Occasionally a black artist would "cross over" when a company marketed his recording to the race and hillbilly markets simultaneously. A black string band from southwest Virginia led by Howard Armstrong and Carl Martin found itself in such a position in 1930, when Vocalion released its disc "Knox County Stomp" and "Vine Street Drag." For hillbilly record purchasers, they were the Tennessee Trio (Vo 5472), whereas the race series billed them as the Tennessee Chocolate Drops (Vo 1517).

Given the general sales of hillbilly and race records, it is not surprising that few musicians made much money directly from their recordings. Groups that made only a single, meagerly selling record—for example, Carroll County's Pipers Gap Ramblers or the Golden Crown Quartet from Norfolk—received little money from the sale of their records. Nor, for that matter, did the record companies gain much money from the release of such discs.

Other musicians did well, of course, particularly those who pressed for royalty rights. The Carter Family received regular royalties from Victor, ARC, and Decca for many years. In addition to royalties from record sales, some musicians were fortunate enough to gain composer rights to original songs that later became powerful sellers. In 1985, Gene Kelly Harrell, son of Kelly Harrell, was still receiving composer royalty statements for his father's song "Way Out on the Mountain," which was copyrighted through (Ralph) Peer International in 1928.

Typically, musicians were offered two forms of payment. They could either take a flat fee, which ranged from $25 to $100 per song, or they could be paid a percentage of the record's sales. Because of the precarious and unpredictable nature of the record business, most musicians opted for a flat fee.[13]

Musicians choosing a flat fee during the Depression often fared better than those who decided upon royalties. For example, guitarist Byrd Moore and Fiddlin' Clarence Greene recorded "Pig Angle" and "Cincinnati Rag" on February 13, 1930, and within six months the recording was issued on Champion 16357 and Superior 2838. Greene's royalty statement from April 1, 1932, reveals that Greene had been advanced $19.22 against future royalties and that both releases had sold a total of seventy-six copies—fifty-three on Champion and twenty-three on Superior. The royalty rate was admittedly meager, approximately one-quarter cent for each disc sold, so Greene was due only thirty-four cents in royalties after nearly one and one-half years of sales. As of April 1, 1932, Greene owed the Gennett Records $18.88.[14]

In addition to the musician's fee for recordings, the record companies generally paid all other expenses. Mrs. Vermillion noted in her letter home that Brunswick was covering their transportation, hotel, and meals. This was standard procedure for most record companies, and the travel fees could be fairly expensive before the advent of field recording sessions. Most of the nonfield sessions were held in northeastern cities like Camden or New York City. The other center for recordings was Gennett's studio in Richmond, Indiana. Recording previously untried groups was a gamble on the record companies' part, one that only occasionally paid off.

Even at field recording sessions, expenses could be stiff. A short trip, such as the one taken by Dr. Lloyd and Howard Maxey from Franklin County, Virginia, to Winston-Salem, North Carolina, for the OKeh Company, was not a financial strain. At the other extreme was Frank Blevins' journey from Lansing, North Carolina, to Columbia's Atlanta field session in 1927. Instead of suggesting a train trip from Asheville or Bristol to Atlanta, A & R man Frank Walker apparently felt extravagant, and the company paid for Blevins and his group to travel round trip by taxi.

For the musicians, at least, money was generally not the final arbiter in their prewar recording careers. Recording was only a small part of the musical expression of many of Virginia's prewar folk artists. Most played only in their spare time or semiprofessionally. Even those who performed full-time generally used recording as a springboard for personal appearances. The real money was in playing for live audiences, which is why Roy Hall and the Blue Ridge Entertainers and Henry Whitter were so eager to exploit their opportunities to record. Even into the 1930s, long after Whitter had stopped recording for OKeh, Gennett, and Victor, he proudly billed himself as a recording artist on his handbills and business cards.

Though long dead, some of these musicians still retain legendary status among older residents in their communities. Eccentric Uncle Eck Dunford is widely remembered in Galax, while some black residents of Lynchburg recall the days when Luke Jordan played on street corners. Even among young people Charlie Poole's reputation and music often enjoy instant recognition in Franklin, Henry, and Pittsylvania counties. Many long-time residents of Ararat, Virginia, recall the tragic day in 1934 when Holland Puckett was stabbed to death in an argument over a poker game. People treasure the memories of these musicians and their old records as nostalgic reminders of youth.

Sixty years ago, a reputation as a recording artist held a far greater significance than it does today. The chances to make records were far fewer, since the

Introduction

industry was dominated by Columbia and Victor. Relatively few of Virginia's folk artists had the opportunity to record. Even today many of the state's pioneer recording artists look proudly on the aural documentation of their early careers.

Bill Hill (Henry County), for instance, returned to music only in 1980 and regrets that he did not make more than his three records for Bluebird in 1937. Hill's age and experience have allowed him to appreciate better the cultural, musical, and historical significance of his early records. Frank Blevins is particularly nostalgic about his 1927 and 1928 Columbia recordings; he was only sixteen years old at the time and didn't fully comprehend the significance of what he was doing.

Blevins's reflections about recording provide a tidy summary of the prewar folk music record industry in Virginia. The business came into itself during a period of increasing sophistication in terms of recording technology, marketing, and the recruitment of musical talent. In the mid-1920s, however, it was a haphazard operation and neither musician nor executive had a clear vision of where their efforts would lead.

When the Carter Family responded to a newspaper ad in 1927, they had no idea that this fledgling industry would become a billion-dollar business or that they were initiating a dynasty in that field. Nor could Melvin Smith of the Silver Leaf Quartette of Norfolk have anticipated a 1979 visit from a young white researcher inquiring of his recording career, which had ceased forty-eight years before.

In many respects, folk musicians from Virginia pioneered and helped to establish the multimillion-dollar country music industry. The history of American country music would be far different were it not for the persistence and entrepreneurship of men like Henry Whitter. Furthermore, black groups such as the Dinwiddie Colored Quartet and the Old South Quartette set the precedents that slowly opened the record industry to participation by Afro-American musicians. In the 1980s we have come to understand and appreciate these recordings and the people behind them as a critically important part of Virginia's vernacular history.

Notes

1. A copy of this letter was supplied by Vermillion's daughter, Mrs. Cleo McNutt, of Gate City, Virginia.

2. For more on the early recording industry, consult Ronald Dethlefson, ed., *Edison Blue Amberol Recordings* (Brooklyn, N.Y.: APM Press, 1981); Robert Dixon and John Godrich, *Recording the Blues* (London: Studio Vista, 1970); and Lawrence Gelatt, *Those Fabulous Phonographs* (New York: Appleton-Century, 1965).

3. What little is known of the Dinwiddie Colored Quartet is summarized by Kip Lornell,

"Happy in the Service of the Lord" : *Afro-American Gospel Quartets in Memphis*. (Urbana: Univ. of Illinois Press, 1988, chapter 1.

4. A complete account of Carson's career was written by Gene Wiggins, *Fiddlin' Georgia Crazy: Fiddlin' John Carson, His Real World, and the World of His Songs* (Urbana: Univ. of Illinois Press, 1986).

5. For more information, see Kinney Rorrer, "The Four Virginians," *Old Time Music* 14 (Autumn 1974): 18.

6. Archie Green, "Hillbilly Music: Source and Symbol," *Journal of American Folklore* 78: 211.

7. Kip Lornell, "Spatial Perspectives on the Field Recording of Traditional American Music: A Case Story From Tennessee in 1928," *Tennessee Folklore Society Bulletin* 46 (1981): 153-59; reprinted in George O. Carney, ed., *Sounds of People and Places: Readings in the Geography of Music*, 2d ed. (Washington, D.C.: Univ. Press of America, 1987). 91-100.

8. BRI 003 "Western Piedmont Blues," brochure notes by Kip Lornell with Mike Mayo and Dell Upton, 1979, underscores this point, as does Kinney Rorrer, *Rambling Blues: The Life & Songs of Charlie Poole* (London: Old Time Music, 1982).

9. For more on Myer, consult BRI 008 "Southwest Virginia Blues," brochure notes by Vaughan Webb, 1988.

10. An account of Harris' life is found in Kip Lornell, " 'My Christian Friends in Bonds of Love': The story of Elder Golden Harris," *Old Time Music* 39 (Winter 1982 to Spring 1984): 19-20.

11. These sales figures appear in Kinney Rorrer, *Rambling Blues: The Life & Songs of Charlie Poole*, pp. 31 and 54.

12. The author is indebted to David Freeman of County Records for supplying these figures.

13. Personal conversation with Gene Kelly Harrell, Roanoke, Virginia, January 1985.

14. Copies of these statements were supplied by Greene's son, Clarence H. Greene of Hudson, North Carolina.

Note on the Discography

Arrangement of Entries

Entries are arranged alphabetically; the main heading for each entry is the name of an artist or group, followed by dates indicating the approximate period during which the artist or group was active in blues, gospel, or country music. When a lead artist is named in the principal label credits, the artist's name (or a group name that incorporates it) is chosen as the main heading; when no individual artist is named in the principal label credits, a group name such as "Floyd County Ramblers" is used as the name of the entry. Artists not named in a main heading are listed in the index of artists.

Some overlapping between entries is inevitable under this arrangement. For example, the entries for Byrd Moore and Melvin Robinette include some identical information because many of their recordings were credited to both. On the other hand, all of the fiddler G.B. Grayson's recordings are co-credited to Henry Whitter; because very little is known of Grayson's life, all of the available information is given in the Whitter entry, and the entry under Grayson's name is a cross-reference to Whitter. In addition "see also" cross references are used to help the reader locate information on closely allied musicians or those who recorded both independently and with others. Several dozen pseudonyms were used by record companies for Virginia folk musicians. Each pseudonym has a separate entry that refers the reader to the performer's real name.

Each entry includes historical and biographical information about the artist or group, followed by a discography (see below). Most entries also include a bibliography, which is usually exhaustive and always cites the most recent or important publications related to the subject artist or group. But a few of the bibliographies are selective; in the case of the Carter Family, for example, there are simply too many ephemeral publications to permit a comprehensive treatment.

Discography

The discography section of each entry is arranged chronologically, by session; a session includes all of the records made on one day. To illustrate the interpretation of the discography, each item (designated a, b, c, etc. in parentheses) in the following abbreviated sample is explained below.

(a) *Richmond, Indiana, 3 December 1930*
(b) Roy Harvey: (c) Roy Harvey, guitar/vocal (1); Jess Johnston, fiddle/guitar (2)/ vocal (3)

(d) GN-17337 (e) Hobo's Pal (1)   (f) Chm 16187, Spr 2658
    GN-17344   When It's Lamplighting Time in the Valley (1, 3)   Chm rejected
    GN-17348   Railroad Blues (2)   Chm 16255, Spr 2626, *CY 523*
(g) [Spr 2626 issued as by John Martin; delete fiddle on GN-17348]

(a) Location and date of recording session.
(b) Name under which recordings from session were released.
(c) Personnel list for the entire session, or series of sessions when the same group recorded together on successive days (indicated by "as above" in succeeding entries). Number in parentheses following the credit for a vocal or instrumental part indicates that it applies only to those releases followed by same number. In this example, the (1) indicates that a vocal by Roy Harvey is heard on the first and second songs; Jess Johnston's guitar is heard only on "Railroad Blues," and his voice on "When It's Lamplighting Time"; Harvey's guitar and Johnston's fiddle are heard on all three selections, except "Railroad Blues," which is a guitar duet.
(d) Control numbers. A three-to-seven-digit matrix number was assigned to the song being recorded. An additional number or letter, following a dash, often appears; this is the number of the performance or "take." (Take numbers were generally assigned even if the performance remained unissued, and are given in the discography whenever available.) Control numbers are often stamped into the wax of the record between the runoff grooves and label; sometimes they are printed on the label.
(e) Song title as it appears on the label. (Note parenthetical number referring to personnel listing above.)
(f) Company name (abbreviated) and number assigned to the original release(s). Prewar record companies sometimes released an identical selection, often under a pseudonym, on more than one label simultaneously. In the example above "Hobo's Pal" was released on both Champion and Superior labels. Following the original releases, company name and release number for any reissue on long-playing disc is listed; reissues are italicized. In some discographies, unissued recordings are listed; these are designated, in place of release numbers, by the word "test," referring to a recording not intended for commercial issue but made to determine how the performers sounded on disc; by the word "rejected" for a selection that the original company found unacceptable for technical or aesthetic reasons; or simply "unissued" when the reasons for not releasing it are unknown.
(g) Additional information such as minor personnel alterations not shown above, labeling of other releases of the same recording, and performer credits for the other side of the disc, is given where needed in brackets at the end of the session.

Key to Record Label Abbreviations

Unless otherwise indicated, these are American companies. Non-American companies or foreign divisions of American companies appear with the country of origin noted in brackets following each abbreviation.

Prewar Labels

ARC   American Record Corporation
Au   Aurora [Canada]
Ba   Banner
Bb   Bluebird
Be   Bell
Br   Brunswick
Br SA Brunswick [Great Britain]
Bs   Black Swan
Bw   Broadway
Ca   Cameo
Ch   Challenge
Chm   Champion
Cl   Clarion
Co   Columbia
Cor   Coral
Cq   Conqueror
Cr   Crown
De   Decca
De FM Decca [South Africa]
De X Decca [Australasia]
Di   Diva
Do   Domino
Ed   Edison
El   Elektradisk
Fa   Famous
Ge   Gennett
He   Herwin
HMV   His Master's Voice [Great Britain]
Ho   Homestead
Je   Jewel
JD   Joe Davis
LA   Lonesome Ace
Li   Lincoln
Me   Melotone [45000 and 92000 series are from Canada]
Min   Minerva [Canada]
MW   Montgomery Ward
Mus   Musicraft
OK   OKeh
Or   Oriole
Pa   Pathe
Pe   Perfect
Ph   Phonola [Canada]
Pm   Paramount
QRS   QRS
RCA   Radio Corporation of America
RCA CNV Radio Corporation of America [Great Britain]
Re   Regal
RZ   Regal Zonophone
RZ G Regal Zonophone [Australasia]
RZ I Regal Zonophone [Ireland]
RZ ME Regal Zonophone [Great Britain]
RZ MR Regal Zonophone [Great Britain]
RZ T Regal Zonophone [Great Britain]
Ro   Romeo
Sil   Silvertone
Spr   Superior
Spt   Supertone
Sr   Sunrise
St   Standard
Str   Starr [Canada]
Sun   Sun [Canada]
TT   Timely Tunes
Va   Varsity

Ve   Velvetone
Vi   Victor
Vo   Vocalion
VT   Velvet Tone

Zo   Zonophone [4000 and 5000 series are from Great Britain]
Zo EE   Zonophone [Australasia]

Postwar Long-play Reissues

AH   Ace of Hearts
ARB   Arbor (Same as Puritan)
AS   Asch
BC   Blues Classics
BF   Bear Family [West Germany]
BI   Biograph
BR   Brunswick
BRI   BRI Records
CAM   Camden
CIO   Club Internacional del Disco [Argentina]
CMF   Country Music Foundation
CMH   CMH [West Germany]
CBS   Columbia Broadcasting System
CO   Columbia
CON   Confidential [Great Britain]
COR   Coral
CT   Country Turtle
CY   County
DU   Davis Unlimited
FL   Flyright [Great Britain]
FM   Franklin Mint
FO   Fontana
FSSM   Folksong Society of Minnesota
FW   Folkways
GJ   Guilde du Jazz [France]
HA   Harmony
HE   Heritage
HEG   Heritage [Great Britain]
HI   Historical
JEMF   John Edwards Memorial Foundation
JO   Joker [Italy]

JT   Jazz Tone
LBC   Library of Congress
MA   Matchbox [Great Britain]
MU   Musicraft
NW   New World
OH   Old Homestead
OJL   Origin Jazz Library
OT   Old Timey
OTC   Old Time Classics
PU   Puritan (Same as Arbor)
RCA   Radio Corporation of America
RCA   Radio Corporation of America [700 series is from France]
RCA INT   Radio Corporation of America [Great Britain]
RBF   RBF (Records, Books, Films)
RO   Rounder
RT   Roots [Austria]
SGR   Seeger
SM   Smithsonian Institution
ST   Stetsen [Great Britain]
STA   Stash
SY   Saydisc [Great Britain]
TL   Time Life
TR   Top Rank [Great Britain]
VA   Vanguard
VE   Vetco
VJ   Vee Jay
VO   Vogue [Great Britain]
VX   Vox [Great Britain]
WO   Wolf [Austria]
YZ   Yazoo

Virginia Recording Artists

Unidentified musicians from Franklin County, Virginia, circa 1920

Allegheny Highlanders
See Charlie Poole

Art, Andy, Bert, and Dave
A pseudonym on Clarion and Velvet Tone for Wade Ward

H.M. Barnes' Blue Ridge Ramblers (ca. 1927–ca. 1932)
H.M. "Hank" Barnes led a string band that toured the East Coast vaudeville circuit during the late 1920s. Barnes himself was not a musician, but lent his name to the group and booked them. The band included two traditional musicians associated with Virginia—Lonnie Austin and Jack Reedy—whose contributions are noted elsewhere in this book.

According to Lonnie Austin's recollections and a diary he kept in 1928 and 1929, the Blue Ridge Ramblers regularly appeared at theaters and hotels throughout North Carolina, West Virginia, Virginia, Maryland, Delaware, Pennsylvania, and New York. Occasionally they performed as far north as Maine and Montreal and as far west as Evansville, Indiana. They played one or two days at smaller locations such as Hinton, West Virginia, or Rocky Mount, North Carolina, and as long as one week in New York City. Nearly all of these jobs were booked through the Loews chain of theaters.

The intense touring and traveling of the group brought about many personnel changes. During the period it recorded, H.M. Barnes', Blue Ridge Ramblers generally included three fiddles, steel guitar, piano, mandolin, banjo, and guitar. Possibly because the musicians were performing on the popular stage, their recorded sides represent one of the early attempts to synthesize swing with old-time music. It is unclear how long the group remained on the vaudeville circuit, though it probably continued to tour into the first years of the Depression.

New York, New York, 28 January 1929
H.M. Barnes' Blue Ridge Ramblers: Frank E. "Dad" Williams, fiddle; Fred Roe, fiddle; Jim Smith, fiddle; Frank Wilson, steel guitar; Harry Brown, mandolin; Jack Reedy, banjo; Henry Roe, guitar; Lonnie Austin, piano; vocal chorus (1)

E-29091	Golden Slippers	Br 313
E-29092	Old Joe Clark	Br 313
E-29093	Repasz Band March	Br 361, Me 18022
E-29094	Lineman's Serenade	Br 327
E-29095	Who Broke the Lock on the Hen-House Door? (1)	Br 310, Br 1027, Spt 2052
E-29096	Blue Ridge Ramblers' Rag	Br 346, Spt 2093

Members of H.M. Barnes' Blue Ridge Ramblers gathered for this photograph about 1929. *Courtesy Blue Ridge Heritage Archive/Clarence H. Greene*

E-29097	Flop Eared Mule Br 346, Spt 2093
E-29098	She'll Be Comin' round the Mountain When She Comes (1) Br 310, Br 1027, Spt 2052
E-29099	Goin' Down the Road Feelin' Bad (1) Br 327

[E-29095 omits fiddles, mandolin, and banjo, and includes Jim Smith as lead vocalist; E-29098 omits two fiddles; Spt issued as by Smoky Mountain Ramblers; Me, a Canadian label, issued as by Le Orchestra Cartier]

New York, New York, 29 January 1929

As above: omit Henry Roe (2); Russell Jones replaces Frank Wilson

E-29250	Honolulu Stomp (2) Br 463
E-29251	Three O'Clock in the Morning (2) Br 463
E-29252	Echoes of Shenandoah Valley Br 397
E-29253	Our Director March Br 361, Me 18022
E-29254	Mandolin Rag Br 397, *CY 548*

Bibliography: Janet Kerr, "Lonnie Austin/Norman Woodlief," *Old Time Music* 17 (Summer 1975): 6-10; Tony Russell, "H.M. Barnes Blue Ridge Ramblers," *Old Time Music* 17 (Summer 1975): 11; Charles Wolfe, "Up North with the Blue Ridge Ramblers: Jennie Bowman's 1931 Tour Diary," *Journal of Country Music* 6, no. 3 (1975): 48-53.

See also Lonnie Austin and Jack Reedy.

Elvin Bigger (ca. 1925–ca. 1940) and Troy Martin (mid-1930s)

Elvin Bigger was a member of the Four Virginians, who recorded for OKeh in 1927. During the 1930s he teamed with Troy Martin to record for the American Record Corporation. He lived in Pittsylvania County, Virginia, and died there in 1969.

Troy Martin was born in Danville, Virginia, about 1910. After performing in south central Virginia, Martin moved to Nashville, Tennessee, and by the early 1950s had become an important songwriter. His writing had a considerable impact on the repertoire of bluegrass musicians Lester Flatt and Earl Scruggs.

New York, New York, 16 May 1936

Elvin Bigger and Troy Martin: Elvin Bigger, vocal/guitar; Troy Martin, vocal/guitar

19265-	Meet Me in the Moonlight ARC unissued
19266-	Give Me Flowers While I'm Living ARC unissued
19267-	Can't Blame Me for That ARC unissued
19270-	Heartbroken Girl ARC unissued
19271-1	I'm Going Home ARC 6-10-53
19272-2	You'll Never Miss Your Mother Till She's Gone ARC 6-10-53

See also Four Virginians.

Dad Blackard's Moonshiners

A pseudonym on Victor for the Shelor Family.

Frank Blevins (1926–1941)

Born in Smyth County, Virginia, on February 25, 1912, Blevins moved with his family to Lansing, North Carolina, at a very early age. His father was a fiddler and by his ninth birthday Blevins was following his father's lead. By 1926 he was making music regularly with his brother, Ed, who played both banjo and guitar.

Between 1926 and 1929 the Blevins Brothers were professional musicians working northwestern North Carolina, southwestern Virginia, and southern West Virginia. At times they augmented their duo with Frank Miller, a neighbor and banjo player. In 1927 and 1928 they went to Atlanta to record for the Columbia Record Company as Frank Blevins and the Tar Heel Rattlers. Their records sold below average, but are considered quintessential string band performances.

When the Depression hit, the Blevinses resettled in Marion to work at a furniture factory. They stayed in Smyth County for several years playing music part-time with such local musicians as Jack Reedy and Corwin Mathews. This group was often billed as the Southern Buccaneers and played many theaters in West Virginia. In 1933 they traveled to neighboring Grayson County to participate in the Whitetop Folk Festival.

The Blevinses continued to play music on a regular basis until Ed's sudden death by blood poisoning about 1939. Within two years their friend, banjo player Jack Reedy, died of an unexpected heart attack. Frank Blevins took the deaths of his brother and Reedy as a sign that music was dangerous to one's health and all but gave up playing the fiddle.

He did remain in the furniture business, however, and moved into managerial ranks. Blevins worked for several companies in Smyth County and West Jefferson, North Carolina, until 1965, when he began his own plant in Greenville, Tennessee. Today he still lives in Greenville and manages his company with the help of his two sons.

Atlanta, Georgia, 8 October 1927
Frank Blevins and the Tar Heel Rattlers: Frank Blevins, fiddle; Ed Blevins, guitar; Miller, banjo/vocal

145158-	Sally Aim [sic]	Co 15765
145159-	I've Got No Honey Babe Now	Co 15765
145160-1	Old Aunt Betsy	Co 15210
145161-	Little Bunch of Roses	Co unissued
145162-	Late Last Night when Willie Came Home	Co unissued
145163-2	Fly Around My Pretty Little Miss	Co 15210, *CO CS 9660*

Unidentified woman, Frank Blevins, Corwin Matthews, and Ed Blevins (seated) performing as "The Southern Buccaneers," about 1936. *Courtesy Corwin Matthews*

Atlanta, Georgia, 17 April 1928
As above
146102-	We Have Met and We Have Parted	Co unissued
146103-	The Drunkard's Doom	Co unissued
146104-1	Don't Get Trouble in Your Mind	Co 15280
146105-1	Nine Pound Hammer	Co 15280

Bibliography: Kip Lornell, "A Talk with Walter Frank Blevins," *The Devil's Box* 21 (Spring 1987): 3-12.

See also Jack Reedy.

Blue Ridge Corn Shuckers

A pseudonym on Victor for Ernest V. Stoneman.

Blue Ridge Highballers (1924–1929)

The leader of this group was fiddle player Charley La Prade, born in Franklin County, Virginia, on November 17, 1888. La Prade moved to Spray, North Carolina, with his family in 1900 and soon went to work in the textile mills. At about the same time, he began playing the fiddle, guitar, and banjo.

About 1918 he moved to Danville, Virginia, for a more lucrative mill job. In 1924 he formed a band with Lonnie Griffith (guitar) and Arthur Wells (banjo) that was known as the Blue Ridge Highballers. The group played for dances and at theaters, and competed at many fiddlers' conventions throughout the region.

With the assistance of Luther B. Clarke, a Danville music store proprietor, the band secured a Columbia recording contract. Their Columbia session consisted primarily of instrumentals, though Clarke himself sang on three selections. These recordings sold well, and the demand for the band's services increased accordingly. In the fall of 1926 they were hired by tobacco warehouse owners to entertain the farmers who came to Danville to sell their products.

In 1927 Griffith and Wells were augmented by John Thomason (fiddle), Lewis Adams (guitar), and Lige Hardy (banjo). That fall the sextet traveled to New York City and recorded for Paramount. This was their final session because these records did not sell well. The musicians gradually dropped out of music, though La Prade himself continued to perform regularly until his death on April 24, 1958.

New York, New York, ca. 23 March 1926
Blue Ridge Highballers: Charley La Prade, fiddle; Arthur Wells, banjo; Lonnie Griffith, guitar

141841-2	Green Mountain Polka	Co 15070, *CY 407, VE 106*
141842-2	Skidd More	Co 15168, *CY 407*

Charley LaPrade of the Blue Ridge Highballers, circa 1927.
Courtesy Dave Freeman (County Records)

Arthur Wells (banjo) and Lonnie Griffith (guitar) of the Blue Ridge Highballers, circa 1927.
Courtesy Kinney Rorrer

THE BLUE RIDGE HIGHBALLERS
(*Led by* CHARLEY LA PRADE, *Fiddler*)

HERE they are — the Blue Ridge Highballers from the highlands of the South! When it comes to playing the mountain dance music and the tunes, melodies and marches famous in the Southern hill country, the Highballers take nobody's dust. Charley La Prade, fiddler of note in a country critical of this type of music, is the organization's leader.

THE BLUE RIDGE HIGHBALLERS

SOLDIER'S JOY — Mountain Dance Music. SKIDD MORE — Mountain Dance Music	15168-D 10-inch 75c
DARNEO — Mountain Dance Music DARLING CHILD — Mountain Dance Music	15132-D 10-inch 75c
GOING DOWN TO LYNCHBURG TOWN — Intro.: Don't Let Your Deal Go Down — Mountain Dance Music WISH TO THE LORD I HAD NEVER BEEN BORN — Vocal — Luther B. Clarke, Accomp. by Blue Ridge Highballers	15096-D 10-inch 75c
SANDY RIVER BELLE — Mountain Dance Music ROUND TOWN GIRLS — Mountain Dance Music	15089-D 10-inch 75c
FLOP EARED MULE — Mountain Dance Music FOURTEEN DAYS IN GEORGIA — Mountain Dance Music	15081-D 10-in. 75c 75c
GREEN MOUNTAIN POLKA — Mountain Dance Music UNDER THE DOUBLE EAGLE — March Medley — Mountain Dance Music	15070-D 10-inch 75c

VIVA-TONAL RECORDING. THE RECORDS WITHOUT SCRATCH

Blue Ridge Highballers as they appear in an advertisement from a 1927 Columbia Records catalogue. *Courtesy Dave Freeman (County Records)*

Blues Birdhead

141843-1	Flop Eared Mule	Co 15081, *CY 407*
141844-2	Darneo	Co 15132, Cl 5139, Ve 7103, *CY 407*
141845-1	Soldier's Joy	Co 15168, *CY 407*
141846-1	Darling Child	CO 15132, Cl 5139, Ve 7101, *CY 407, CO CS 9660*
141847-	Flying Cloud	Co unissued
141848-1	Under the Double Eagle	Co 15070, *CY 407*
141849-2	Fourteen Days in Georgia	Co 15081, *CY 407*
141850-2	Sandy River Belle	Co 15089, *CY 407*
141851-2	Round Town Gals	Co 15089, *CY 407*
141852-	Hop Light Ladies	Co unissued

New York, New York, ca. 24 March 1926
As above: add Luther C. Clarke, vocal (1)

141853-2	The Bright Sherman Valley (1)	Co 15069
141854-1	I'll Be All Smiles Tonight (1)	Co 15069
141855-2	Wish to the Lord I'd Never Been Born (1)	Co 15096, *CY 407*
141856-1	Going Down to Lynchburg Town	Co 15096, *CY 407*

[Ve and Cl issued as by the Smokey Blue Highballers; Reverse of Ve 7103 and Ve 1701 unknown]

New York, New York, ca. October 1927
As above: omit Luther B. Clarke; add John Thomason, fiddle; Lewis Adams, guitar; Lige Hardy, banjo

2861-2	Red Wing	Pm 3083, Bw 8159
2865-2	Jule Girl	Pm 3083, Bw 8159
2867-2	Are You Angry with Me, Darling	Pm 3077, Bw 8185
2868-1	I'm Tired of Living Here Alone	Pm 3077, Bw 8185

Bibliography: Kinney Rorrer, brochure notes to "The Blue Ridge Highballers: Original Recordings of 1926," CY 407.

Blues Birdhead (late 1920s)

Named "Blues Birdhead" by officials of the OKeh Company, James Simons was a harmonica player living in Norfolk at the time of these recordings. The details of his life remain obscure.

Richmond, Virginia, 13 October 1929
Blues Birdhead: James Simons, harmonica; unknown piano

403111-A	Mean Low Blues	OK 8824, Cl 5195, VT 7132, *MA 209, RT 320*
403112-A	Harmonica Blues	OK 8824, Cl 5194, VT 7120, *MA 209, RT 320*

[Reverse of VT and Cl by Boyd Senter. VT and Cl issued as by Harmonica Tim. Blues

Birdhead may be the harmonica player on OK 8737, recorded earlier the same day in Richmond, and issued as by the Bubbling-Over Five.]

Dock Boggs (1918–1970)

Born near Norton, Virginia, on February 7, 1898, Moran Lee "Dock" Boggs was an idiosyncratic banjo player and vocalist with ambitions of becoming a professional musician. Although he went to work in the coal mines in 1910, he was always thinking of ways to further his musical career. Beginning in the mid-1920s, Boggs worked with a group, the Cumberland Mountaineers, on a musical circuit in southwestern Virginia and eastern Kentucky that included tent shows, theaters, and coal camps. About February 1927, he was auditioned by a talent scout from the Brunswick record company and invited to New York to record his heavily black-influenced banjo tunes and songs.

His initial records did not sell well. This did not entirely discourage Boggs, however, for in 1929 Richlands, Virginia, businessman William A. Myer recorded him for Myer's own fledgling label, Lonesome Ace. These records had extremely limited distribution, and by the 1930s Boggs had slipped into musical semiretirement.

During the renewed interest in folk music in the 1960s Boggs was located and interviewed by Mike Seeger. Some of Seeger's recordings of Boggs were issued on Folkways. He returned to performing music and touring throughout the country before his death in 1970.

New York City, 10 March 1927
Dock Boggs: Dock Boggs, vocal and banjo; G.H. "Hub" Mahaffey, guitar (1)

E-21795-6	Country Blues	Br 131, *FW RBF 654, FW FA 2953*
E-21797-8	Sammie, Where Have You Been So Long (1)	Br 131, *FW RBF 654, CY 511*
E-21799-80	Down South Blues (1)	Br 118, *FW RBF 654*
E-21801-	Sugar Baby (1)	Br 118, *FW RBF 654, FW FA 2953*
E-21811-2	Danville Girl	Br 132, *FW RBF 654*
E-21813-4	Pretty Polly	Br 132, *FW RBF 654, BR 59001, COR MH 174, MCA VIM 3013*
E-21815-	New Prisoner's Song (1)	Br 133, Vo 5144, *FW RBF 654*
E-21817-8	Hard Luck Blues (1)	Br 133, Vo 5144, *FW RBF 654*

Chicago, Illinois, ca. September 1929
As above: delete Mahaffey; add Emry Arthur, guitar

21403-2	False Hearted Lover's Blues	LA 1, *FW RBF 654*
21404-3	Old Rub Alcohol Blues	LA 1, *FW RBF 654*

Dock Boggs in the late 1930s, photographed in Wise County, Virginia.
Courtesy Blue Ridge Heritage Archive/Ed Ward

21405-2   Will Sweethearts Know Each Other There   LA 2, *FW RBF 654*
21406-3   Lost Love Blues   LA 2, *FW RBF 654*

Bibliography: Barry O'Connell, "Dock Boggs, Musician and Coal Miner," *Appalachian Journal* 11 (Autumn-Winter 1983-84); Barry O'Connell, brochure notes to "Dock Boggs," RBF 654; Mike Seeger, brochure notes to "Dock Boggs: Legendary Banjo Player and Singer," FW FH 5458.

Buck Mountain Band (late 1920s)
See Wade Ward.

Bull Mountain Moonshiners (late 1920s)
Little is known of this group except that they were from southwestern Virginia, possibly Wise or Lee County. Its members included Charles and William McReynolds, who were grandfathers of the noted bluegrass duo Jim and Jesse McReynolds. Charles McReynolds was born in Coeburn (Wise County) on February 19, 1873, and died there on January 30, 1952.

Bristol, Tennessee, 1 August 1927
Bull Mountain Moonshiners: Charles McReynolds, fiddle; William McReynolds, banjo; Howard Green, guitar; Charlie Greer, guitar; Bill Dean, vocal

39748-2   Sweet Marie   Vi unissued
39749-2   Johnny Goodwin   Vi 21141 *CMF 011-L*
[Reverse of Vi 21141 by the Tenneva Ramblers]

Jack Burdette and Bert Moss
A pseudonym on Superior for Byrd Moore and Melvin Robinette.

Caldwell Brothers
A pseudonym on Supertone for the Sweet Brothers.

Sam Caldwell
A pseudonym on Supertone for Herbert Sweet.

Buster Carter (ca. 1924–ca. 1938) and Preston Young (1928–1940)
Preston Young and Buster Carter are linked because of their long-standing musical partnership and their Columbia recordings. Born in Franklin County on February 9, 1907, Young first learned music from his uncle, Walter Spencer,

who played the autoharp. He then picked up a guitar, but after meeting Charlie Poole about 1928, Young was inspired to take up the banjo.

About 1930 he joined with fiddler Posey Rorer and another of his friends, guitarist Buster Carter, to form a string band that was quintessential south central Virginia. Each member was a veteran musician and the trio soon felt it was ready to record. Their model was Charlie Poole, with whom Rorer had fiddled for many years. Like Poole they traveled to New York to audition for Columbia; unfortunately their recording career was severely hindered by the Depression, which was in full force by mid-1931.

Young continued to play music after returning to Henry County. His records sold poorly, so Young turned to radio work as an outlet for his talent. He sometimes played over the radio in nearby High Point, North Carolina, but his primary income was provided by working with sheet metal, carpentry, and other skilled trades.

The Depression forced Young away from music; by 1940 his instruments had been sold and he had quit music altogether. Young lived in Martinsville until his death about 1978, about the time that his one-time partner, Buster Carter, passed away.

New York, New York, 26 June 1931

Buster Carter and Preston Young: Posey Rorer, fiddle; Buster Carter, banjo/vocal (1); Preston Young, guitar/vocal (2)

151643-2	Its Hard to Love and Can't Be Loved (2)	Co 15690
151644-	Wish That Gal Were Mine	Co unissued
151645-2	I'd Rather Be Rosy Nell	Co unissued
151646-	We'll Be Married When the Sun Goes Down	Co unissued
151647-1	It Won't Hurt No More (1, 2)	Co 15702
151648-2	A Lazy Farmer Boy (1)	Co 15702, *FW FP251, FW FA 2951*
151649-1	What Sugar Head Likker Will Do (1)	Co 15758
151650-1	Bill Morgan and His Gal (1, 2)	Co 15758
151651-1	I'll Roll in My Sweet Baby's Arms (1, 2)	Co 15690, *OT 101*
151652-1	She's a Darn Good Gal	Co unissued

[No banjo audible on 151648 or 151649]

Bibliography: Tony Russell, "Good Old Times Makin' Music: The Preston Young Story," *Old Time Music* 7 (Winter 1972/3): 4-7.

Carter Family (1926–1943)

With firm roots in Scott County, Virginia, the Carter Family has had a profound impact on American country music. The original trio consisted of Alvin

Preston Young (guitar), Posey Rorer (fiddle), and Buster Carter (banjo) recorded together for Columbia in the early 1930s. *Courtesy Kinney Rorer*

Pleasant Carter (born April 15, 1891, in Maces Spring, Virginia), his wife, Sara (born July 21, 1898, in Coeburn, Virginia), and her sister, Maybelle (born May 10, 1909, in Copper Creek, Virginia). The Addington sisters began playing music in their teens; A.P. was known as a fine singer. In 1915 Sara Addington and A.P. Carter were married and moved to Maces Springs, Virginia.

By 1926 the Carters and Maybelle Addington had pooled their musical resources and began performing around Scott County. A year later the trio traveled to nearby Bristol, Tennessee, to audition for the Victor Company. Their successful audition led to a recording career that lasted until 1941.

During the years following their initial recordings, the Carters toured throughout Virginia and the surrounding states. Early in their career they often performed at schools and small auditoriums. As the Carter Family's popularity grew, the scope of their touring increased. And unlike most musical artists, they continued to record through the Depression. Their solidarity as a musical trio remained constant well into the 1930s, despite the gradual disintegration of A.P. and Sara's marriage about 1932.

The Carter Family was also involved with radio broadcasts, and in 1938 they made a bold move to Texas in order to broadcast over the powerful radio stations located just over the Mexican border. Much of this broadcasting was done over XERA, which beamed its signal to millions of listeners across North America. Their border radio stint lasted three years and ended just as World War II swept across Europe and Asia.

In 1941 and 1942 the trio, which was now often augmented by members of their extended family, spent much time working out of Charlotte, North Carolina, where they also had a regular show on WBT. The original trio, though, continued to record for a variety of labels until their final session in fall 1941. By 1943 the original Carter Family trio had disbanded.

By this time several members of the extended family—especially A.P. and Sara's children, Joe and Janette, and Maybelle's three daughters, Helen, Anita, and June—had also become more involved with music on a professional level. Their music reflected changes in popular country music as they included more contemporary honky-tonk sounds in addition to some of the traditional tunes.

In the 1950s, there were occasional reunions. A.P., Sara, and other members of the family recorded sessions for a local company, which were issued on the Acme, Bell, and Pine Mountain labels. On November 7, 1960, A.P. passed away and was followed by Maybelle on October 23, 1978, and Sara on January 8, 1979. Today Joe and Janette Carter still live in Scott County and operate a performance center, the Carter Family Fold, devoted to traditional music.

The Carter Family, circa 1929 (probably at Hiltons, Virginia). From left: Maybelle, Sara, A.P. Carter. *Courtesy Dave Freeman (County Records)*

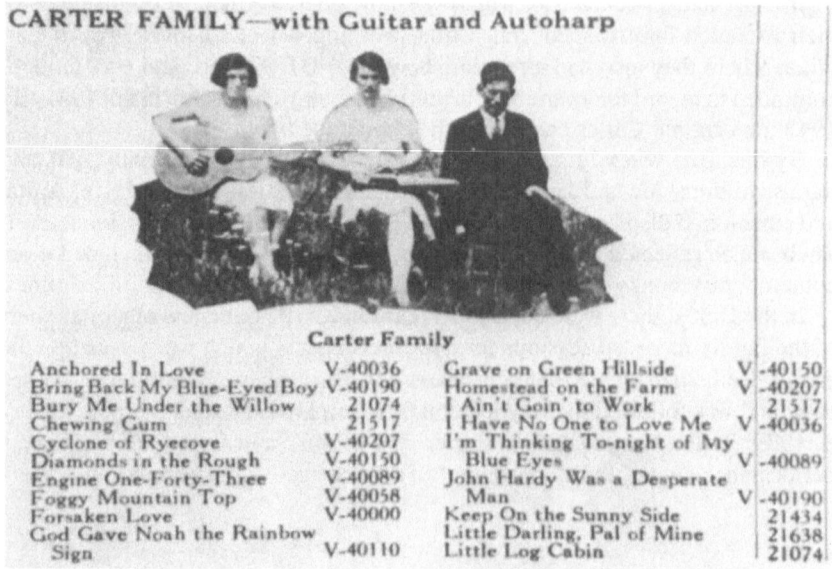

As adapted in 1929 Victor catalogue. *Courtesy Kinney Rorrer*

Carter Family 39

Bristol, Tennessee, 1 August 1927

The Carter Family: A.P. Carter, vocal (1); Sara Carter, vocal/autoharp/guitar (2); Maybelle Carter, guitar/vocal (3)

39750-1	Bury Me under the Weeping Willow	Vi unissued
39750-2	Bury Me under the Weeping Willow (1, 3) Vi 21074, Bb 6053, MW 7020, *RCA RCX 7100, RCA LPM 2772, RCA RA 5321, RCA RA 5513, RCA RA-5641, CMF-011-L*	
39751-1	Little Log Cabin by the Sea Vi unissued	
39751-2	Lttle Log Cabin by the Sea (1) Vi 21074, Bb 6271, *RCA RCX 7100, RCA RA 5389, RCA RA 5641, CMF-011-L*	
39752-1	Poor Orphan Child Vi unissued	
39752-2	Poor Orphan Child (1) Vi 20877, MW 7445, *RCA LPM 2772, RCA RA 5321, RCA RA 5513, RCA RA 5641, CMF-011-L*	
39753-1	The Storms Are on the Ocean Vi unissued	
39753-2	The Storms Are on the Ocean (1, 3) Vi 20937, Bb 6176, MW 7021, *RCA RA-5641, ACM 15, CMF-011-L*	

Bristol, Tennessee, 2 August 1927

As above

38754-1	Single Girl, Married Girl Vi unissued	
39754-2	Single Girl, Married Girl (1, 3) Vi 20937, MW 7445, *FW FP253, FA2953, RCA RA 5389, RCA RA 5641, CMF-011-L*	
39755-1	The Wandering Boy (1, 3) Vi 20877, MW 7446, *CAM ACL10047, RCA RA 5641, CMF-011-L*	

Camden, New Jersey, 9 May 1928

As above

45020-1	Meet Me by the Moonlight Alone Vi unissued	
45020-2	Meet Me by the Moonlight Alone (1) Vi 23731, Bb 5096, Sr 3274, El 2174, MW 7149, *RCA RCX 7100, RCA RA 5641, ACM 15*	
45021-1	Little Darling Pal of Mine Vi unissued	
45021-2	Little Darling Pal of Mine (1) Vi 21638, Bb 5301, Sr 3382, El 2172, MW 4427, *RCA 7100, RCA RA 5389, RCA RA 5641*	
45022-1	Keep on the Sunny Side (1, 3) Vi 21434, Bb 5006, Sr 3172, El 1964, MW 4225, Zo 4270, Zo EE179, *RCA LPM 2772, RCA RA 5321, RCA RA 5513, RCA LPM 6015, RCA RA 5641, CAM CXS-9020*	
45023-1	Anchored in Love Vi unissued	
45023-2	Anchored in Love (1) Vi 40036, Bb 5406, Sr 3427, MW 4740, Zo 4228, Zo 5753, Zo EE205, RZ ME33, RZ T5753, HMV MH184, *CMH 107, RCA RA 5641*	

THE CARTER FAMILY

10-inch, List Price 75¢

V-40229	When the Roses Bloom in Dixieland / No Telephone in Heaven
V-40207	The Homestead on the Farm / The Cyclone of Ryecove
V-40190	John Hardy Was a Desperate Little Man / Bring Back My Blue-Eyed Boy to Me
V-40150	Diamonds in the Rough / The Grave on the Green Hillside
V-40126	Sweet Fern / Lulu Wall
V-40110	Little Moses / God Gave Noah the Rainbow Sign
V-40089	Engine One-Forty-Three / I'm Thinking To-Night of My Blue Eyes
V-40058	My Clinch Mountain Home / The Foggy Mountain Top
V-40036	I Have No One to Love Me (But the Sailor on the Deep Blue Sea) / Anchored in Love
V-40000	Wildwood Flower / Forsaken Love
21638	Will You Miss Me When I'm Gone? / Little Darling, Pal of Mine
21517	Chewing Gum / I Ain't Goin' to Work Tomorrow
21434	River of Jordan / Keep on the Sunny Side
21074	Bury Me Under the Weeping Willow / Little Log Cabin By the Sea
20937	Single Girl, Married Girl / The Storms Are on the Ocean
20877	The Poor Orphan Child / The Wandering Boy

Maybelle, A.P., and Sara Carter in a 1929 Victor release sheet.
Courtesy Dave Freeman (County Records)

Carter Family 41

Camden, New Jersey, 10 May 1928
As above
45024-1   John Hardy Was a Desperate Man   Vi unissued
45024-2   John Hardy Was a Desperate Man   Vi 40190, Bb 6033, Zo 40190, MW 4741, *FW FP251, FA2951, RCA RCX 7101, RCA RA 5641*
45025-1   I Ain't Gonna Work Tomorrow (1, 3)   Vi 21517, MW 7019, *RCA RCX 7101, RCA RA 5641*, ACM 15
45026-1   Will You Miss Me When I'm Gone (1)   Vi 21638, MW 4228, *RCA LPM 2772, RCA RA 5641*
45027-1   River of Jordan   Vi unissued
45027-2   River of Jordan (1, 3)   Vi 21434, Bb 5058, Sr 3143, El 1984, MW 4430, Zo 4270, Zo EE179, *CMH 107, RCA DSP 2046, RCA RA 5642*, ACM 8
45028-1   Chewing Gum   Vi unissued
45028-2   Chewing Gum (1, 3)   Vi 21517, MW 7019, *RCA RCX 7101, RCA RA 5642*, ACM 15
45029-1   Wildwood Flower (2)   Vi-40000, Bb 5356, Sr 3437, MW 4432, *RCA 20369, RCA RA 5321, RCA RA 5531, RCA RA 5642, CAM-92, CAM CAL-586*
45030-1   I Have No One to Love Me   Vi unissued
45030-2   I Have No One to Love Me (But the Sailor on the Deep Blue Sea) (1, 3)   Vi 40036, Bb 5356, Sr 3437, MW 4320, MW 4740, Zo 4228, Zo 5753, Zo EE205, RZ ME28, RZ T5753, RZ G22465, *RCA RA 5642, RCA DPS 2046, CMH 107*
45031-1   Forsaken Love   Vi unissued
45031-2   Forsaken Love (1)   Vi 40000, MW 4734, *RCA RA-5321, RCA RA 5513, RCA RA 5642, CAM 92, CAM CAL 586*
[Reverse of MW 4320 by the Floyd County Ramblers]

Camden, New Jersey, 14 February 1929
As above
49856-1   Sweet Fern   Vi unissued
49856-2   Sweet Fern (1, 2)   Vi 40126, Bb 5927, MW 4437, RZ G22826, *RCA 20369, RCA RA 5642, CAM 92, CAM CAL-586*
49857-1   My Clinch Mountain Home (1, 2)   Vi 40058, Bb 5301, MW 4432, Sr 3382, El 2172, Zo 4226, Zo 5493, Zo EE226, RZ ME27, RZ T5493, RZ IZ325, HMV MH185, *RCA RCX 7101, RCA LPM 2772, RCA RA 5321, RCA RA 5513, RCA RA 5642*
49858-1   God Gave Noah the Rainbow Sign (1, 3)   Vi 40110, Bb 5272, MW 4427, Sr 3353, El 2146, *RCA RA 5642, CAM 92, CAM CAL 586*
49859-1, 2   I'm Thinking Tonight of My Blue Eyes   Vi unissued
49859-3   I'm Thinking Tonight of My Blue Eyes (1)   Vi 40089, Bb 5122, Sr 3203, El 2032, MW 4230, *RCA RA 5321, RCA RA 5513, RCA RA 5642, CAM 92, CAM CAL-586*

49860-1   Little Moses   Vi unissued
49860-2   Little Moses (1, 2)   Vi 40110, Bb 5924, MW 5010, *FW FP252, FW FA2952, CAM 92, CAM CAL-586, RCA 5642*
49861-1   Lulu Walls   Vi unissued
49861-2   Lulu Walls (1, 3)   Vi 40126, Bb 5927, Zo 4239, RZ G22826, MW 4437, *CAM 92, CAM CAL-586, RCA 5642*
49846-1   Grave on the Green Hillside   Vi unissued
49846-2   Grave on the Green Hillside (1, 3)   Vi 40150, MW 7021, Zo 4249, *CAM 92, CAM CAL-586, RCA RA 5642*

[49861 entitled "Lulu Walls" on CAM 92]

Camden, New Jersey, 15 February 1929
As above
49864-1   Don't Forget This Song   Vi unissued
49864-2   Don't Forget This Song (1, 2)   Vi 40238, MW 7022, Zo 4347, Zo EE263, *CMH 107, RCA RA 5642, ACM 15*
49865-1   Foggy Mountain Top   Vi unissued
49865-2   Foggy Mountain Top (1, 3)   Vi 40058, MW 4743, Zo 4226, Zo 5493, Zo EE210, RZ ME27, RZ T5493, RZ IZ325, HMV MH 185, *RCA LPM 2772, RCA RA 5321, RCA RA 5513, RCA RA 5642*
49866-1   Bring Back My Blue Eyed Boy to Me   Vi unissued
49866-2   Bring Back My Blue Eyed Boy to Me (1, 3)   Vi 40190, Bb 6271, MW 4741, *CMH 107, RCA RA 5642, ACM 15*
49867-1   Diamonds in the Rough   Vi unissued
49867-2   Diamonds in the Rough (1, 2, 3)   Vi 40150, Bb 6033, MW 4434, *CAM 92, CAM CAL-586, RCA 5642, RCA RCX 7102, RCA 20369*
49868-1   Engine 143   Vi unissued
49868-2   Engine 143 (1, 3)   Vi 40089, Bb 6223, MW 4743, *FW FP251, FW FA2951, RCA RCX 7102, RCA LPV 532, RCA RD 7870, RCA RA 5643*

[Reverse Zo EE210 by the McCravy Brothers]

Atlanta, Georgia, 22 November 1929
As above
56566-1   Homestead on the Farm (1, 3)   Vi 40207, MW 7023, Zo 4286, Zo EE240, *RCA LPM 2772, RCA RA 5321, RCA RA 5513, RCA 5642*
56567-1
 and -2   Cyclone of Rye Cove   Vi unissued
56567-3   Cyclone of Rye Cove (1, 3)   Vi 40207, MW 7023, Zo 4286, *CMH 107, RCA RA 5642, ACM 15*
56568-1
 and -2   Motherless Children   Vi unissued
56568-3   Motherless Children (3)   Vi 23641, Bb 5924, MW 5010, Zo EE361, *RCA LPM 2772, RCA RA 5513, RCA RA 5643, RCA RA 5321*

Carter Family   43

Atlanta, Georgia, 24 November 1929

As above
56581-1   When the Roses Bloom in Dixieland   Vi unissued
56581-2   When the Roses Bloom in Dixieland (1, 3)   Vi 40229, Bb 5716, MW
               4544, Zo 4322, Zo EE26, *RCA RA 5643*
56582-1   No Telephone in Heaven   Vi unissued
56582-2   No Telephone in Heaven (1, 3)   Vi 40229, Bb 5257, MW 4430, Sr
               3353, El 2146, Zo 4322, Zo EE240, *RCA RA 5643, ACM 8*
56583-1   Western Hobo   Vi unissued
56583-2   Western Hobo (2, 3)   Vi 40255, Bb 6223, MW 7147, *RCA RCX
               7102, RCA RA 5389, RCA RA 5643, ACM 15*
56584-1   Carter's Blues (2)   Vi 23716, Bb 6036, MW 5012, RZ G22795, *RCA
               RCX 7102, RCA RA 5643, ACM 15*
56585-1, 2 Wabash Cannonball   Vi unissued
56585-3   Wabash Cannonball   Vi 23731, Bb 8350, MW 7444, RZ G24157,
               *RCA 20369, RCA RCX 7109, RCA RA 5321, RCA RA 5513, RCA RA
               5643, CAM 92, CAM CAL-586*

Atlanta, Georgia, 25 November 1929

As above
56586-1   A Distant Land to Roam   Vi unissued
56586-2   A Distant Land to Roam (1, 2, 3)   Vi 40255, Bb 5543, MW 7020,
               CAM CAL 2473, RCA RA 5643
56587-1   Jimmie Brown the Newsboy   Vi unissued
56587-2   Jimmie Brown the Newsboy   Vi 23554, MW 5027, ZO EE297, *RCA
               RCX 7109, RCA RA 5389, RCA RA 5643*
56588-1   Kitty Waltz (2, 3)   Vi 40277, Bb 5990, MW 4434, Zo EE238, *CAM
               92, CAM CAL 586, RCA RA 5643*
56589-1   Fond Affection   Vi unissued
56589-2   Fond Affection (2, 3)   Vi 23585, Bb 6176, MW 4744, Zo 4364, *RCA
               RCX 7109, RCA RA 5389, RCA RA 5643, ACM 15*

Memphis, Tennessee, 24 May 1930

As above
59979-1   The Cannonball (1)   Vi 40317, Bb 6020, MW 4742, *RCA RCX 7110,
               RCA RA 5389, RCA RA 5643, ACM 15*
59980-1   Lover's Farewell   Vi unissued
59980-2   Lover's Farewell (1, 3)   Vi 40277, Bb 6036, MW 5012, Zo EE238,
               RCA DPS2046, RCA RA 5643, ACM 15
59981-1   There's Someone A-Waiting for Me   Vi unissued
59981-2   There's Someone A-Waiting for Me (1)   Vi 23554, Zo EE297, *RCA
               RCX 7109, RCA RA 5643, ACM 15*
59982-1   Little Log Hut in the Lane   Vi unissued
59982-2   Little Log Hut in the Lane (1, 3)   Vi 40328, MW 7022, Zo 4347, Zo
               EE263, *CMH 107, RCA RA 5643, ACM 15*

59983-1	When the Springtime Comes Again Vi unissued
59983-2	When the Springtime Comes Again (1, 3) Vi 40293, Bb 5122, MW 4227, El 2032, Zo EE256, Sr 3023, *RCA RA DPS2046, RCA RA 5643, ACM 15*
59984-1	When the World's on Fire Vi unissued
59984-2	When the World's on Fire (1) Vi 40293, Bb 1836, Bb 33-0537, Bb 5006, Sr 3127, MW 4229, Zo EE256, *RCA VRA 5005, RCA RA 5644, CAM CAL 815, CAM CAS 816, ACM 8*
59985-1	I Have an Aged Mother Vi unissued
59985-2	I Have an Aged Mother (1, 3) MW 7446, *CMH 107, RCA DPS 2046, RCA RA 5644, ACM 8*
59986-1	Dying Soldier Vi unissued
59986-2	Dying Soldier (3) Vi 23641, MW 4735, Zo EE361, *RCA RA 6544, ACM 15*
59987-1	Worried Man Blues Vi unissued
59987-2	Worried Man Blues (1, 3) Vi 40317, Bb 6020, MW 4742, Vi 27497, RZ G22795, *RCA RCX 7110, RCA LPV 507, RCA VRA 5005, RCA RA 6544, CAM ACL1 0047*

Memphis, Tennessee, 24 November 1930
As above

64705-1	Lonesome Valley Vi unissued
64705-2	Lonesome Valley (1, 3) Vi 23541, Bb 6117, MW 4735, Zo EE295, *RCA RA 5644, ACM 8*
64706-1	On the Rock Where Moses Stood Vi unissued
64706-2	On the Rock Where Moses Stood (1, 3) Vi 23513, Bb 6055, MW 4739, Zo 4739, RZ G22617, *CAM 92, CAM CAL-586, RCA RA 5644, TL CW 06*
64707-1	Room in Heaven for Me Vi unissued
64707-2	Room in Heaven for Me (1, 3) Vi 23618, Bb 5993, MW 4733, RZ G22827, *CMH 107, RCA RA 5644, ACM 8*

Memphis, Tennessee, 25 November 1930
As above

64714-1	Lonesome Pine Special Vi unissued
64714-2	Lonesome Pine Special (1, 2, 3) Vi 23716, MW 4737, *CAM CAL 2473, RCA RCX 7110, RCA RA 5339, RCA RA 5644*
64715-1	No More the Moon Shines on Lorena Vi unissued
64715-2	No More the Moon Shines on Lorena (1, 3) Vi 23523, MW 5027, Zo 4328, *RCA DPS2046, RCA RA 5644, CAM ACL1 0501*
64716-1	On My Way to Canaan's Land Vi unissued
64716-2	On My Way to Canaan's Land (1, 3) Bb 8167, *CAM CAL 816, RCA RA 5339, RCA DPS2046, RCA RA 5644, ACM 8*
64717-1	Where Shall I Be Vi unissued

Carter Family

64717-2 Where Shall I Be (1, 3)   Vi 23523, Bb 6055, MW 4229, Zo 4328, RZ G22617, *RCA DPS2046, RCA RA 5644, CAM CAS 1554, ACM 15*
64718-1 Sow 'Em on the Mountain   Vi unissued
64718-2 Sow 'Em on the Mountain (1)   Vi 23585, Bb 5468, MW 4744, *RCA RCX 7110, RCA RA 5644, ACM 8*
64719-1 Darling Nellie across the Sea   Vi unissued
64719-2 Darling Nellie across the Sea (1, 3)   Vi 23513, MW 4739, *RCA RA 5644, ACM 15*
64720-1 Birds Were A-Singing of You   Vi unissued
64720-2 Birds Were A-Singing of You (1, 2, 3)   Vi 23541, Bb 6117, MW 4226, Zo EE295, *RCA RA 5644, ACM 15*

Charlotte, North Carolina, 25 May 1931
As above
69345-1 Weary Prodigal Son   Vi unissued
69345-2 Weary Prodigal Son (1, 3)   Vi 23626, MW 7443, Zo EE330, *ACM 8, RCA RA 5645*
69346-1 My Old Cottage Home   Vi unissued
69346-2 My Old Cottage Home (1, 2)   Vi 23599, Bb 6000, RZ G22828, MW 5011, *CAM ACL1 0047, RCA DPS2046, RCA RA 5645*
69347-1 When I'm Gone (1, 2, 3)   Vi 23569, Bb 6053, MW 4736, RZ G22654, *RCA RA 5646, ACM 15*
69348-1 Sunshine in the Shadows   Vi unissued
69348-2 Sunshine in the Shadows (1, 3)   Vi 23626, Bb 5468, MW 7148, Zo 4375, Zo EE330, *CMH 107, RCA DPS2046, RCA RA 5645, CAM CAS 2554*
69349-1 Let the Church Roll On   Vi unissued
69349-2 Let the Church Roll On (1, 3)   Vi 23618, MW 4733, *CAM CAL 816, RCA RA 5646, RCA DPS2046, ACM 8*

Charlotte, North Carolina 26 May 1931
As above
69350-1 Lonesome for You   Vi unissued
69350-2 Lonesome for You (1, 2)   Vi 23599, Bb 6000, MW 5011, RZ G22828, *RCA RA 5645, ACM 22*
69351-1 Can't Feel at Home   Vi unissued
69351-2 Can't Feel at Home (1, 3)   Vi 23569, Bb 6259, MW 4736, Zo 4366, *RCA RA 5645, ACM 8*

Louisville, Kentucky, 10 June 1931
As above: add Jimmie Rodgers, guitar/vocal (4)

69412-1 Why There's a Tear in My Eye (2, 4)   Bb 6698, MW 7138, RZ ME33, RZ MR2374, RZ MR2429, *RCA LPM 2865, RCA RA 5645, RCA RA 5463, RCA RD 7644, ACM 22*

69413-1   The Wonderful City   Vi unissued
69413-2   The Wonderful City (2, 4)   Bb 6810, MW 7137, RZ MR2455, RZ G23184, *RCA LPM 2865, RCA RD 7644, RCA RA 5464, RCA RA 5645*

[Reverse of all issues by Jimmie Rodgers alone]

Louisville, Kentucky, 11 June, 1931

As above
69427-1, -2,
    and -3   Jimmie Rodgers Visits the Carter Family   Vi unissued
69428-1, -2,
    and -3   The Carter Family Visits Jimmie Rodgers (The Carter Family Interview Jimmie Rodgers)   Vi unissued

Louisville, Kentucky, 12 June 1931

As above
692427-4   Jimmie Rodgers Visits the Carter Family (1, 2, 3, 4)   Vi 23574, MW 4720, Zo EE369, RZ ME34, HMV MH188, *FM 34, RCA LPM 2865, RCA RA 5464, RCA RA 5645, RCA RD 7644*
692428-4   The Carter Family and Jimmie Rodgers in Texas (1, 2, 3, 4)   Bb 6762, MW 7137, RZ ME34, RZ MR3164, MHV MH188, *RCA LPM 2865, RCA RA 5001, RCA RD 7644, RCA RA 5464, RCA RA 5645, DPL 2-0075*

[Both 69427-4 and 69428-4 contain speaking by all of the participants; reverse of Bb 6762 by the Monroe Brothers; others by Jimmie Rodgers]

Atlanta, Georgia, 23 February 1932

As above: omit Jimmie Rodgers

71609-1   Mid the Green Fields of Virginia (1, 3)   Vi 23686, Bb 5243, El 2126, MW 4737, Sr 3326, Zo EE350, *RCA LPM 2772, RCA RA 5321, RCA RA 5513, RCA RA 5645*
71610-1   Happiest Day of All   Vi unissued
71610-2   Happiest Day of All (1, 3)   Vi 23701, Bb 6106, MW 4738, RZ G23169, *CMH 107, CAM ACL1 0501, RCA RA 5646, TL CW 06*
71611-1   Picture on the Wall (1, 3)   Vi 23686, Bb 5185, El 2078, Sr 3265, Vi 20-3259, Zo EE350, MW 4228, *RCA LPM 2772, RCA RA 5321, RCA RA 5513, RCA RA 5646*
71612-1   Amber Tresses (1, 2, 3)   Vi 23701, Bb 5185 MW 4738, Sr 3265, Zo 4379, *RCA DPS2046, RCA RA 5646, OTC 6001, ACM 22*

Atlanta, Georgia, 24 February 1932

As above
71613-1   I Never Loved But One (1, 2, 3)   Vi 23656, Bb 6257, Zo 4366, MW 4734, *RCA RA 5646, ACM 22*

Carter Family 47

71614-1	Tell Me That You Love Me (1, 2, 3)	Vi 23656, Bb 5406, MW 4230, RZ G22465, *RCA RA 5646, ACM 22*
71615-1	Where We'll Never Grow Old (1, 2, 3)	Vi 23672, Bb 5058, El 1984, MW 4349, MW 4732, Sr 3143, *RCA RA 5646, SM P8 15640, ACM 8*
71616-1	We Will March through the Streets of the City	Vi unissued
71616-2	We Will March through the Streets of the City (1, 2, 3)	Vi 23672, Bb 5161, El 2058, MW 4336, MW 4732, Sr 3242, *CMH 107, RCA RA 5646, ACM 8*

[Reverse of MW 4336 by the McGravys; reverse of MW 4349 by Ed McConnell]

Camden, New Jersey, 12 October 1932

As above

59017-1	Sweet as the Flowers in Maytime	Vi unissued
59017-2	Sweet as the Flowers in Maytime (1, 3)	Vi 23761, Bb 5096, El 2011, MW 4226, Sr 3174, Zo 4375, *CMH 107, CAM ACL1 0047, RCA RA 5646*
59018-1	Will the Roses Bloom in Heaven (1, 2, 3)	Vi 23748, Bb 5161, El 2058, MW 7149, Sr 3242, *RCA RA 5646, CAM CAS 2554*
59019-1 and -2	On a Hill Lone and Gray	Vi unissued
59019-3	On a Hill Lone and Gray (1, 2, 3)	Bb 5961, MW 4545, RZ G22657, *RCA RA 5648, RCA DPS2046, OTC 6001*
59020-1	My Little Home in Tennessee	Vi unissued
59020-2	My Little Home in Tennessee (1, 3)	*RCA CNV 102, RCA RA 5646, CAM CAL 2473*
59021-1	Sun of the Soul	Vi unissued
59021-2	Sun of the Soul (1, 2, 3)	Vi 23776, Bb 5543, MW 7148, RZ G22470, *RCA DPS2046, RCA RA 5646, OTC 6001, ACM 22*
59022-1	If One Won't Another One Will (2)	Vi 23761, MW 7444, *LBC 2, RCA DPS2046, RCA RA 5646, ACM 22*
59023-1	Broken Hearted Lover	Vi unissued
59023-2	Broken Hearted Lover (1, 3)	Vi 23791, MW 4433, *RCA RCX 7111, RCA RA 5389, RCA RA 5646, OTC 6001, ACM 22*

[MW 4433 titled "Broken Hearted Sweetheart"]

Camden, New Jersey, 13 October 1932

As above

59024-1	Two Sweethearts (1, 2, 3)	Vi 23791, Bb 6106, MW 4433, RZ G23169, *OTC 6001, RCA RCX 7711, RCA RA 5389, RCA RA 5647, ACM 22*
59025-1	Winding Stream (1, 2, 3)	Vi 23807, MW 7443, *RCA LPM-2772, RCA RA 5647*
59026-1	I Won't Mind Dying (1, 2)	Vi 23807, MW 7358, *RCA RA 5647, ACM 8*

59027-1 Spirit of Love Watches over Me (1, 2, 3)   Vi 23748, Bb 5243, El
         2126, MW 4227, Sr 3326, *CAM ACL1 0501, RCA RA 59028-1*
59028-1 Church in the Wildwood (1, 2, 3)   Vi 23776, Bb 5993, MW 4225, RZ
         G22827, *CAM CAL 767, ACM 8, RCA RA 5647*

[Some copies of MW 7358 may be mistitled "See That My Grave Is Kept Green"]

Camden, New Jersey, 17 June 1933
As above
76278-1 Give Me Roses While I Live (1, 2, 3)   Vi 23821, MW 7356, *RCA RA
         5647, ACM 8*
76701-1 Give Me Roses While I Live   Vi unissued
76279-1 I Never Will Marry (1, 2, 3)   Bb 8350, MW 7356, RZ G24157, *CAM
         CAS 2554, RCA RCX 7111, RCA RA 5339, RCA RA 5647*
76702-1 I Never Will Marry   Vi unissued
76280-1 On the Sea of Galilee (1, 2, 3)   Vi 23845, MW 7355, *CAM CAL 767,
         CAM ACL1 0047, RCA DPS2046, RCA RA 5647*
76703-1 On the Sea of Galilee   Vi unissued
76281-1 Home by the Sea (1, 2, 3)   MW 7146, MW 7357, RCA CNV 103,
         CAM CAL 2473, RCA RA 5647, RCA LPT 3037
76704-1 Home by the Sea   Vi unissued
76282-1 When the Roses Come Again (1, 3)   RCA CNV 103, *CAM CAL 2473,
         RCA RA 5647*
76705-1 When the Roses Come Again   Vi unissued
76283-1 I Loved You Better Than You Knew (1, 2, 3)   Vi 23835, MW 7357,
         RCA RA 5647, ACM 22
76706-1 I Loved You Better Than You Knew   Vi unissued
76284-1 This Is Like Heaven to Me (1, 2, 3)   Vi 23845, MW 7358, *RCA RA
         5321, RCA RA 5513, RCA RA 5648, RCA LPM 2772*
76707-1 This Is Like Heaven to Me   Vi unissued
76285-1 See That My Grave Is Kept Clean (1, 3)   Vi 23835, Zo 4379, *ACM 8,
         RCA RA 5647*
76708-1 See That My Grave Is Kept Clean   Vi unissued
76286-1 Old Rugged Cross   Vi rejected
76709-1 Old Rugged Cross   Vi unissued
76287-1 Will the Circle Be Unbroken   Vi rejected
76710-1 Will the Circle Be Unbroken   Vi unissued
76288-1 Over the Garden Wall (1, 2, 3)   MW 7354, *RCA LPM 2772, RCA RA
         5647*
76711-1 Over the Garden Wall   Vi unissued
76289-1 Gold Watch and Chain (1, 3)   Vi 23281, MW 7354, *FM 33, RCA RA
         5648, ACM 22*
76712-1 Gold Watch and Chain   Vi unissued
76290-1 School House on the Hill (1, 2, 3)   RCA CNV 101, *CAM CAL 2473,
         RCA RA 5648*
76713-1 School House on the Hill   Vi unissued

Carter Family   49

76291-1	Will My Mother Know Me There (1, 2, 3) MW 7355, *RCA RA 5648, ACM 8*	
76714-1	Will My Mother Know Me There Vi unissued	
76292-1	Faded Flowers Vi unissued	
76715-1	Faded Flowers *RCA RA 5648*	
76293-1	Poor Little Orphaned Boy Vi unissued	
76716-1	Poor Little Orphaned Boy (1, 3) *CAM ACL1 0047, RCA DPS2046, RCA RA 5648*	

[One side of MW 7358 is labeled "See That My Grave Is Kept Clean," but no copy thus far traced actually plays 76285-1; the performance is actually "I Wouldn't Mind Dying" 59026-1]

Camden, New Jersey, 8 May 1934
As above
83129-1   Cowboy Jack (2, 3)   Bb 8167, MW 4545, *RCA LPM 2772, RCA RA 5321, RCA RA 5513, RAC RA 5648*
83130-1   I'll Be All Smiles Tonight (1, 2, 3)   Bb 5529, MW 4497, *CMH 107, RCA RA 5648, ACM 22*
83131-1   Away Out on the Old Saint Sabbath (1, 3)   Bb 5817, MW 4544, *CAM ACL1 0501, RCA DPS2046, RCA RA 5648*
83132-1   Cuban Soldier   Vi rejected
83133-1   Darling Little Joe (1, 3)   RCA CNV 102, *CAM CAL 2473, RCA RA 5648*
83134-1   Happy or Lonesome (1, 3)   Bb 5650, MW 4550, RZ G22470, *RCA RCX 7111, RCA RA 5648, ACM 22*
83135-1   One Little Word (1, 3)   Bb 5771, MW 4546, RZ G22482, *RCA RA 5648, ACM 22*
83136-1   Darling Daisies (3)   Bb 5586, MW 4496, MW 7146, RZ G22469, *RCA DPS2046, RCA RA 5648, ACM 22*
83137-1   East Virginia Blues #1 (2, 3)   Bb 5650, MW 4550, Vi 27494, *RCA LPV 507, RCA VRA 5005, RCA DPS2046, RCA RA 5648, ACM 22*
83138-1   What Does the Deep Sea Say   Vi rejected
83139-1   Lover's Return (1, 2, 3)   Bb 5586, MW 4496, MW 7147, RZ G22469, *OTC 6001, RCA RA 5648, RCA DPS2046, ACM 22*
83140-1   It'll Aggravate Your Soul (1)   Bb 5817, MW 4541, Zo 4541, *CMH 107, LBC 12, RCA RA 5648, TL CW 06, ACM 22*
83141-1   Hello Central, Give Me Heaven (3)   Bb 5529, MW 4497, *CAM CAS 2554, RCA DPS2046, RA 5649*
83142-1   I'm Working on a Building (1, 3)   Bb 5716, MW 4541, Zo 4541, *OTC 6001, RCA DPS2046, RCA RA 5649, ACM 8*
83143-1   You've Been Fooling Me, Baby (2, 3)   Bb 5771, MW 4548, RZ G22482, *RCA RA 5649, ACM 22*

Camden, New Jersey, 1 December 1934

As above

87020-1	Longing for Old Virginia (3)	Bb 5856, MW 5018, RZ G22596, *RCA LPM 2772, RCA RA 5649*
87021-1	March Winds Gonna Blow My Blues Away (1, 3)	Bb 5590, MW 4548, *RCA RA 5649, ACM 22*
87022-1	There'll Be Joy, Joy, Joy (1, 3)	Bb 5911, MW 4547, *CAM CAL 816, ACL1 0047, RCA RA 5339, RCA RA 5649, RCA DPS2046*
87023-1	Home in Tennessee (1, 3)	RCA CNV 104, *CAM CAL 2473, RCA RA 5649*
87024-1	Are You Tired of Me, My Darling (1, 3)	Bb 5956, MW 4546, RZ G22658, *CAM CDN 5111, RCA RA 5649*
87025-1	I Cannot Be Your Sweetheart (1, 3)	RCA CNV 104, *CAM CAL 2473, RCA RA 5649*
87026-1	My Heart's Tonight in Texas (1, 3)	Bb 5908, MW 4549, RZ G22501, *CAM CDN 5111, RCA RA 5649*
87027-1	Be Careful Boys	Vi rejected
87028-1	My Virginia Rose	Vi rejected
87029-1	There's No Hiding Place Down Here (1, 3)	Bb 5961, MW 4547, RZ G22567, *CAM CAS 2554, RCA DPS2046, RCA RA 5649*
87030-1	Cowboy's Wild Song to His Herd (3)	Bb 5908, MW 4549, RZ G22657, *CAM ACL1 0501, CAM CDN 5111, RCA RA 5649*
87031-1	A Lad from Old Virginia	Vi rejected
87032-1	Lonesome Day	Vi rejected
87033-1	Evening Bells Are Ringing (1, 2, 3)	Bb 5856, MW 5018, RZ G22596, *RCA LPM 2772, RCA RA 5321, RCA RA 5513, RCA RA 5649*
87034-1	Little Adobe Shack	Vi rejected
87035-1	Mountains of Tennessee (1, 2, 3)	Bb 5956, MW 4542, RZ G22658, *CAM ACL1 0501, CAM CDN 5111, RCA RA 5649*
87036-1	My Texas Girl	Vi rejected
87037-1	I'll Be Home Someday (1, 2, 3)	Bb 5911, MW 4543, *CAM CAL 2554, RCA RA 5650*
87038-1	Faded Coat of Blue (1, 2, 3)	Bb 5974, MW 4543, RZ G22656, *CMH 107, RCA RA 5650*
87039-1	Sailor Boy (1, 3)	Bb 5974, MW 4542, RZ G22656, *RCA RA 5650*

New York, New York, 5 May 1935

As above

17476-1	Glory to the Lamb (1, 2, 3)	Ba 33465, Me 13432, Or 8484, Pe 13155, Ro 5484, Cq 8529, Vo/OK 03027, Me 92043, Co 20268, Co 37669, *HA HL 7396*
17477-1	Behind These Stone Walls (1, 3)	ARC 6-03-51, Cq 8633, *HA HL 7422*

Carter Family

17478-1 Sinking in the Lonesome Sea   ARC unissued
17478-2 Sinking in the Lonesome Sea (1, 2, 3)   ARC 7-12-63, Cq 8644, Vo/OK 03160, Co 20333, Co 37756, *HA HL 7422, TL CW 06*

New York, New York, 6 May 1935

17471-1 He Took a White Rose from Her Hair   ARC unissued
17471-2 He Took a White Rose from Her Hair (1, 3)   BA 33462, Me 13429, Or 8481, Pe 13152, Ro 5481, Cq 8530, Me 92040, *HA HL 7344*
17472-1 Can the Circle Be Unbroken (Bye and Bye)   ARC unissued
17472-2 Can the Circle Be Unbroken (Bye and Bye) (1, 3)   Ba 33465, Me 13432, Or 8484, Pe 13155, Ro 5484, Cq 8529, Vo/OK 03027, Me 92043, Co 20268, Co 37669, *HA HL 7280, HA HS-11332, FM 33, SM P8 15640, TL CW 06*
17473-1 Let's Be Lovers Again   ARC unissued
17473-2 Let's Be Lovers Again (1, 2, 3)   ARC 35-09-23, Cq 8539, Vo/OK 04442, Me 92087
17474-1 Your Mother Still Prays (For You, Jack) (1, 3)   Ba 33462, Me 13429, Or 8481, Pe 13152, Ro 5481, Cq 8530, Me 92040
17475-1 Kissing Is a Crime (1, 3)   ARC 6-05-53, Cq 8643, *HA HL 7300, TL CW 06*

New York, New York, 7 May 1935
As above
17479-1 Don't Forget Me Little Darling (1, 3)   ARC 6-01-59, Cq 8636, Vo/OK 04390, Co 20235, Co 37636, *HA HL 7422*
17480-1 Sad and Lonesome Day   ARC unissued
17480-2 Sad and Lonesome Day (2, 3)   ARC 7-04-53, Cq 8735, *HA HL 7344*
17481-1 By the Touch of Her Hand   ARC unissued
17481-2 By the Touch of Her Hand (1, 3)   ARC 6-09-59, Cq 8644, *HA HL 7422*
17482-1 East Virginia Blues #2   ARC unissued
17482-2 East Virginia Blues #2 (1, 3)   Ba 33463, Me 13430, Or 8482, Pe 13153, Ro 5482, Cq 8535, Me 92041, *HA HL 7422, TL CW 06*
17483-1 My Old Virginia Home (1, 2, 3)   ARC 6-03-51, Cq 8633, *HA HL 7344*
17484-1 My Virginia Rose Is Blooming   ARC unissued
17484-2 My Virginia Rose Is Blooming (1, 2, 3)   ARC 7-02-58, Cq 8691, Cq 9663, Vo/OK 05475
17489-1 My Texas Girl   ARC unissued
17489-2 My Texas Girl (1, 2, 3)   ARC 6-09-59, Cq 8691, *HA HL 7344, TL CW 06*
17490-1 No Other's Bride I'll Be   ARC unissued
17490-2 No Other's Bride I'll Be (1,2, 3)   ARC 7-08-69, Cq 8733, *HA HL 7344*
17491-1 Gathering Flowers from the Hillside   ARC unissued

17491-2	Gathering Flowers from the Hillside (1, 3) ARC 6-01-59, Cq 8636, Vo/OK 04390, Co 20235, Co 37636, *HA HL 7280, HA HS 11332*
17492-1	Gospel Ship ARC unissued
17492-2	Gospel Ship (1, 3) ARC 6-07-56, Cq 8692, *HA HL 7280, HA HS 11332*
17493-1	Little Black Train (1, 3) ARC 7-07-62, Cq 8815, Vo/OK 03112, *HA HL 7396, RBF 19*

New York, New York, 8 May 1935
As above

17498-1	Keep on the Sunny Side (1, 2, 3) ARC 6-07-56, Cq 8692, *HA HL 7280, HA HS 11332*
17499-1	River of Jordan ARC unissued
17499-2	River of Jordan (1, 3) BA 33466, Me 13433, Or 8485, Pe 13156, Ro 5485, Cq 8541, Me 92044, *HA HL 7396, CMH 107*
17500-1	Lonesome Valley (1, 2, 3) ARC 7-07-62, Cq 8815, Vo/OK 03112, *HA HL 7280, HA HS 11332, RBF 19*
17501-1	God Gave Noah the Rainbow Sign (1, 2, 3) ARC 6-11-59, Cq 8693, *HA HL 7396*
17502-1	Single Girl, Married Girl (2) ARC 7-04-53, Cq 8733
17503-1	The Fate of Dewey Lee (1, 2, 3) Ba 33463, Me 13430, Or 8482, Pe 13153, Ro 5482, Cq 8535, Me 92041, *CMH 116*
17504-1	Wildwood Flower ARC unissued
17504-2	Wildwood Flower (1, 2, 3) ARC 5-11-65, Cq 8542, *Ha HL 7280, HA HS 11332, FM 33*

New York, New York, 9 May 1935

17505-1	Sea of Galilee (1, 2, 3) Ba 33466, Me 13433, Or 8485, Pe 13156, Ro 5485, Cq 8541, Me 92044, *HA HL 7300*
17506-1	Don't Forget This Song (1, 3) ARC 7-01-54, Cq 8734, *CMH 107*
17507-1	My Clinch Mountain Home (1, 2, 3) ARC 7-08-69, Cq 8806, *FM 33, HA HL 7280, HA HS 11332*
17508-1	The Storms Are on the Ocean ARC unissued
17508-2	The Storms Are on the Ocean (1, 2, 3) ARC 7-12-63, Cq 8806, Vo/OK 03160, Co 20333, Co 37756, *HA HL 7396*
17509-1	Will You Miss Me When I'm Gone (1, 2, 3) Ba 33464, Me 13431, Or 8483, Pe 13154, Ro 5483, Cq 8540, Vo/OK 02990, Me 92042, *HA HL 7280*
17510-1	Broken Hearted Lover (1, 2, 3) Ba 33464, Me 13431, Or 8483, Pe 13154, Ro 5483, Cq 8540, Vo/OK 02990, Me 92042, *HA HL 7344*

New York, New York, 10 May 1935
As above

17519-1	Little Darling, Pal of Mine (1, 3) ARC 5-11-65, Cq 8542, *HA HL 7280, HA HS 11332*

Carter Family

17520-1	The Homestead on the Farm ARC unissued
17520-2	The Homestead on the Farm (2) ARC 7-02-58, Cq 8735, Cq 9663, Vo/OK 05475, Pe 16-101
17521-1	Cannon Ball Blues ARC unissued
17521-2	Cannon Ball Blues (1, 2, 3) ARC 7-05-55, Cq 8816, *HA HL 7422*
17522-1	Meet Me by Moonlight Alone ARC unissued
17522-2	Meet Me by Moonlight Alone (1, 2, 3) ARC 7-01-54, Cq 8734
17523-1	On the Rock Where Moses Stood ARC unissued
17523-2	On the Rock Where Moses Stood (1, 2, 3) ARC 6-11-59, Cq 8693, *HA HL 7396*
17524-1	Lula Walls ARC unissued
17524-2	Lula Walls (1, 2, 3) ARC 6-05-53, Cq 8643, *HA HL 7280, HA HS 11332*
17525-1	I'm Thinking Tonight of My Blue Eyes ARC unissued
17525-2	I'm Thinking Tonight of My Blue Eyes (1, 2, 3) ARC 35- 09-23, Cq 8539, Vo/OK 04442, Me 92087, *HA HL 7422*
17526-1	Worried Man Blues ARC unissued
17526-2	Worried Man Blues (1, 2, 3) ARC 7-05-55, Cq 8816, *HA HL 7280, HA HS 11332*

[Reverse Pe 16-101 by Roy Acuff]

New York, New York, 8 June 1936

As above

61128-A	My Dixie Darling (1, 3) De 5240, De 46086, MW 8000, Me 45229, De X1206, *AH AH58, DE ED 2788, DE DL 4404, DE DL 74404, TL CW 06, ST 3022*
61129-A	Give Me Your Love and I'll Give You Mine De unissued
61229-B	Give Me Your Love and I'll Give You Mine (1, 3) De 5318, MW 8001, Br SA1136, *CMH 112*
61130-A	Are You Lonesome Tonight De 5240, De X1206, MW 8000, Me 45229, Br SA1138, *CMH 112*
61131-A	The Last Move for Me De unissued
61131-B	The Last Move for Me (1, 3) De 5386, MW 8002, *CMH 112*
61132-A	The Wayworn Traveller (1, 3) De 5359, MW 8003, *DE ED 2788, DE DL 4404, DE DL 74404, AH AH58, ST 3022*
61133-A	Just Another Broken Heart (1, 3) De 5254, MW 8004, Me 45230, De X1223, *DE DL 4557, AH AH112*
61134-A	When Silver Threads Are Gold Again (1, 3) De 5304, De X1353, MW 8005, Me 45230, *CMH 112*
61135-A	There's No One Like Mother to Me (1, 3) De 5242, De X1325, De FM5139, Me 45231, *MCA VIM 4012*
61136-A	In a Little Village Churchyard De unissued
61136-B	In a Little Village Churchyard (1, 3) De 5386, MW 8002, Br SA1138, *CMH 112*

61137-A	Jealous Hearted Me (2, 3)	De 5241, De 46005, MW 8007, Me 45231, *DE ED 2788, DE DL 4404, DE DL 74404, AH 58, TL CW 06, ST 3022*
61138-A	My Native Home (2, 3)	De 5241, MW 8007, Me 45260, *DE DL 4557, AH AH112*
61139-A	Sweet Heaven in My View	De unissued
61339-B	Sweet Heaven in My View (2, 3)	De 5318, MW 8001, *DE ED 2788, DE DL 4404, DE DL 74404, AH 58, ST 3002*

New York, New York, 9 June 1936

As above

61140-A	No Depression (In Heaven)	De unissued
61140-B	No Depression (In Heaven) (1, 2, 3)	De 5242, MW 8006, Me 45260, *AH 112, DE DL 4557*
61141-A	Bonnie Blue Eyes (1, 2, 3)	De 5304, MW 8005, De X1353, Me 45258, *CMH 112*
61142-A	My Honey Lou (1, 3)	De 5263, MW 8008, Me 45258, *CMH 112*
61143-A	In the Shadow of the Pine (1, 2, 3)	De 5359, MW 8003, *CMH 112, MCA VIM 4012*
61144-A	Answer to Weeping Willow	De 5254, De X1223, Me 45232, Br SA1136, MW 8004, *MCA VIM 4012*
61145-A	You've Been a Friend to Me (1, 3)	De 5283, De X1325, MW 8009, Br SA1139, *DE DL 4404, DE DL 74404, AH 58, TL CW 06, ST 3022*
61146-A	Where the Silvery Colorado Wends Its Way (1, 2, 3)	De 5263, De X1265, MW 8008, Me 45232, *CMH 112*
61147-A	Lay My Head beneath the Rose (2, 3)	De 5283, De 46005, Br SA1139, Me 45232, *CMH 112*

New York, New York, 17 June 1937

As above

62280-A	The Broken Down Tramp (1, 3)	De 5518, Me 45255, Cor 64019, *CMH 112*
62881-A and -B	Lover's Lane	De unissued
62881-C	Lover's Lane (3)	De 5430, MW 8023, *MCA VIM 4012*
62882-A	Hold Fast to the Right (1, 3)	De 5494, MW 8028, Me 45247, Min 14085
62882-B	Hold Fast to the Right	De unissued
62883-A	Lord I'm in Your Care (1, 3)	De 5494, MW 8028, Me 45247, Min 14085, *CMH 112*
62283-B	Lord I'm in Your Care	De unissued
62290-A and -B	Funny When You Feel That Way	De unissued

Carter Family 55

62290-C	Funny When You Feel That Way (1, 2, 3) De 5411, MW 8022, *DE DL 4404, DE DL 74404, AH 58, ST 3022*
62291-A and -B	In the Shadow of Clinch Mountain De unissued
62291-C	In the Shadow of Clinch Mountain (1, 2, 3) De 5430, MW 8023, *MCA VIM 4012*
62292-A	Hello Stranger De unissued
62292-B	Hello Stranger (2, 3) De 5479, MW 8027, Me 45250, *DE DL 4404, DE DL 74404, AH 58, FM 33, TL CW 06, ST 3022*
62293-A	Never Let the Devil Get the Upper Hand of You De unissued
62293-B	Never Let the Devil Get the Upper Hand of You (1, 2, 3) De 5479, MW 8027, Me 45250, *DE DL 4557, AH 112*
62294-A	When This Evening Sun Goes Down (2, 3) De 5467, MW 8026, Me 45251, *MCA VIM 4012*
62295-A	Jim Blake's Message (1, 2, 3) De 5467, MW 8026, Me 45251, De FM5134, *DE DL 4557, AH 112*
62296-A	Honey in the Rock De unissued
62296-B	Honey in the Rock (1, 2, 3) De 5452, MW 8024, Cor 64019, *CMH 112*
62297-A	Look How This World Has Made a Change (1, 2, 3) De 5451, MW 8024, *MCA VIM 4012*

New York, New York, 18 June 1937
As above

62288-A	Little Girl That Played upon My Knee De unissued
62288-B	Little Girl That Played upon My Knee (1, 2, 3) De 5677, Me 45310, *MCA VIM 4012*
62289-A	You Better Let That Liar Alone De unissued
62289-B	You Better Let That Liar Alone (1, 2, 3) De 5518, Me 45255, *DE DL 4457, AH 112*
62298-A	Farewell Nellie De unissued
62298-B	Farewell Nellie (1, 2, 3) De 5677, Me 45310, *MCA VIM 4012*
62299-A and -B	The Only Girl I Ever Cared About De unissued
62299-C	The Only Girl I Ever Cared About (1, 2, 3) De 5411, MW 8022, *CMH 112*
62300-A	Goodbye to the Plains (1, 3) De 5532, De X2184, De FM5135, Me 45265, *CMH 112*
62301-A	My Home's across the Blue Ridge Mountains (1, 2, 3) De 5532, De X2184, De FM5135, Me 45265, *AH 112, DE DL 4557*
62302-A	Dark Haired True Lover De unissued
62302-B	Dark Haired True Lover (1, 2, 3) De 5447, MW 8025, *MCA VIM 4012*
62303-A	He Never Came Back De unissued

62303-B   He Never Came Back (1, 2, 3)   De 5447, MW 8025, *MCA VIM 4012, TL CW 06*

New York, New York, 8 June 1938
As above
64086-A   Happy in Prison (1, 3)   De 5779, MW 8066, Me 45281, *CMH 112*
64087-A   Walking in the King's Highway (1, 3)   De 5579, MW 8066, Me 45281, *DE DL 4557, AH 112*
64088-A   St. Regious Girl (3)   De 5649, MW 8067, De FM 5133, *DE DL 4557, AH 112*
64089-A   Just a Few More Days (1, 3)   De 5632, MW 8068, Me 45292, *MCA VIM 4012*
64090-A   Bring Back My Boy (1, 3)   De 5649, MW 8067, De FM 5133, *DE DL 4557, AH 112, CMH 107*
64091-A   It Is Better Farther On (1, 3)   De 5692
64092-A   Charlie and Nellie (3)   DE 5702
64093-A   Cuban Soldier (1, 3)   De 5662, MW 8069, *DE DL 4557, AH 112*
64094-A   Heart That Was Broken for Me (1, 2, 3)   De 5662, MW 8069
64095-A   You're Nothing More to Me (3)   De 5722
64096-A   Stern Old Bachelor (3)   De 5565, MW 8070, Me 45283, *DE DL 4404, AH 58, DE DL 74404, ST 3022*
64097-A   Little Joe (1, 3)   De 5632, MW 8068, Me 45292, *DE DL 4404, AH 58, DE DL 74404, ST 3022*
64098-A   Reckless Motorman (2, 3)   De 5722, *DE DL 4557, AH 112*
64099-A   You Denied Your Love (2, 3)   De 5702, *BR OE9168*
64100-A   Oh Take Me Back (2, 3)   De 5565, MW 8070, Me 45283, *DE DL 4404, AH 58, DE DL 74404, ST 3022*
64101-A   You Are My Flower (2, 3)   De 5692, *DE DL 4404, DE DL 74404, AH 58, BR OE9168, ST 3022*
64102-A   Who's That Knocking at My Window (2, 3)   De 5612, MW 8071, Me 45275, *MCA VIM 4012*
64103-A   They Call Her Mother (2, 3)   De 5596, MW 8072, Me 45280
64104-A   Coal Miner's Blues (2, 3)   De 5596, De 46086, MW 8072, Me 45280, *BR OE9168, DE DL 4404, DE DL 74404, AH 58, ST 3022*
64105-A   Young Freeda Bolt (2, 3)   De 5612, MW 8071, De FM 5134, Me 45275

Chicago, Illinois, 3 October 1940
As above
C-3349-1   Little Poplar Log House on the Hill (1, 3)   OK 06078, Cq 9568, Co 20253, Co 37654, *HA HL 7344*
C-3350-1   The Dying Mother (1, 3)   Cq 9569, *HA HL 7300*
C-3351-1   Buddies in the Saddle (1, 3)   Cq 9570, *HA HL 7300*
C-3352-1   Heaven's Radio (1, 3)   OK 05931, Cq 9666, *HA HL 7300*

Carter Family 57

C-3353-1   Beautiful Home (1, 3)   Cq 9568, *HA HL 7396*
C-3354-1   There'll Be No Distinction There (1, 3)   OK 05982, Cq 9572, *HA HL 7396*
C-3355-1   Give Him One More as He Goes (2, 3)   Cq 9664, *HA HL 7300*
C-3356-1   Lonesome for You Darling (2, 3)   OK 05843, Cq 9575, *HA HL 7422*
C-3357-1   Blackie's Gunman (2, 3)   OK 06313, Cq 9570, *TL CW 06*

Chicago, Illinois, 4 October 1940
As above
C-3358-1   You've Got to Righten the Wrong   OK 05982, Cq 9867, *TL CW 06*
C-3359-1   Meeting in the Air (2, 3)   OK 05931, Cq 9666, *HA HL 7300*
C-3360-1   My Home among the Hills (2, 3)   OK 06078, Cq 9867, Co 20253, Co 37654, *HA HL 7344, TL CW 06*
C-3361-1   Black Jack David (2, 3)   OK 06313, Cq 9574, *HA HL 7422, TL CW 06*
C-3362-1   Look Away from the Ocean (2, 3)   OK 06030, Cq 9572, Cq 9665, *HA HL 7396*
C-3363-1   We Shall Rise (1, 3)   OK 06030, Cq 9664, *HA HL 7344*
C-3364-1   I Found You among the Roses (1, 2)   Cq 9575, *HA HL 7300*
C-3365-1   Bear Creek Blues   Cq 9574, *HA HL 7300, TL CW 06, BRI 008*
C-3366-1   I'll Never Forsake You (3)   OK 05843, Cq 9569, *HA HL 7344*
C-3367-1   Beautiful Isle o'er the Sea (3)   Pe 12-102, *HA HL 7396, TL CW 06*
C-3368-1   It's a Long Long Road to Travel Along (2, 3)   Cq 9665, *HA HL 7300*
[Reverse of Pe 16-102 by the Coon Creek Girls]

New York, New York, 14 October 1941
As above
066780-1   Why Do You Cry Little Darling (2, 3)   Bb 33-0502, *CAM CDN 5111, RCA RA 5650*
066781-1   You Tied a Love Knot in My Heart (2, 3)   RCA CNV 105, *CAM CAL 2473, RCA RA 5650*
066782-1   Lonesome Homesick Blues (3)   Bb 33-0502, *CAM CDN 5111, RCA RA 5650, RCA CPM1 2763*
066783-1   Wabash Cannonball   Vi rejected, *RCA CMP1 2763*
067991-1   Dark and Stormy Weather (1, 2, 3)   Bb 8868, *RCA RA 5650*
067992-1   In the Valley of the Shenandoah   Bb 8868, *RCA DPS2046, RCA RA 5650*
067993-1   Girl on the Greenbriar Shore (3)   Bb 8947, *RCA RA 5650*
067994-1   Something Got a Hold of Me (1, 2)   Bb 8947, *RCA DPS2046, RCA RA 5650, ACM 8*
067995-1   Fifty Miles of Elbow Room (1, 3)   Bb 9026, *CAM ACL1 0501, RCA RA 5650*
067996-1   Keep on the Firing Line (1, 3)   Bb 9026, *CAM ACL1 0047, RCA RA 5650*

067997-1   Waves on the Sea (1, 3)   Bb 33-0512, *RCA DPS2046, RCA RA 5650*
067998-1   Rambling Boy (1, 2, 3)   Bb 33-0512, *RCA RA 5389, RCA RA 5650, RCA DPS2046*
067999-1   You're Gonna Be Sorry You Let Me Down (1, 2, 3)   RCA CNV 105, *CAM CAL 2473, RCA RA 5650*

Bibliography: John Atkins, ed., "The Carter Family," *Old Time Music Booklet 1* (London: Old Time Music, 1973); John Atkins, brochure notes to "The Carter Family on Border Radio," JEMF 101; John Atkins, "The Carter Family," in Bill Malone and Judith McCulloh, eds., *Stars of Country Music* (Urbana: Univ. of Illinois Press, 1975), pp. 95-121; Archie Green, "The Carter Family's 'Coal Miner's Blues,' " *Southern Folklore Quarterly* 25 (December 1961): 226-37.

Harry Carter

A pseudonym on Supertone for Byrd Moore and on Superior for Byrd Moore and Melvin Robinette.

Oscar Carver

A pseudonym on Conqueror for Byrd Moore.

Chumber's Breakdown Gang

A pseudonym on QRS for the Highlanders.

Clark and Howell

A pseudonym on Supertone for Byrd Moore and Melvin Robinette.

Clark Brothers

A pseudonym on Champion for the Sweet Brothers.

John Clark

A pseudonym on Champion for Herbert Sweet.

Conley and Logan

A pseudonym on Challenge for Walter "Kid" Smith.

Dinwiddie Colored Quartet (ca. 1898–ca. 1904)

At the turn of the century, the Dinwiddie Colored Quartet sang to raise money in support of the John A. Dix Industrial School, Dinwiddie, Virginia. The group was formed by Charles B. Cheshire for the purpose of fundraising, and over a two-year period they helped bring several hundreds of thousands of dollars into the school's coffers. Following Cheshire's death in about 1902, the singers continued to perform on the vaudeville stage before disbanding in 1904. The Dinwiddie Colored Quartet was the second black folk group in the entire country to record for a commercial record company. The first was the Standard Quartette, which had recorded some six years earlier for Columbia.

New York, New York, 29 October 1902
Dinwiddie Colored Quartet: possibly Sterling Rex, first tenor voice; J. Clarence Meredith, second tenor voice; Harry B. Cruder, first bass voice; J. Marshall Thomas, second bass voice

1714-	Down on the Old Camp Ground	Vi 1714, Monarch 1714, *LBC 1*
1715-	Poor Mourner	Vi 1715
1716-	Steal Away	Vi 1716

New York, New York, 31 October 1902
As above
1724-	My Way Is Cloudy	Vi 1724
1725-1	Gabriel's Trumpet	Vi 1725, Monarch, 1725, *VJM VLP 2*
1726-	We'll Anchor Bye-and-Bye	Vi 1726

[These 78s are single-sided releases]

Bibliography: Kip Lornell, *"Happy in the Service of the Lord": Afro-American Gospel Quartets in Memphis, Tennessee* (Urbana: Univ. of Illinois Press, 1988), p. 15.

Dixie Mountaineers

See Ernest V. Stoneman.

Down South Boys

A pseudonym on Varsity for the Norfolk Jubilee Quartet.

Eckford Dunford (ca. 1880–ca. 1950)

"Uncle Eck" Dunford was a fiddle player, guitarist, raconteur, and amateur photographer who lived in Galax, Virginia. During the mid-to-late 1920s he performed with Ernest V. Stoneman and his Dixie Mountaineers. Dunford participated in several recording sessions with Stoneman for Victor. Because of his close affiliation with Stoneman and the small number of selections actually issued under Dunford's own name, these recordings are listed under Stoneman's entry.

See also Ernest V. Stoneman.

Dykes Magic City Trio (ca. 1925–1933)

Formed in the middle 1920s by John Dykes, this group performed for many social functions in and around Scott County for about seven years. Dykes Magic City Trio was founded around the fiddling of John Dykes, who was born about 1880. The autoharp of Myrtle Vermillion and G.H. "Hub" Mahaffey's guitar and singing provided a nice foil for this low-key group.

John Dykes himself was living in Kingsport, Tennessee, during the 1920s. This was a boom period for Kingsport, which seemed to grow like magic—hence the city's nickname and the group's name. Mrs. Vermillion was born in 1901 in Scott County, Virginia, not far from Gate City. She came from a very musical family, was a cousin of Sara Addington Carter, and learned to play the autoharp in her teens. Mahaffey is supposed to have been born and raised in Norton, Virginia (Wise County).

The group came together to entertain their neighbors. At some point John Dykes had played with Dock Boggs around Norton, Virginia, which is how the band came to record. When Brunswick auditioned musicians in Ashland, Kentucky, in March 1927, Boggs suggested that Dykes' group try out. Brunswick liked their sound, and the entire group took the train to New York City to record.

Following the recording session, they stayed together for several years. The main reason that the group broke up was that Mrs. Vermillion was starting a family, so that she was simply not able to devote as much time to music and gradually moved away from playing. Some of her children learned to play music, too, and have continued to play since her death in the middle 1960s. It is unclear what happened to Dykes, though he apparently died in the late 1940s. Hub Mahaffey continued to play music for many years and died in Bluff City, Tennessee, about 1984.

New York, New York, 9 March 1927

Dykes Magic City Trio: John Dykes, fiddle; Myrtle Vermillion, autoharp; Hub Mahaffey, guitar/vocal

E21803/4	Frankie	Br 127, Vo 5143, *OH 191*
E21805/6	Poor Ellen Smith	Br 127, Vo 5143, *OH 191*
E21807/8	Cotton Eyed Joe	Br 120, *OH 191*
E21809/10	Twilight Is Stealing	Br 130, *OH 191*

New York, New York, 10 March 1927

As above

E21831/2	Tennessee Girls	Br 120, *OH 191*
E21833/4	Huckleberry Blues	Br 129, *OH 191*
E21835/6	Free Little Bird	Br 129, *CY 503*, *OH 191*

Dykes Magic City Trio, circa March 1927. John Dykes (fiddle), Myrtle Vermillion (autoharp), Hub Mahaffey (guitar). *Courtesy Blue Ridge Heritage Archive/Cleo McNutt*

E21837/8   Shortening Bread   Br 125, *OH 191*
E21839/40   Ida Red   BR 125, *OH 191*
E21841/2   Callahan's Reel   Vo 5181, *OH 191*
E21843/4   Red Steer   Vo 5181, *OH 191*

New York, New York, 11 March 1927
As above
E21845/6/7   Golden Slippers   Br 128
E21848/9   Hook and Line   Br 128
E21850/1/2   Far Beyond the Blue Sky   Br 130
[Br 130 includes a vocal trio, presumably by the three musicians.]

Bibliography: Tony Russell, "Dykes Magic City Trio," *Old Time Music* 29 (Summer 1978): 18-19; Charles Wolfe, "Dykes Magic City Trio," *Old Time Herald* Vol. 1, 3 (Feb.-April 1988): 4-9; brochure notes to "Dykes Magic City Trio," *OH 191*.

Excelsior Quartet (ca. 1920–ca. 1932)

This group was apparently community-based at its inception, but during the early 1920s the Excelsior Quartet moved into the commercial ranks. According to the May 27, 1922, issue of the *Norfolk Journal and Guide*, it was touring the mid-Atlantic states with the black blues and vaudeville singer Mamie Smith, as part of her stage company. It is quite possible that their recordings were the result of this theater work. Nothing more concrete is known about the Excelsior Quartet beyond the fact that they were performing together as late as 1932.

New York, New York, ca. 22 March 1922
Excelsior Quartet: James Brown, tenor voice; Theodore Lee, lead voice; Samuel Pierce, baritone voice; William Gibson, bass voice

70568-B   Kitchen Mechanic Blues   OK 4481, OK 8033
70569-B   Roll Them Bones   OK 8033
          Jelly Roll Blues   OK 4481
[Despite the listing of this session in *Blues and Gospel Records 1902-1943*, its existence is disputed by several discographers.]

New York, New York, ca. 25 March 1922
As above
7827   Jelly Roll Blues   Ge 4881, Str 9250, *SY 206*
7828   Kitchen Mechanic Blues   Ge 4881, Str 9250, *SY 206*

New York, New York, ca. 10 April 1922
As above
70600-A   Nobody Knows the Trouble I See   OK 4636

Excelsior Quartet, circa 1920. From left, James Brown, Willie Gibson, Theodore Lee; seated, Samuel Pierce. *Courtesy Norfolk Journal & Guide*

70601-A	Going Up to Live with God (Golden Slipper) [sic]	OK 4619
70602-C	Walk in Jerusalem Just Like John	OK 4619
70608-B	I Am the King of the Sea	OK 4701
70611-B	Good Lord, I Done Done	OK 4701
70612-A	Sinners Crying, Come Here Lord	OK 4636
70613-A	Over the Green Hill	OK 8035
70614-A	Down by the Old Mill Stream	OK 8035
	Goodbye, My Coney Island Baby	OK 8038
	If Hearts Win Tonight, You Lose	OK 8038

New York, New York, ca. May 1922
Excelsior Norfolk Quartette: as above

        Coney Island Babe   Bs 2060, Pm 12131
        Jelly Roll Blues   Bs 2060, Pm 12131

Bibliography: Vaughan Webb, Brochure notes to "Hampton Roads Quartet Tradition," BRI 009.

Fletcher and Higgins

A pseudonym on Clarion and Velvet Tone for Roy Harvey and Earl Shirkey.

Floyd County Ramblers (1926–1931)

Based in Floyd County, Virginia, in the late 1920s, this group consisted of friends and neighbors living in the Check/Bent Mountain community. They had known one another and played together for several years, including performances over Roanoke radio station WDBJ, when the community was shocked by the brutal murder of Freeda Bolt on December 17, 1929. Bolt was killed on Bent Mountain by Buren Harmon, and the grisly crime inspired a ballad that the Floyd County Ramblers played over WDBJ.

    This song brought them to the attention of the Victor Record Company, which invited them to New York City to record "The Murder of Freeda Bolt" and several other tunes. Their record of this tragedy sold well locally and is still treasured by Floyd County residents.

    Unfortunately, the Depression had all but knocked out the record industry and the Floyd County Ramblers never recorded again. Its members remained in the area and often played together over the years, though not on a regular basis. Sam McNeil remained the most musically active of the group, teaching most of his children to play some stringed instrument. The last surviving member of the Floyd County Ramblers, Walter Boone, still lives in Salem, Virginia.

The Four Virginians 65

New York, New York, 29 August 1930
Floyd County Ramblers: Sam McNeil, banjo; John Willie Boone, guitar/tenor vocal (1); Walter Boone, harmonica/lead vocal (2); Banks McNeil, fiddle

63610-3	The Story of Freeda Bolt (1, 2)	Vi 40307, *BRI 004*
63611-2	Step Stone (1, 2)	Vi 40331, Bb 5107, E1 2023, Sr 3190
63612-2	Ragtime Annie	Vi 23759, TT 1561
63613-2	Sunny Tennessee (1, 2)	Vi 40307, *CY 502*
63614-2	Granny, Will Your Dog Bite?	Vi 23759, TT 1561, *CY 531*
63615-2	Aunt Dinah's Quilting Party (1, 2)	Vi 40331, Bb 5107, E1 2023, Sr 3190

[TT 1561 issued as by the Virginia Ramblers]

Bibliography: Doug DeNatale, brochure notes to "Native Virginia Ballads," BRI 004, pp. 13, 14.

David Foley
A pseudonym on Challenge for G.B. Grayson and Henry Whitter.

The Four Virginians (1925–ca. 1935)
This string band was based in Pittsylvania County and consisted of Richard Bigger (fiddle), Elvin Bigger (guitar), Fred Richards (guitar), and Leonard Jennings (tiple). Each man worked at one of the local textile mills and played music as a sideline. The band was formed in 1925 and played for programs in theaters, dances, and other community occasions.

After two years of playing together the group was inspired by the success of Charlie Poole to try to make recordings. On impulse the group traveled to Camden, New Jersey, to audition for Victor, which did not greet them warmly. They continued to New York City only to find that OKeh records was about to hold a recording session in Winston-Salem, North Carolina, in September 1927.

The group successfully auditioned for OKeh and made six sides while in Winston-Salem. The group's recordings sold in modest numbers, and they were not invited by OKeh to record again. The Four Virginians did remain together, however, through the middle 1930s.

Of the group members, only Fred Richards' whereabouts are unknown. Elvin Bigger passed away in 1969, followed by Leonard Jennings (ca. 1982). Richard Bigger is still an active fiddler and lives in Pittsylvania County.

Winston-Salem, North Carolina, 21 September 1927
Four Virginians: Richard Bigger, fiddle; Leonard Jennings, tiple; Elvin Bigger, guitar/vocal (1); Fred Richards, guitar

The Four Virginians in 1927. Standing, Richard Bigger and Fred Richards; seated, Leonard Jennings and Elvin Bigger. *Courtesy Kinney Rorrer*

Golden Crown Quartet

81367-A	Swing Your Partner	OK 45181
81368-A	Promenade All	OK 45201
81369-B	New Coon in Town	OK 45181
81370-	Chasing Squirrels	OK unissued
81371-B	One Is My Mother (1)	OK 45163
81372-A	Two Little Lads (1)	OK 45163

[Reverse of OK 45201 by the Scottsdale String Band]

Bibliography: Kinney Rorrer, "The Four Virginians," *Old Time Music* 14 (Autumn 1974): 18.
See also Elvin Bigger and Fred Richards.

Harry Gay
See Tarter and Gay

Norman Gayle
A pseudonym on Champion for G.B. Grayson and Henry Whitter.

Georgia Sacred Singers
A pseudonym on Herwin for the Norfolk Jubilee Quartet.

Gold Palm Quartet
A pseudonym on Velvet Tone, Diva, and Clarion for the Silver Leaf Quartet of Norfolk.

Golden Crown Quartet (1919–ca. 1955)
Formed in 1919 by singers from the Berkley section of Norfolk, Virginia, this quartet began its career as a representative of St. Mark's Church. It was organized by Deacon William White and was one of the first local groups to sing over radio station WTAR about 1925. During the late 1920s the Golden Crowns sang in churches throughout Tidewater. In 1929 they traveled to Richmond, Virginia, and were recorded by OKeh Records. The one released recording had little impact upon their career, which continued for at least another twenty-five years.

The Golden Crown Quartet struggled through the Depression and war years, benefiting from the tremendous surge of interest in quartets during the decade following 1945. In 1949 they recorded for the Score label and by 1950 they owned two cars that were used to travel to jobs. The Golden Crown Quartet also broadcast over WGH during this same period. As the interest in quartets declined, bookings diminished and by the mid-1950s the group had disbanded.

Richmond, Virginia, 13 October 1929
Golden Crown Quartet: James Holley, first tenor voice; Wilson Taylor, second tenor voice; Samuel Benton, baritone voice; Maynard Bennett, bass voice

403107-A	The Sign of Judgement	OK 8739
403108-B	I Love to Sing	OK unissued
403109-A	What Are They Doing in Heaven Today?	OK unissued
403113-A	Scandalize My Name	OK 8739

Bibliography: Vaughan Webb, brochure notes to "Hampton Roads Quartet Tradition" BRI 009.

Golden Gate Quartet (1934–Present)

Formed in the middle 1930s by four students at Norfolk, Virginia's Booker T. Washington High School, the Golden Gate Quartet is one of the best known and most enduring black gospel ensembles. Among its earliest members were Orlandus Wilson (bass), Henry Owen (tenor), Bill Langford (tenor), and Willie Johnson (baritone). The Golden Gates began as a mainstream black gospel quartet whose initial inspiration was the Mills Brothers, but their innovative arrangements soon caught the public's ear.

By 1935 the Golden Gate Quartet was singing over local radio stations and performing throughout Tidewater. They were synthesizing a new style of singing known as "jubilee," which soon proved popular. In late 1935 they began an engagement over WBT in Charlotte, North Carolina, a 50,000-watt station that reached much of the eastern United States. It was this extended radio program that brought them to the attention of Victor Records, which first brought the Golden Gate Quartet into its temporary studios in Charlotte's Pope Hotel in 1937.

After their initial recording session, the Golden Gate Quartet's career took wings. They began recording regularly and in December of 1938 appeared at John Hammond's famous "Spirituals to Swing" concert. This Carnegie Hall program introduced them to New York's high society. Eventually they made New York City their home base. In January 1941 the Golden Gate Quartet performed at Franklin D. Roosevelt's inauguration ceremony. They were also appearing daily over the CBS network radio and singing throughout the country.

World War II brought several important changes: the group switched to the OKeh label, and two group members, Willie Johnson and Orlandus Wilson, were drafted by the armed services. Immediately after the war, the entire black gospel quartet scene heated up and the Golden Gates were once more in the middle of it. They continued to record regularly for Columbia, Sittin' In With, Mercury, and Apollo, toured extensively, and appeared in several commercial films. The Golden Gate Quartet remained at the top of their field until the middle 1950s.

Golden Gate Quartet, circa 1937. Peg Ford (?), Henry Owen, Clyde Reddick (?), Willie Johnson. *Courtesy Ray Funk*

By 1955 the group had gone through numerous personnel changes and was faced with changing tastes in popular music. That year included the Golden Gates' first tour of Europe, which was wildly successful. They quickly shifted much of their attention to Europe and by 1959 the Golden Gate Quartet had moved their base of operation to Paris. The group is still headquartered in Paris and tours the Continent regularly. In recent years they have also appeared in Africa, but have not performed in the United States for many years. The only remaining early member of the Golden Gate Quartet is its current leader, Orlandus Wilson.

Charlotte, North Carolina, 4 August 1937
Golden Gate Jubilee Quartet: Willie Johnson, baritone voice; Henry Owen, tenor voice; William Langford, tenor voice; Orlandus Wilson, bass voice

011931-1	Golden Gate Gospel Train	Bb 7126, MW 7493, *RCA CL 42111*
011932-1	Gabriel Blows His Horn	Bb 7126, Vi 20-2921, *RCA CL 42111*
011933-1	Bedside of a Neighbor	Bb 7278, Vi 20-3308, MW 7441
011934-1	Jonah	Bb 7154, Vi 27322, Vi 20-2073, MW 7440
011935-1	Preacher and the Bear	Bb 7205, Vi 27322, *RCA CL 42111, JO 4043*
011936-1	Born Ten Thousand Years Ago	Bb 7205, *RCA CL 42111, JO 4043*
011937-1	Behold the Bridegroom Cometh	Bb 7154, Vi 20-3308, MW 7440
011938-1	Go Where I Send Thee	Bb 7340, Vi 20-2134, *RCA CL 42111, JO 4043*
011939-1	Won't That Be One Happy Time	Bb 7340
011940-1	Job	Bb 7376, Vi 27323, Vi 20-2134, *RCA CL 42111, JO 4043*
011941-1	Bonnett	Bb 7264, *RCA CL 42111*
011942-1	Massa's in the Cold, Cold Ground	Bb 7264, *RCA CL 42111, JO 4043*
011943-1	Stand in the Test of Judgement	Bb 7376, Vi 20-2797
011944-1	Found a Wonderful Savior	Bb 7278, MW 7441

Charlotte, North Carolina, 24 January 1938
As above

018622-1	Carolina in the Morning	Bb 7415
018623-1 and -2	Motherless Child	Bb 7463, MW 7496
018624-1	Travelin' Shoes	Bb 7463, Vi 20-2073, MW 7496, *RCA CL 42111*
018625-1	John, the Revelator	Bb 7631, Vi 27324, MW 7912, *RCA CL 42111, JO 4043*
018626-1	Remember Me	Bb 7564
018627-1 and -2	Pure Religion	Bb 7564, MW 7493
018628-1	Dipsy Doodle	Bb 7415, *RCA CL 42111, JO 4043*
018629-1	Swanee River	Bb 7676, RZ MR2867
018630-1 and -2	Lead Me On and On	Bb 7617, MW 7494, *RCA CL 42111, JO 4043*

Golden Gate Quartet

018631-1	Sweet Adeline	Bb 7676, RZ MR2867, *RCA CL 42111*
018632-1	Sampson	Bb 7513, Vi 27324, MW 7495, *RCA CL 42111*
018633-1 and -2	I Was Brave	Bb 7513, MW 7495
018634-1	Take Your Burden to God	Bb 7617, MW 7494, *RCA CL 42111*
018635-1 and -2	Ol' Man River	Bb 8190

[Reverse of Bb 7631 and MW 7912 by the Evening Four]

New York, New York, 10 August 1938

As above

023459-1	When They Ring the Golden Bells	Bb 7897, MW 7864, *RCA CL 42111, JO 4043*
023460-1	My Lord Is Writing	Bb 7804, MW 7596
023461-1	Rock My Soul	Bb 7804, Vi 20-2921, MW 7596
023462-2	Climbing Up	Bb unissued
023463-1	Bye and Bye Little Children	Bb 7848, MW 7594
023464-1	God Almighty Said	Bb 7848, MW 7594
023465-1	Let That Liar Alone	Bb 7835, MW 7595
023466-1	To the Rock	Bb 7835, MW 7595, *RCA CL 42111*
023467-1	Saints Go Marching In	Bb 7897, Vi 20-2797, MW 7864, *RCA CL 42111, JO 4043*
023468-1	When I Grow Too Old	Bb unissued
023469-1	Sweetheart	Bb unissued
023470-1	My Bonnie	Bb unissued
023471-1	Jingle Bells	Bb unissued
023472-1	Wait for Sunshine	Bb unissued

New York, New York, 15 November 1938

As above

028962-1	Cheer the Weary Traveler	Bb 8019, MW 7867
028963-1	I Heard Zion Moan	Bb 7962, MW 7865
028964-1	Noah	Bb 7962, MW 7865, *RCA CL 42111, JO 4043*
028965-1	Lord, Am I Born to Die?	Bb 7994, MW 7866
028966-1	What Are They Doing in Heaven Today?	Bb 7994, MW 7866
028967-1	Packing Up—Getting Ready to Go	Bb 8019, MW 7867, *RCA CL 42111*

Rock Hill, South Carolina, 2 February 1939

As above

031974-1	Troubles of the World	Bb 8087, MW 7868
031975-1	Lis'n to de Lambs	Bb 8123, MW 7869
031976-1	Dese Bones Gonna Rise Again	Bb 8123, MW 7869
031977-1	Everything Moves by the Grace of God	Bb 8087, MW 7868
031978-1	This World Is in a Bad Condition	Bb 8160, Vi 20-3159

031979-1	Precious Lord	Bb 8190
031980-1	Noah	Bb 8160, Vi 27323, *RCA CL 42111*
031918-1 and -2	Ol' Man Mose	Bb 10154, *RCA CL 42111*
031982-1	Change Partners	Bb 10154

Rock Hill, South Carolina, 6 October 1939
As above: add William Langford, guitar (1)

042900-1	What a Time	Bb 8286, MW 8774, *RCA CL 42111*
042901-1	Alone	Bb 8286, MW 8774
042902-1	He Said He Could Calm the Ocean	Bb 8328, MW 8776, *RCA CL 42111, JO 4043*
042903-1	Hide Me in Thy Bosom	Bb 8362, MW 8778, *RCA CL 42111*
042904-1	If I Had My Way	Bb 8306, MW 8775
042905-1	I Looked Down the Line and I Wondered	Bb 8348, Vi 20-3159, MW 8777, *RCA CL 42111, JO 4043*
042906-1	Way Down in Egypt Land	Bb 8306, MW 8775
042907-1	Our Father	Bb unissued, *CAM CAL 308, RCA CL 42111*
042908-1	You'd Better Mind	Bb 8348, MW 8777, *RCA CL 42111*
042909-1	I'm a Pilgrim	Bb 8392, MW 8778, *RCA CL 42111*
042910-1	Everytime I Feel the Spirit	Bb 8328, MW 8776, *RCA CL 42111, JO 4043*
042911-1	Whoa Babe	Bb 8579, MW 8779
042912-1	Stormy Weather (1)	Bb 8579, MW 8779, *RCA CL 42111*
042913-1	The Devil with the Devil	Bb 8594, MW 8780
042914-1	Julius Caesar	Bb 8594, MW 8780
042915-1	Timber	Bb 8620, MW 8781, *RCA CL 42111*
042916-1	Jonah in the Whale (1)	Bb 8620, MW 8781, *RCA CL 42111*

New York, New York, 24 December 1939
As above

	Gospel Train	*VA VRS8524, VA VSD48, VA JY504, FO TFL 5188, FO FJL402, TR 35065, CID SJ2, GJ J1249, JT J1249, VA VJD550, VX VST26340*
	I'm on My Way	*VA VRS8524, VA VSD48, VA VY504, FO TFL5188, CID SJ2, GJ J1249, JT J1249, VA VJD550, VX VST26340*

New York, New York, 26 December 1939
As above

046124-1	My Walking Stick (1)	Bb 8565, MW 8783
046125-1	Darling Nellie Gray (1)	Bb 8565, MW 8783
046126-1	Whats New? (1)	Bb 10569
046127-1	My Prayer	Bb 10569

Golden Gate Quartet

046128-1 What Did Jesus Say? Bb 8388, MW 8782
046129-1 The Valley of Time Bb 8388, MW 8782, *RCA CL 42111*

New York, New York, 18 April 1941

Golden Gate Quartet: omit William Langford; add Clyde Reddick, tenor voice; unknown drums

30282-1 Daniel Saw the Stone OK 6204
30283-2 Jezebel OK 6204, Co 37835
30284-1 Time's Winding Up OK 6238, Co 30044, Co 37477
30285- Nicodemus OK unissued

New York, New York, 25 May 1941

As above
30548-2 The Sun Didn't Shine OK 6345, Co 30043, Co 37476
30549-1 Blind Barnabas OK 6345, Co 30043, Co 37476, Co 37834
30550-2 Anyhow OK 6238, Co 30044, Co 37477
30551-1 Didn't It Rain OK 6529, Co 30042, Co 37475

New York, New York, 3 December 1941

As above: omit drums; add unknown guitarist (1)

31849-1 Toll the Bell Easy (1) Co 30160
31850-1 He Never Said a Mumbling Word OK 6529, Co 30042, Co 37475
31851-2 Moses Smote the Waters (1) Co 36937
31852- Handwriting on the Wall (1) OK unissued

New York, New York, 25 March 1942

As above
32620-1 Run On (1) OK 6713
32621- Sabbaths Have to End (1) OK unissued
32622-2 Dip Your Fingers in the Water (1) OK 6712
32623- My Time Done Come (1) OK unissued

New York, New York, 5 March 1943

As above
33183-1 Stalin Wasn't Stallin' OK 6712

New York, New York, 19 May 1943

As above
33216-1 Comin' In on a Wing and a Prayer OK 6713
33217- Hit the Road to Dreamland OK unissued

[Reverse of Co 30160, Co 36937, Co 37834, and Co 37835 are postwar recordings by this group]

Bibliography: Peter Grendysa, brochure notes to "The Golden Gate Quartet—35 Historic Recordings," RCA CL 42111; Vaughan Webb, brochure notes to "Hampton Roads Quartet Tradition," BRI 009.

Alex Gordon
A pseudonym on Conqueror for Frank Jenkins' Pilot Mountaineers—see Ernest V. Stoneman.

Grant Brothers (ca. 1924–mid 1930s)
Claude and Jack Grant were brothers born near Bristol, Tennessee, just after the turn of the century. Claude played the guitar and sang, while his brother picked the mandolin. By the early 1920s the Grants had joined the medicine show of Doc Pagett and were touring throughout eastern Tennessee.

Although the brothers joined Padgett's troupe as comedians, they also added a musical component to the daily shows. About 1924 the brothers formed the Tenneva Ramblers, a name derived from the diminution of Tennessee and Virginia. Along with fiddler Jack Pierce of Smyth County, Virginia, the Grants toured throughout southwestern Virginia playing music in vaudeville theaters and with several medicine shows. This basic trio was often augmented by Claude Slagle, a banjo player who owned a fleet of cabs in Bristol, Tennessee.

In 1927 the Tenneva Ramblers met Jimmie Rodgers in Asheville, North Carolina. Rodgers joined the group and accompanied them to Bristol in August 1927, where the Tenneva Ramblers made their first recordings and Rodgers made his solo debut. Before long Rodgers split from the group to pursue his own career.

By the early 1930s the Tenneva Ramblers were broadcasting regularly over Bristol radio station WOPI. They also performed in schools throughout the coal-mining areas of southwestern Virginia and the lower Shenandoah Valley between Bristol and Wytheville.

Throughout the 1930s and into the 1940s the Grants continued their entertainment career. They performed over radio stations such as WCYB in Bristol and Johnson City's WJHL and continued touring the theater circuit. By 1954, however, they stopped playing music full-time and moved on to other lines of work. Jack Grant died in 1968; while Claude lived in Bristol until his death in 1976.

Bristol, Tennessee, 4 August 1927
Tenneva Ramblers: Claude Grant, guitar/vocal; Jack Grant, mandolin; Jack Pierce, fiddle; Claude Slagle, banjo (1)

The Grant Brothers and Jimmie Rodgers, photographed in Asheville, North Carolina, May 1927. From left, Jack Grant, Jimmie Rodgers, Jack Pierce, Claude Grant. *Photo from personal collection of Claude Grant, Archive of Appalachia, East Tennessee State University*

39770-2   The Longest Train I Ever Saw (1)   Vi 20861, *PU 3001, CMF-011-L*
39771-2   Sweet Heaven, When I Die (1)   Vi 20861, *PU 3001*
39772-2   Miss Liza, Poor Gal   Vi 21141, *PU 3001*
[Reverse of Vi 21141 by the Bull Mountain Moonshiners]

Atlanta, Georgia, 18 February 1928
As above
41908-2   Darling, Where Have You Been So Long? (1)   Vi 21645, *PU 3001*
41909-2   If I Die a Railroad Man (1)   Vi 21406, *PU 3001, RCA LPV 532*
41910-2   I'm Goin' to Georgia (1)   Vi 21645, *PU 3001*
41911-2   The Curtain of Night   Vi 21289, *PU 3001*
41912-2   The Lonely Grave   Vi 21289, *PU 3001*
41913-2   Seven Long Years in Prison (1)   Vi 21406, *PU 3001, RCA LPV 548*

Johnson City, Tennessee, 15 October 1928
Grant Brothers and Their Music: presumably as above

147178-1   When a Man Is Married   Co 15322
147179-1   Goodbye, My Honey, I'm Gone   Co 15460
147180-2   Tell It to Me   Co 15322, *RO 1033*
147181-2   Johnson Boys   Co 15460
[Add vocal chorus on 147180]

Bibliography: David Samuelson, brochure notes to "The Tenneva Ramblers—Great Original Recordings 1927-28," PU 3001.

See also Smyth County Ramblers.

G.B. Grayson (ca. 1900–1930)
See Henry Whitter.

Hall Family (late 1920s)
This family group was from Orange County, Virginia, and performed over WRVA, Richmond's 50,000-watt station, between about 1927 and 1930. Two members of the family, possibly the parents, played guitar and mandolin, while the youngest daughter, Marjorie, sang. Their lone OKeh recording session came about because of their radio work.

Richmond, Virginia, 17 October 1929
Hall Family: Marjorie Hall, vocal; unknown guitar and mandolin

403165-A   Little Stranger   OK unissued
403166-B   Molly Bland   OK unissued

Roy Hall (1935-1943) and Jay Hugh Hall (1935-1950)

Both Roy Hall (born January 6, 1907) and his brother Jay Hugh (born November 13, 1910) were reared in Haywood County, North Carolina. They began playing guitars in their early teens and, like many of their contemporaries, spent time working in textile mills. Their hope was to make music a full-time career, a dream they pursued by playing throughout western North Carolina during the Depression.

By April 1937 they had left the mills to work as the Hall Brothers on radio station WSPA in Spartanburg, South Carolina. On WSPA they played with other Carolina-based artists such as Clyde Moody and Wade Mainer, who were also pursuing radio and live performance dates. The Halls were very much influenced by similar performers, especially the Delmore Brothers.

By mid-1938 Roy and Jay Hugh were no longer a regular team, and Roy formed the first edition of his Blue Ridge Entertainers. He stayed in Spartanburg briefly before moving on to WWNC in Asheville and WBIG in Greensboro. Roy Hall's peripatetic life style soon brought the group to WAIR in Winston-Salem, where they settled into a regular half-hour daily program and built up a substantial local following.

Late in 1939 the group made a permanent move to Roanoke in order to broadcast over WDBJ on shows sponsored by Dr. Pepper. They made innumerable live appearances as well as performing twice daily over WDBJ. Hall also started the "Blue Ridge Jamboree," a Saturday night stage show featuring some of the biggest names in American country music. The group was so popular that they often broke up into two separate units; one led by Roy, the other under the command of Jay Hugh, who rejoined his brother in the fall of 1940.

The Halls were at the height of their popularity when Roy was tragically killed in a car accident on May 16, 1943. World War II had already taken several band members into the armed services, and Roy's death brought an end to the Blue Ridge Entertainers. Jay Hugh remained in music until 1950 and lived in Roanoke until his death in April 1974.

Charlotte, North Carolina, 16 February 1937
Hall Brothers: Roy Hall, guitar/vocal; Jay Hugh Hall, guitar/vocal

BS-07039	When It Gets Dark	Bb 6925, MW 7236
BS-07040	McDowell Blues	Bb 7363, MW 7238
BS-07041	Whistle Honey Whistle	Bb 6925, MW 7236
BS-07042	Never Alone	Bb 7801, MW 7239
BS-07043	Spartanburg Jail	Bb 7363, MW 7238
BS-07044	Hitch Hike Blues	Bb 7801, MW 7239
BS-07045	Little Mohee	Bb 6843, MW 7237, *RCA LPV 548*

Roy Hall and Jay Hugh Hall as shown in a Bluebird Record catalogue from the late 1930s. *Dave Freeman (County Records)*

BS-07046   Way Out There   Bb 6843, MW 7237
BS-07047   Little Girl You've Done Me Wrong   Bb 7103, MW 7240
BS-07048   My Girl Has Gone and Left Me   Bb 7103, MW 7240
BS-07049   I'll Remember You Love in My Prayers   MW 7241
BS-07050   Kingdom Land   MW 7241

Charlotte, North Carolina, 27 February 1938
As above: add Steve Ledford, fiddle (1)

BS-018773   It Was Only a Dream   Bb 7642
BS-018774   An Old Man's Story   Bb 8923
BS-018775   Alcatraz Prisoner   Bb 7642
BS-018776   Your Love Was Not Mine (1)   Bb 7728
BS-018777   Constant Sorrow (1)   Bb unissued
BS-018778   The Wrong Road (1)   Bb 7728, *CY 406*

Rock Hill, South Carolina, 26 September 1938
As above: omit fiddle

BS-027703   The Great Speckled Bird   Bb unissued
BS-027704   Waiting for the Boatman   Bb unissued
BS-027705   Don't Go Away Unsaved   Bb unissued
BS-027706   Lover's Goodbye   Bb unissued
BS-027707   Alcatraz Prisoner—Part 2   Bb unissued
BS-027708   The Elevated Railroad in the City   Bb 8923

Columbia, South Carolina, November 1938
Roy Hall and His Blue Ridge Entertainers: Roy Hall, guitar/vocal; Tommy Magness, fiddle; Clato Buchanan, tenor banjo; Talmadge Aldridge, guitar; Bob Hopson, guitar

SC-84   Come Back Little Pal   Vo 04842, *CY 406*
SC-88   Good for Nothing Gal   Vo 04627
SC-89   The Lonely Blues   Vo 04627
SC-90   Where the Rose Never Fades   Vo 04771, Cq 9184, *CY 406*
SC-91   Answer to the Great Speckled Bird   Vo 04771, Cq 9184
SC-95   Sunny Tennessee   Vo 04842
SC-97   Lonesome Dove   Vo 04717, Cq 9230, *CY 406*
SC-101   Wabash Cannon Ball   Vo 04717, Cq 9230, *CY 406*

[This session encompassed a total of eighteen numbers by Hall and his band. The gaps in the matrix numbers account for these selections, the titles for which are unknown except for "Orange Blossom Special."]

Atlanta, Georgia, 5 February 1940
The Happy-Go-Lucky Boys: Jay Hugh Hall, vocal/guitar; Clyde Moody, guitar/vocal; Steve Ledford, fiddle

BS-047522 Darling I'm Still in Love with You   Bb 8528, MW 8719
BS-047523 No Letter in the Mail Today   Bb 8467, MW 8719
BS-047524 Come Back Sweetheart   Bb 8467, MW 8720
BS-047525 I Hope She's Satisfied   Bb 8528, MW 8720
BS-047526 Happy-Go-Lucky Breakdown   Bb 8391, MW 8718
BS-047527 Whatcha Gonna Do with the Baby   Bb 8391, MW 8718
[BS-047526 omits vocals]

Atlanta, Georgia, 9 October 1940
Roy Hall and His Blue Ridge Entertainers: Roy Hall, guitar/vocal (1); Bill Brown, steel guitar; Clayton Hall, banjo/vocal (2); Saford Hall, fiddle; Wayne Watson, bass; vocal chorus (3)

BS-054572 New "San Antonio Rose" (1)   Bb 8561
BS-054573 She's Winkin' at Me (1, 2)   Bb 8702
BS-054574 I'd Die Before I'd Cry over You (1, 2)   Bb 8561
BS-054575 Your Heart Should Belong to Me (1, 2)   Bb 8702
BS-054576 Don't Let Your Sweet Love Die (1, 2)   Bb 8656, *CY 406*
BS-054577 Can You Forgive? (1, 2)   Bb 8656, *CY 406, RCA LPV 569*
BS-054578 Loving You Too Well (1, 2)   Bb 8676, *CY 406*
BS-054579 I Played My Heart and Lost (1, 2)   Bb 8676
BS-054580 Rubber Dolly (3)   Bb 8617
BS-054581 Bye Bye Baby, Bye Bye (3)   Bb 8617
BS-054582 Little Sweetheart Come and Kiss Me (1, 2)   Bb 8794, *CY 406*
BS-054583 'Neath the Bridge at the Foot of the Hill (1, 2)   Bb 8794, *CY 406*

Atlanta, Georgia, 1 October 1941
Roy Hall and His Blue Ridge Entertainers: Roy Hall, guitar/vocal; Tommy Magness, fiddle; Bill Brown, steel guitar; Clayton Hall, banjo; Wayne Watson, bass; Glenwood Howell, vocal (1)

BS-071048 Until I Return to You   Bb 8906
BS-071049 Natural Bridge Blues (1)   Bb 8863, *CY 406*
BS-071050 I Wonder If the Moon Is Shining   Bb 8959
BS-071051 I Wonder Where You Are Tonight   Bb 8959, *CY 406*
BS-071052 I'm Glad We Didn't Say Goodnight   Bb 33-0515
BS-071053 My Sweet Mountain Rose   Bb 8906
BS-071054 The Best of Friends Must Part Some Day   Bb 33-0515, *CY 406*
BS-071055 Polecat Blues   Bb 8863, *CY 406*

Bibliography: Kip Lornell, brochure notes to "Early Roanoke Country Radio," BRI 010; Ivan Tribe, brochure notes to "Roy Hall and His Blue Ridge Entertainers," CY 406, and "Roy Hall and His Blue Ridge Entertainers," *Bluegrass Unlimited* (September 1978): 44-50.

Hampton Institute Quartette (ca. 1885–late 1950s)

Although this group recorded in 1941, its roots can be traced to the 1880s, when Hampton Institute (now Hampton University) formed its first quartet to promote the school and to raise money. Following the lead of Fisk University, the early Hampton Institute Quartette and its affiliated jubilee singing troupes toured extensively, including cross-country trips prior to the turn of the century.

By 1890 the Hampton Institute Quartette had been established as an entity separate from other singing groups associated with Hampton. The group served as ambassadors for the school and performed for business and political leaders across the United States. This hectic schedule reached a peak in 1929 when the quartet gave 258 programs.

The quartet was so important to Hampton Institute that the school maintained several quartets simultaneously. Their primary group was composed of alumni singers; students formed a junior group and the Armstrong Quartette. Thus, Hampton could always count on at least one group representing the school by performing on the road. During the 1930s the Hampton Institute Senior Quartette toured Europe. Within the United States, the Quartette was also used to promote racial harmony as well as to raise money.

Given its long history and the general popularity of quartets, it is surprising that the Hampton Institute Quartette did not record commercially until 1939. These records came during a conservative period, when commercial record companies were recording very few previously unrecorded groups. The reputation of the Hampton Institute Quartette almost certainly influenced Victor to take the chance.

The Hampton Institute Quartettes continued to perform until the middle 1950s, even recording a few selections for Musicraft in the late 1940s. By 1956 the general interest in such groups had waned, and by 1960 Hampton Institute stopped sponsoring a quartet, thus ending a tradition that had continued for approximately 75 years.

New York, New York, ca. June 1939

Hampton Institute Quartet: unaccompanied male vocal quartet

GM-555-B Goin' To Shout All Over God's Heaven   Mus 230
GM-557-E I Want to be Ready   Mus 233
GM-559-C Little David, Play On Your Harp   Mus 231
GM-560-C I Want to Go to Heaven When I Die   Mus 234
GM-561-A Ezekiel Saw de Wheel   Mus 232
GM-563-C De Ole Ark A-Moverin' (*sic*) Along   Mus 234
GM-564-D Mary and Martha Jes Gone 'Long   Mus 232
GM-565-A In Bright Mansions Above   Mus 231
GM-566-A Reign, Massa Jesus, Reign   Mus 230
GM-568-C Ole-Time Religion   Mus 233

Hampton Institute Quartette, 1942. From left, Lorenzo White (Hampton Institute staff), Robert Hall, George Hamilton, Mrs. Roosevelt, Charles Flax, Jeremiah Thomas, William Byrd. *Courtesy Norfolk Journal and Guide*

New York, New York, 23 April 1941
Hampton Institute Quartette: Probably Robert Hall, first tenor voice; George Hamilton, second tenor voice; Charles Flax, baritone voice; William Byrd, bass voice

BS065032-1 Were You There   RCA unissued
BS065033-1 Roll de Ole Chariot   RCA unissued
BS065034-1 De Band of Gideon   RCA unissued
BS065035-1 Keep Inching Along   RCA 27473
BS065036-1 Go Down Moses   RCA 27472
BS065037-1 Swing Low, Sweet Chariot   RCA 27470

New York, New York, 24 April 1941
As above
BS065039-1 My Lord What a Morning   RCA 27471
BS065040-1 There's No Hiding Place Down Here   RCA 27472
BS065041-1 Old Time Religion   RCA unissued
BS065042-1 'Tis Me   RCA 27471
BS065043-1 Nobody Knows the Trouble I've Seen   RCA 27473
BS065044-1 Steal Away   RCA 27470
BS065045-1 We're Walkin' in the Light   RCA unissued
BS065046-1 Deep River   RCA unissued

[These discs were issued as Victor album set P-78 entitled "Swing Low Spirituals."]

Bibliography: Vaughan Webb, brochure notes to "Hampton Roads Quartet Tradition," *BRI 009*.

Kelly Harrell (1924–1942)

Crockett Kelly Harrell was born in Wythe County, Virginia, on September 13, 1889. Harrell grew up in Fries and as a youth began working at one of the local textile mills. One of his fellow workers was Henry Whitter, another pioneering hillbilly recording artist. Inspired by Whitter's success, Harrell took the train to New York City early in 1925 and recorded four selections for Victor with the support of anonymous studio musicians. Later that year he accompanied Whitter to Asheville, North Carolina, where both men recorded for the OKeh Company. In June 1926 the persistent Harrell returned to New York City and recorded for Victor, once more backed by unknown musicians.

    Discouraged by the modest sales of his recordings and lured by the higher wages being offered by the Fieldcrest Mills in Henry County, Harrell moved east late in 1926. He quickly located a local band, which was soon dubbed the Virginia String Band, to support his singing. At this point his recording career began anew when he contacted Victor again.

    The musical revival succeeded as his sympathetic, working band provided him with fine backing. These recordings also sold modestly, though well enough for Victor to call him back several times between 1927 and 1928. On one of these sessions, Harrell was joined by another vocalist, Danville wholesale grocer Henry Norton, with whom he sang two duets.

Unfortunately, Harrell's recording career was cut short by the Depression. The group continued performing locally into the early 1930s, while its members worked in Henry County's mills. Despite the loss of his Victor contract, Harrell remained interested in recording. He contacted other companies during the 1930s, but no one was willing to take a chance on him. On July 9, 1942, Harrell had a heart attack while at work and died before reaching the hospital.

New York, New York, 7 January 1925
Kelly Harrell: Kelly Harrell, vocal; unknown fiddle, guitar, harmonica (1)

31584-2	New River Train	Vi 19596, *BF 15508*
31585-2	Rovin' Gambler	Vi 19596, *BF 15508*
31856-2	I Wish I Was a Single Girl Again (1)	Vi 19563, *BF 15508*
31857-3	Butcher's Boy	Vi 19563, *BF 15508*

Asheville, North Carolina, 25 August 1925
As above: delete unknown instruments; add Henry Whitter, guitar/harmonica

9270-A	I Was Born about 10,000 Years Ago	OK 40486, *BF 15508*
9271-A	Wild Bill Jones	OK 40486, *BF 15508*
9272-A	Peg and Awl	OK 40544, *BF 15508*
9273-A	I Was Born in Pennsylvania	OK 40544, *BF 15508*
9276-A	I'm Going Back to North Carolina	OK 40505, *BF 15508*
9277-A	Be at Home Soon Tonight, My Dear Boy	OK 40505, *BF 15508*
9279-A	The Wreck on the Southern Old 97	OK 7010, *BF 15508*
9280-A	Blue Eyed Ella	OK 7010, *BF 15508*

[OK 7010 is a special 12" disc]

New York, New York, 8 June 1926
As above: delete Henry Whitter; add unknown fiddle, guitar, harmonica (1), train whistle (2)

31584-6	New River Train (1, 2)	Vi 20171, *BF 15508, CMH 106*
31585-6	Rovin' Gambler	Vi 20171, MW 4367, *BF 15508*
31586-6	I Wish I Was a Single Girl Again	Vi 20242, *BF 15508*
31587-5	Butcher's Boy	Vi 20242, *BF 15508, BRI 002*

[Reverse of MW 4367 by Masters' Hawaiians]

New York, New York, 9 June 1926
As above
35667-3	O! Molly Dear Go Ask Your Mother	Vi 20280, *BF 15509*

Kelly Harrell

35668-3	Broken Engagement	Vi 20280, *BF 15509*
35669-3	The Dying Hobo	Vi 20527, *BF 15509*
35670-3	Beneath the Weeping Willow Tree	Vi 20535, *BF 15509*
35671-3	My Horses Ain't Hungry	Vi 20103, *BF 15509*
35672-3	Bright Sherman Valley	Vi 20527, *BF 15509*

New York, New York, 10 June 1926
As above
35673-3	The Cuckoo She's a Fine Bird	Vi 40047, *BF 15509*
35674-3	Hand Me Down My Walking Cane	Vi 20103, MW 4330, *BF 15509, CMH 106*
35675-3	Bye and Bye You Will Forget Me	Vi 20535, *BF 15509*

[Vi 40047 issued as by Virginia String Band; reverse MW 4330 by Bud Billings Trio]

Camden, New Jersey, 22 March 1927
As above: delete unknown instruments; add Posey Rorer, fiddle; R.D. Hundley, banjo; Alfred Steagall, guitar

38231-2	Oh, My Pretty Monkey	Vi 40047, *BF 15509*
38232-1	I Love My Sweetheart the Best	Vi 20867, *BF 15509*
38233-2	Henry Clay Beattie	Vi 20797, *BF 15509, CY 502, CY 408*
38234-1	I Want a Nice Little Fellow	Vi 20867, *BF 15509*

Camden, New Jersey, 23 March 1927
As above
38235-2	My Name Is John Johanna	Vi 21520, *BF 15510*, FW FP251, FW FA2951, *CY 408*, RCA LPV 548
38236-2	In the Shadow of the Pine	Vi 20657, *BF 15510, CY 408, CY 504*
38237-2	Charles Giteau	Vi 20797, *BF 15510*, FW FP251, FW FA2951, *CY 408, CY 504*
38238-1	I'm Nobody's Darling on Earth	Vi 20657, *BF 15510, CY 408*
38239-2	My Wife, She Has Gone and Left Me	Vi 21520, *BF 15510, CY 408*

[Vi 21520 issued as by Kelly Harrell (Virginia String Band)]

Charlotte, North Carolina, 12 August 1927
Kelly Harrell and Henry Norton: delete Posey Rorer, fiddle; add Henry Norton, vocal/banjo; Lonnie Austin, fiddle

39800-2	Row Us over the Tide	Vi 20935, *BF 15510, CY 408, CY 508*
39801-2	I Have No Loving Mother Now	Vi 20935, *BF 15510, CY 408*
39807-3	For Seven Long Years I've Been Married	Vi 21069, *BF 15510, CY 408*
39808-2	Charley, He's a Good Old Man	Vi 21069, *BF 15510, CY 408*, RCA 552

[Vi 21069 omits Henry Norton]

Camden, New Jersey, 18 February 1929
Kelly Harrell: Kelly Harrell, vocal; [?] Gorodetzer, fiddle; Alfred Steagall, guitar

49869-1 and -2	Are You Going to Leave Your Old Home Today?	Vi unissued
49870-2	The Henpecked Man	Vi 23689, *BF 15510, CY 408*

Camden, New Jersey, 19 February 1929
As above: delete [?] Gorodetzer; add Sam Freed, fiddle; Roy Smeck, harmonica (1) / Jew's harp (2)

49873-2	She Just Kept Kissing On (1, 2)	Vi 40095, *BF 15510*
49874-2	All My Sins Are Taken Away (1, 2)	Vi 40095, *BF 15510*
49875-2	Cave Love Has Gained the Day	Vi 23689, *BF 15510, CY 408*
49876-2	I Heard Somebody Call My Name	Vi 23747, *BF 15510*

[Reverse Vi 23747 by Bill Palmer's Trio]

Bibliography: Kinney Rorrer, brochure notes to "Kelly Harrell," CY 408; Tony Russell, "Kelly Harrell and the Virginia Ramblers," *Old Time Music* 2 (Autumn 1971): 8-11; Richard Weize, brochure notes to "The Complete Kelly Harrell," BF 15508-10.

Elder Golden Harris (ca. 1915–1964)

Golden Pierce Harris was born in Indian Valley, Virginia (Floyd County), on May 5, 1897. This was an area rich in string band music and from an early age Golden played old-time dance music on the fiddle. In 1921 he was "united" with the Primitive Baptist Church and within two years had become an Elder. Unlike most Primitive Baptists, who do not play or approve of stringed instruments, Harris combined his two passions.

During the 1920s he supported his family by farming the rich land in Floyd County. For several years he lay ill with tuberculosis, but was cured after taking Dr. Pierce's Golden Medical Discovery, a locally produced remedy. Following his recovery he continued to work the land and assist the church.

For reasons that are not entirely clear, Golden Harris and a musical compatriot, Monroe Simpkins, traveled to New York City in 1931 to record. This was in the midst of the Depression, not an auspicious time to launch a recording career. Following an audition for the Brunswick Company, however, two of Elder Harris's fiddle-accompanied hymns were released on Brunswick's Melotone label. Though Simpkins claims also to have recorded six banjo solos at the same session, there is no evidence of this.

After their adventure in New York City the duo returned to their lives in Floyd County. Despite the dismal sales of the Melotone recording, both men continued in the music business part-time. In the early to mid-1930s they hand-manufactured phonographs under the Blue Ridge Phonograph Company imprint. Dur-

Elder Golden P. Harris promoted his small Floyd County record company in the early 1930s by distributing these flyers. *Courtesy Blue Ridge Heritage Archive*

ing this period, Harris also traveled back to New York City, recorded two more sides that he released on his own label and sold from his Indian Valley home.

During World War II he moved to nearby Radford to work in a defense-related job. He remained in this small Montgomery County city until his death on January 19, 1964. At the time of his death Harris was still an active Elder and musician.

New York, New York, 19 March 1931
Golden P. Harris: Golden P. Harris, fiddle/vocal

| E36489 | I'll Lead a Christian Life | Me 12178 |
| E36490 | No Sorrow There | Me 12178 |

New York, New York, ca. 1933
| 149-2 | My God the Springs of All My Joys | Harris 101-A |
| 150-1 | My Christian Friends in Bonds of Love | Harris 101-B |

[Harris 101 issued as Elder G.P. Harris. This record apparently had more than one pressing because copies exist with a different label and an alternative titling "Dunlap" and "Bottomly"]

Bibliography: Kip Lornell, " 'My Christian Friends in Bonds of Love': The Story of Elder Golden Harris," *Old Time Music* 39 (Winter 1982/Spring 1984): 19-21.

Sim Harris
A pseudonym on Oriole and Homestead for Ernest V. Stoneman.

Pete Harrison's Bayou Boys
A pseudonym on Velvet Tone and Clarion for Charlie Poole and band.

Roy Harvey (ca. 1905–late 1940s)
Roy Harvey was born on March 24, 1892, in Monroe County, West Virginia, and began playing the guitar shortly after the turn of the century. In his late teens Harvey began working for the local railroads and relocated between Bluefield and Princeton, West Virginia, to take a job as an engineer with the Virginia Railway. A 1923 strike cost him this position and he was operating a streetcar in Bluefield when he met Posey Rorer and Charlie Poole in 1925.

The three men quickly became friends and musical comrades. At this time Poole's regular guitarist, Norman Woodlieff, was forced to curtail his playing owing to tuberculosis. His condition became worse, and Poole offered the job to Harvey; by the fall of 1926 the West Virginian had become a North Carolina Rambler.

Harvey remained with Charlie Poole until 1930 when the Depression all but shut down the recording industry. During these four years, Harvey rambled with Poole and also led several of his own recording sessions for Columbia, Brunswick, Gennett, and Paramount. In addition he played on a session for Columbia featuring the Weaver Brothers. Music provided Harvey with a fulltime living well into the 1930s. Immediately after Poole's death in 1931, Harvey traveled north to record for Champion Records on what was to be his final session.

Harvey moved to Beckley, West Virginia, about 1933 and joined the town's police force in 1937. He moved to Smyrna Beach, Florida, in 1942 for a job with the Florida East Coast Railroad. Harvey virtually abandoned music in the late 1940s and, by the time of his death by cancer in July 1958, his music career was long behind him.

New York, New York, 17 September 1926
Roy Harvey accompanied by the North Carolina Ramblers: Roy Harvey, guitar/vocal; Charlie Poole, banjo; Posey Rorer, fiddle

14639-	Minstrel Hall	Co unissued
14670-2	The Brave Engineer	Co 15174

New York, New York, 11 May 1927
Roy Harvey and Posey Rorer: delete Charlie Poole

144122-	Blue Eyes	Co unissued
144123-1	Dark Eyes	Co 15714
144124-	San Antonio	Co unissued
144125-	Blue Eyed Ella	Co unissued
144126-	Walking on the Streets of Glory	Co unissued
144127-	Learning McFadden to Waltz	Co unissued
144128-2	Willie, Poor Boy	Co 15714
144129-	Jack and May	Co unissued
144130-	What Is Home without Love	Co unissued
144131-1	When the Bees Are in the Hive	Co 15155

New York, New York, 12 May 1927
As above

144138-	Sweet Sunny South	Co unissued
144139-2	Daisies Won't Tell	Co 15155

New York, New York, 25 July 1927
Roy Harvey accompanied by the North Carolina Ramblers: add Charlie Poole, banjo; possibly Bob Hoke, banjo/mandolin

144520-2	The Wreck of the Virginian #3	Co 15174, *HI 8005*

Roy Harvey in the late 1930s. *Courtesy Kinney Rorrer*

Roy Harvey

New York, New York, 17 September 1927

As above: Bob Hoke, banjo/mandolin/vocal (1)

GEX-880	Please Papa Come Home	Ge 6303, Chm 15394, Spt 9251, Sil 8161, Ch 390, *BI 6005*
GEX-881	That Old Clay Pipe (1)	Ge 6303, *BI 6005*
GEX-882/C	Write a Letter to My Mother	Ge 6288, Chm 15394, Spt 9251, Sil 8161, Ch 390
GEX-883	Poor Little Joe	Ge 6288, Chm 15414, Ch 394, Spr 3250
GEX-884/A	We Will Outshine the Sun	Ge 6350, Spt 9269, Sil 5182, Sil 8173
GEX-885	Walking on the Streets of Glory (1)	Ge 6350, Chm 15412, Spt 9269, Sil 5182, Sil 8173, Ch 401, Spr 3250
GEX-886	I Cannot Call Her Mother (1)	Spt 9246, Sil 5181, Sil 8147
GEX-887	Pearl Bryant (1)	Spt 9246, Sil 5181, Sil 8147

[Ge 6303 and Ge 6350 issued as by Roy Harvey and Bob Hoke; Chm 15394 issued as by George Runnels and Ed Sawyers; Chm 15412 issued as by George Runnels and Howard Hall (reverse by Welling and McGhee); Chm 15414 issued as by George Runnels (reverse by John McGhee); Spts and Sils issued as by the Three Kentucky Serenaders, except Spt 9251, which was issued as by the Kentucky Serenaders; Chs issued as by James Ragan, except Ch 390 and Ch 401, which were issued as by James Ragan and Oliver Beck; reverse Ch 394 by Grayson and Whitter; reverse Ch 401 by Welling and McGhee]

Chicago, Illinois, October 1927

North Carolina Ramblers and Roy Harvey: as above

20078-2	Take Back My Ring	Pm 3064, Bw 8118
20079-1	Willie My Darling (1)	Pm 3064, Bw 8118
20080-2	Give My Love to Nell (1)	Pm 3065, Bw 8080
20081-2	My Mother and My Sweetheart (1)	Pm 3065, Bw 8080
20082-2	She's Only a Bird in a Gilded Cage (1)	Pm 3079, Bw 8133
20083-2	Bill Mason	Pm 3079, Bw 8133
20084-2	Kitty Blye (1)	Pm 3072, Bw 8158, *BI 6005*
20085-	Three Leaves of Shamrock	Pm unissued
20086-1 and 2	I'm Glad I'm Married	Pm 3136, Bw 8206
20087-1 and 2	Sweet Sunny South	Pm 3136, Bw 8206
20088-	Maggie Dear, I'm Called Away	Pm unissued
20089-2	Blue Eyes (1)	Pm 3072, Bw 8185, *JEMF 103*

[Pm 3136 issued as by the North Carolina Ramblers/Roy Harvey; Bw 8080 and Bw 8158 issued as by the Wilson Ramblers; some copies of Bw 8158 issued as by the Stone Mountain Entertainers; Bw 8118 issued as by the Plainsmen and Rufus Hall; Bw 8183 issued as by Rufus Hall and the Plainsmen; Bw 8206 issued as by the Plainsmen; 20086 has a vocal solo by Bob Hoke]

Bernice Coleman (guitar) and Ernest Branch (banjo) recorded with Roy Harvey in the early 1930s. *Courtesy Dave Freeman (County Records)*

Roy Harvey

Ashland, Kentucky, 16 February 1928
Roy Harvey and the North Carolina Ramblers: as above

AL-268	The Bluefield Murder (1)	Br 250, *Bl 6005*
AL-271	I'll Be There, Mary Dear (1)	Br 234, Au 22032
AL-275	What Is Home without Love (1)	Br 268
AL-276 and 7	As We Parted by the Gate	Br 234, Au 22032
AL-279	There's a Mother Old and Gray Who Needs Me Now (1)	Br 223
AL-280	There'll Come a Time	Br 223
AL-282 and 3	Sweet Refrain	Vo 5243
AL-285	Budded Roses (1)	Br 268
AL-288 and 9	Take Me Back to Home and Mother (1)	Vo 5243
AL-290	George Collins	Br 250, *Bl 6005*

Johnson City, Tennessee, ca. 18 October 1928
Roy Harvey and Earl Shirkey: Roy Harvey, vocal/guitar; Earl Shirkey, vocal (yodeling)

147226-2	Steamboat Man	Co 15326
147227-1	When the Roses Bloom Again for the Bootlegger	Co 15326
147228-1	Poor Little Joe	Co 15376
147229-2	We Parted at the Gate	Co 15376

Johnson City, Tennessee, 26 March 1929
As above

148130-2	The Yodeling Mule	Co 15406, Ve 2490, Cl 5430
148132-	When I'm Gone	Co unissued
148133-	My Mother and My Sweetheart	Co unissued
148134-1	The Cowboy's Lullaby	Co 15467, RZ 22059
148135-2	Bootlegger's Dream of Home	Co 15429
148136-1	The Railroad Blues	Co 15406, Ve 2490, Cl 5430, *PU 3002, ARB 201*
148137-2	Keep Bachelor's Hall	Co 15429
148138-1	Kitty Waltz Yodel	Co 15467, RZ 22059, *PU 3002, ARB 201*

[Cl and Ve issued as by Joe Fletcher and Arthur Higgins]

New York, New York, ca. 9 May 1929
Fred Newman: Roy Harvey, guitar/vocal; Odell Smith, fiddle; Lonnie Austin, fiddle; Charlie Poole, banjo; Lucy Terry, piano

2913-2	San Antonio	Pm 3177, Pm 3267, Bw 8288
2914-2	What Is Home without Babies	Pm 3177, Pm 3267, Bw 8288

Roy Harvey (left) and Leonard Copeland, who recorded together for Columbia Records in 1929. *Courtesy Kinney Rorrer*

Roy Harvey

Johnson City, Tennessee, 22 October 1929
Roy Harvey and Leonard Copeland: Roy Harvey, guitar; Leonard Copeland, guitar; omit Copeland, add Earl Shirkey and Harvey, vocal (1)

149216-2	Just Pickin'	Co 15514, *YZ 1024*
149217-2	Beckley Rag	Co 15414
149218-2	Underneath the Sugar Moon	Co 15582
149219-1	Lonesome Weary Blues	Co 15582, *CY 523*
149226-1	The Virginian Strike of '23 (1)	Co 15535
149227-2	The Little Lost Child (The Policeman's Little Child) (1)	Co 15642
149228-2	My Yodeling Sweetheart	Co 15490, Ve 2591, Cl 5431
149229-1	I'm Longing to Belong to Someone (1)	Co 15490
149230-2	We Have Moonshine in the West Virginia Hills (1)	Co 15462, *OH 141*
149231-2	A Hobo's Pal (1)	Co 15535

[149226 through 149231 issued as by Roy Harvey and Earl Shirkey; Cl and Ve issued as by Joe Fletcher and Arthur Higgins]

Atlanta, Georgia, 22 April 1930
As above

150337-2	Greasy Wagon	Co 15637
150338-2	Mother's Waltz	Co 15637
150339-	Monroe County Blues	Co unissued
150340-	Back to the Blue Ridge	Co unissued
150341-	Down to the Trail to Home Sweet Home (1)	Co unissued
150342-	The Pal That I Love (1)	Co unissued
150343-	Peggy O'Neil (1)	Co unissued
150345-	When I Lost You (1)	Co unissued
150352-	Learning MacFayden to Dance (1)	Co unissued
150353-	Eileen (1)	Co unissued
150354-	Lamp Lighting Time in the Valley	Co unissued
150355-	There's a Mother Old and Gray	Co unissued

[150354 and 150455 are a solo vocal and guitar by Roy Harvey]

New York, New York, 9 September 1930
Roy Harvey: omit Copeland and Shirkey; add Odell Smith, fiddle

150781-2	Just Goodbye, I'm Going Home	Co 15609
150782-1	Lilly Reunion	Co 15609

Richmond, Indiana, 3 December 1930
As above: Roy Harvey, guitar/vocal (1); Jess Johnston, fiddle/guitar (2)/vocal (3)

GN-17337	Hobo's Pal (1)	Chm 16187, Spr 2658
GN-17338	There'll Be a Change in Business (1)	Chm rejected

GN-17339   Wreck of the C & O Sportsman (1)   Chm rejected
GN-17340   The Lilly Reunion (1)   Chm rejected
GN-17341   No Room for a Tramp (1)   Chm 16187
GN-17342   Little Seaside Village   Chm 16213, Spr 2658
GN-17343   Milwaukee Blues   Spr 2626
GN-17344   When It's Lamplighting Time in the Valley (1, 3)   Chm rejected
GN-17345   My Smoky Mountain Home (1)   Chm rejected
GN-17346   When the Bees Are in the Hives (1)   Chm 16213, MW 4947, *BI 6005*

Richmond, Indiana, 4 December 1930
As above
GN-17347   The Dying Brakeman (3)   Chm 16255
GN-17348   Railroad Blues (2)   Chm 16255, Spr 2626, *CY 523*
GN-17349   Jefferson Street Rag (2)   Chm 16781, Chm 45011, *CY 523*
GN-17350   Guitar Rag (3)   Chm 16871, Chm 45011
[Spr 2626 issued as by John Martin, delete fiddle on GN-17348]

Richmond, Indiana, 3 June 1931
West Virginia Ramblers: Roy Harvey, guitar/vocal (1); Jess Johnston, fiddle/vocal (2); Bernice Coleman, fiddle/vocal (3); Ernest Branch, banjo/vocal (4)

N-17782   By a Cottage in the Twilight (1, 2)   Chm 16780, Spr 2684
N-17783   Goodbye Mary Dear (1, 2)   Chm 16331, Chm 45035
N-17784   Blue Eyes (1, 2)   Chm 16294, Spr 2779
N-17785   Goodbye Sweetheart Goodbye (1, 2)   Chm 16294, Spr 2684
N-17786   Gambling Blues (1)   Chm 16281
N-17787   John Hardy Blues (1)   Chm 16281
N-17788   California Murder (1)   Chm rejected
N-17789   The Great Reaping Day (1, 2)   Chm 16662, Chm 45117
N-17790   You're Bound to Look Like a Monkey (1, 2, 3, 4)   Chm 16331, Spr 2779
N-17791   Someone Owns a Cottage (4)   Chm 16286, Spr 2688
N-17792   O Dem Golden Slippers   Chm 16757, Chm 45017
N-17793   Birdie (1, 2)   Chm 16449
[Spr 2684 and Spr 2779 issued as by the Railroad Boys; Spr 2688 issued as by Dave Walker; Chm 45035 titled "Goodbye Maggie, Goodbye Darling"]

Richmond, Indiana, 4 June 1931
As above
N-17794   Lulu Love (4)   Chm 16286
N-17795   Little Foot Prints (4)   Spr 2688
N-17796   Yellow Rose of Texas   Chm rejected
N-17797   The Only Girl I Ever Loved (3)   Chm 16456
N-17798   The Ring My Mother Wore (3)   Chm 16456

N-17799	Where the Whippoorwill Is Whispering Goodbye (1) Chm 16312, Spr 2701, MW 4947
N-17800	Called to the Foreign Fields (1) Chm 16312
N-17801	My Mother and My Sweetheart (1, 2) Chm 16780, Chm 45035, *BI 6005*
N-17802	Flowers Now Chm rejected
N-17803	The Wreck of the C & O Sportsman (1) Spr 2701

Bibliography: Norm Cohen, "Notes on Some Old Time Musicians from Princeton, West Virginia," *JEMF Quarterly*, 8, Part 2 no. 26 (Summer 1972): 94-104; Kinney Rorrer, *Rambling Blues: The Life & Songs of Charlie Poole* (London: Old Time Music, 1982).

See also Charlie Poole and Posey Rorer.

Uncle Ben Hawkins (and His Gang)

A pseudonym on Champion and Supertone for Ernest V. Stoneman.

Highlanders

See Charlie Poole.

Hill Brothers and Simmons (1934–1938)

Although Bill Hill, Dewey Hill, and Willie Simmons were all born in Surry County, North Carolina, they have strong ties to Henry County, Virginia. Bill and Dewey Hill were brothers who grew up on their parents' farm about twelve miles south of Mount Airy. Most of their siblings played some type of music; Bill picked the autoharp and fiddle, Dewey played the guitar. Willie Simmons was a neighbor and singer who played no instruments.

In 1932 Bill moved to Stanleytown, Virginia, to work for the Stanley Furniture Company. For a short time Dewey joined him, but by 1935 Dewey had returned to Surry County. Bill Hill remained in Henry County, playing with local bands and performing over WBTM in Danville, Virginia.

Despite the conservative nature of record companies during the middle 1930s, when the companies relied heavily upon proven sellers, Dewey Hill wrote to Victor asking for an audition. The Victor Company wrote back encouraging them to come to Charlotte, North Carolina, in August 1937 for a personal audition. With the assistance of Willie Simmons, the brothers practiced for several weeks before their audition, which they passed.

Within a year after this session, both Bill's and Dewey's lives changed. Dewey and his wife began a family; shortly thereafter, Bill followed suit. The trio performed together occasionally, but not with its former regularity.

Bill Hill and Dewey Hill managed to keep their hands in music throughout their lives. Dewey remained in Ararat, North Carolina, though he maintained

The Hill Brothers and Simmons, circa 1935, in Henry County, Virginia. Bill Hill (fiddle), Willie Simmons (autoharp), Dewey Hill (guitar). *Courtesy Blue Ridge Heritage Archive*

regular radio programs on WBOB in Galax, Virginia, and WPAQ in Mount Airy, and also sometimes worked with shape-note singing schools. He was still playing when he passed away on September 23, 1975. His death was preceded by that of Willie Simmons on April 10, 1964.

Bill Hill, however, still lives and plays music in Henry County. He recommenced performing on a regular basis following his retirement in 1980. Today he fronts a band, Bill Hill and the Sounds of Country, that plays in a four-county area surrounding Martinsville.

Charlotte, North Carolina, 6 August 1937
Hill Brothers and Simmons: Bill Hill, autoharp (1)/fiddle (2)/vocal (3); Dewey Hill, guitar/vocal/harmonica (4); Willie Simmons, vocal

013015-1	Just Over in the Glory Land (1)	Bb 7223, MW 7372
013016-1	I'm Glad I Counted the Cost (1)	Bb 7372
013017-1	I am on My Way to Heaven (1)	Bb 7223, MW 7373, *CY 508*
013018-1	Looking to My Prayers (2, 3, 4)	MW 7373
013019-1	Sweetheart, I Have Grown So Lonely	MW 7374
013020-1	In the Hills of Old Virginia (1, 4)	MW 7374

[Bbs issued as by Hill Brothers with Willie Simmons]

Bibliography: Kip Lornell, "The Hills: Alive with the Sound of Music," *Old Time Music* 43 (Winter 1987-Spring 1988) 15-18.
See also E.R. Nance Family.

Ezra Hill and Henry Johnson

A pseudonym on Champion for Byrd Moore and Melvin Robinette.

Hillbillies (1924–1933)

In May 1924 Tony Alderman, Joe Hopkins and his brother Al, and John Rector formed a string band to perform at their homes in Galax, Virginia, and to try their hands at commercial recordings. Rector had just come back from New York City, where he had recorded with Henry Whitter for OKeh. Not satisfied with the results, Rector wanted to put together a stronger band and then approach OKeh once more.

The band worked throughout Carroll County for several months, then traveled to New York City, where they made some test recordings. In January 1925 they were back in New York in front of OKeh executive Ralph Peer, who liked the band and facetiously dubbed them "The Hill Billies." Thus Hopkins and his friends became the first recording band to use this term as part of their name.

One immediate result of their OKeh recordings was a chance to perform over Washington, D.C., radio station WRC. This powerful station broadcast their

The Hillbillies, circa 1928 (possibly in a New York City photo studio).
Courtesy Dave Freeman (County Records)

Hillbillies 101

music throughout the East Coast, which resulted in a series of extensive tours that took them from the Deep South to the Northeast.

By 1927 they were playing in New York City and broadcasting over WJZ. In 1928 they performed in vaudeville shows and theaters in New York, New Jersey, and Pennsylvania. Even the Depression, which knocked many entertainers out of work, did not stop the Hillbillies, who continued to find employment.

Washington, D.C., closer to their mountain home, became their base of operation. They were easily able to fulfill obligations in New York City and the South from this more central location. Washington society embraced them, too, as they were invited to play for President Calvin Coolidge. In 1928 the Hillbillies made a fifteen-minute movie short, "The Hill Billies," which was shown throughout the South.

During this period the group expanded and changed personnel. Charlie Bowman and Ed Belcher worked with them as fiddlers, while Frank Wilson was occasionally added on the guitar. Smyth County banjo player Jack Reedy was also frequently heard on the group's recordings and as a member of their entertainment act.

Things went well until 1932, when the entrepreneurial Al Hopkins was killed in a car crash. He was the spiritual and professional leader of the group and with his passing the group fell apart. By 1933 they had disbanded, moving on to other musical jobs or entirely unrelated careers.

New York, New York, 25 November 1924
Southwest Virginians String Orchestra: Elvis Alderman, fiddle; Al Hopkins, piano; John Rector, banjo; Joe Hopkins, guitar

       Lonesome Road Blues   Vi trial

New York, New York, ca. January 1925
The Hillbillies: as above: add Al Hopkins, vocal

S-73-117A   Old Joe Clark   OK 40376
S-73-118A   Silly Bill   OK 40294
S-73-119A   Cripple Creek   OK 40336
S-73-120A   Whoa! Mule   OK 40376
S-73-121A   Sally Ann   OK 40336
S-73-122A   Old Time Cinda   OK 40294

New York, New York, ca. April 1926
As above: omit Al Hopkins, vocal

E2938-39W   Mountaineers Love Song   Vo 15367, Vo 5115
E2942-43W   Old Joe Clark   Vo 15369, Vo 5117

The Hillbillies, circa 1928 (possibly in New York City). From left, Tony Alderman, Al Hopkins, Frank Wilson, Jack Reedy (?), and Ed Belcher. *Courtesy Dave Freeman (County Records)*

Hillbillies 103

E2944-45W Silly Bill   Vo 15369, Vo 5117, *CY 405*
E2950-51W Cripple Creek   Vo 15367, Vo 5115
E2952-53W Mississippi Sawyers   Vo 15368, Vo 5116
E2958-59W Long Eared Mule   Vo 15368, Vo 5116

New York, New York, ca. April 1926
Charlie Bowman: Charlie Bowman, fiddle; Joe Hopkins, guitar; Al Hopkins, piano/vocal (1); John Hopkins, ukulele

E2966-67W The Hickman Rag   Vo 15337, Vo 5118, *RO 1033*
E2968-69W Possum Up a Gum Stump, Cooney in the Hollow (1)   Vo 15377, Vo 5188

New York, New York, 21 October 1926
The Hillbillies: Charlie Bowman, fiddle/banjo (1); Joe Hopkins, guitar; John Hopkins, ukulele (2); Al Hopkins, piano (3) /vocal effects (4); Elvis Alderman, fiddle (5); Henry Roe, guitar (6); Fred Roe, fiddle (7)

E3972-73W Fisher's Hornpipe (1, 2, 3, 5, 6, 7)   Vo 5017, *CY 405*
E3974-75W Cackling Hen   Vo 5020
E3976-77W East Tennessee Blues   Vo 5016, Br 103
E3978-79W Governor Alf Taylor's Fox Chase (4)   Vo 5016, Br 106
[Brs issued as by Al Hopkins and His Buckle Busters]

New York, New York, 22 October 1926
As above
E3980-81W Walking in the Parlor (1, 2, 3, 5)   Vo 5024
E3982-83W Blue-Eyed Girl (1, 2, 3, 5)   Vo 5017, *CY 525*
E3984-85W Cinda (1, 2, 3, 5)   Vo 5025, Br 105, *CY 405*
E3986-87W Bristol, Tennessee Blues (6, 7)   Vo 5023, Br 104, *CY 405*
E3988-89W Round-Town Girls (3, 5, 7)   Vo 5023, Br 103, *CY 405*
E3990-91W Buck-Eyed Rabbits (1, 2, 3, 5)   Vo 5023, Br 104, *CY 525*
E3992-93W Cumberland Gap (1, 2, 3, 5)   Vo 5024
E3994-95W Sourwood Mountain (1, 2, 3, 5)   Vo 5022
E3996-97W Ragged Annie (1, 2, 3, 5)   Vo 5022
E3998-99W Texas Gals (1, 2, 3, 5)   Vo 5021, *CY 405*
[Brs issued as by Al Hopkins and His Buckle Busters]

New York, New York, 23 October 1926
As above
E4000-01W Going Down the Road Feeling Bad (1, 2, 3, 5)   Vo 5021
E4002-03W Sally Ann (1, 2, 3, 5)   Vo 5019, Br 105, *CY 405, VE 104*
E4004-05W Betsy Brown (1, 2, 3, 5)   Vo 5018
E4006-07W Kitty Wells (1, 2, 3, 5)   Vo 5018

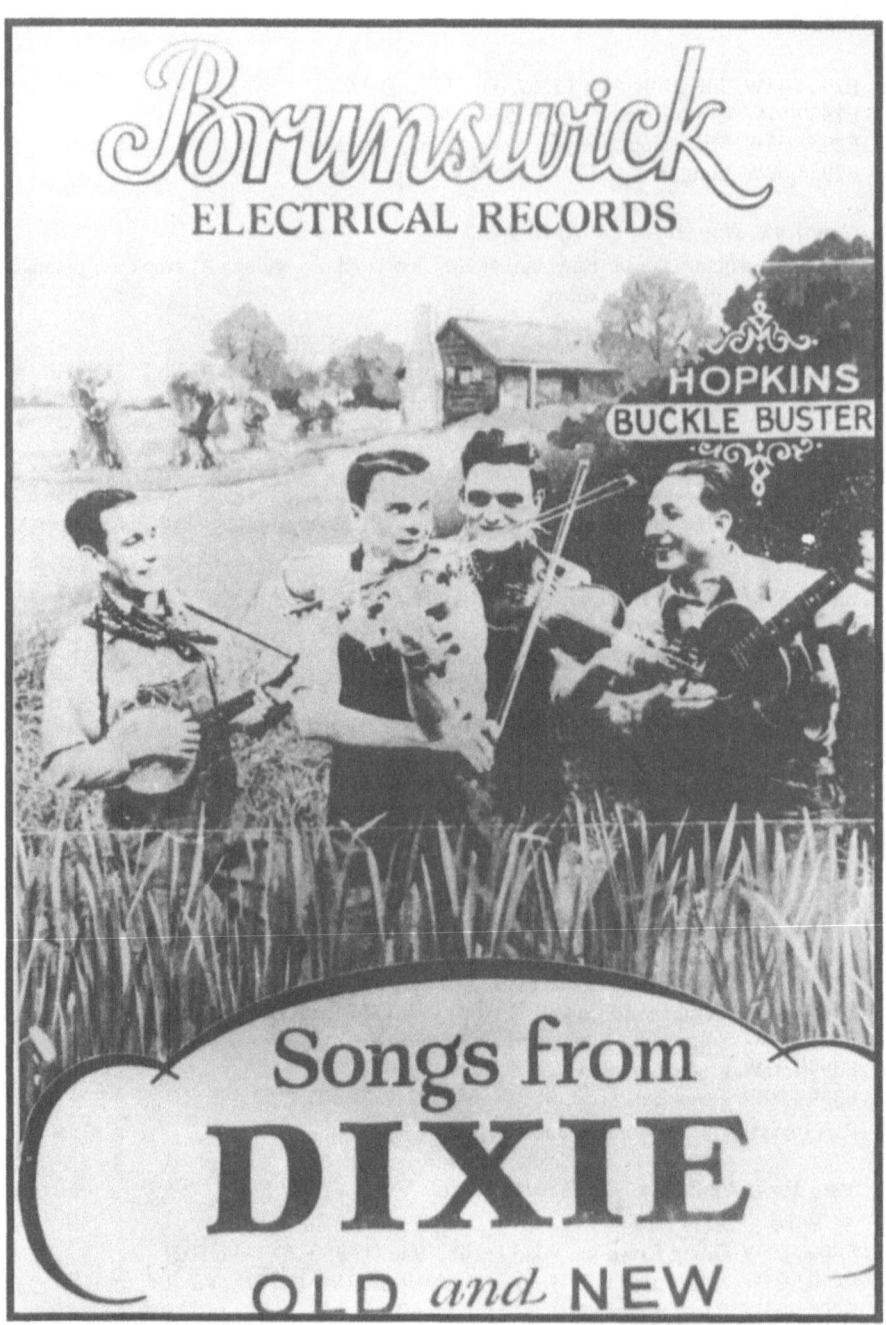

The Hillbillies (also known as Al Hopkins & his Buckle Busters) were the subject of this Brunswick Record catalogue from 1928. *Courtesy Dave Freeman (County Records)*

Hillbillies

E4008-09W Kitty Waltz (1, 2, 3, 5)   Vo 5019, Br 106
E4010-11W Donkey on the Railroad Track (1, 2, 3, 5)   Vo 5020

[Br issued as by Al Hopkins and His Buckle Busters; E4000-01W has vocal trio by the Hopkins brothers]

New York, New York, 12 May 1927

The Hillbillies: Charlie Bowman, fiddle (1); Elvis Alderman, fiddle (2); Elbert Bowman, guitar; Joe Hopkins, ukulele; Jack Reedy, banjo (3); Al Hopkins, vocal

E23110-11   Blue Ridge Mountain Blues (1, 2)   Br 180

[E23110-11 has vocal quartet]

New York, New York, 13 May 1927

As above
E23116-17   Sweet Bunch of Daisies (1)   Vo 5178, Br 174
E23118-19   Daisies Won't Tell (1)   Vo 5178, Br 174
E23120-21   Down to the Club (1)   Br 184
E23122-23   Sleep, Baby, Sleep (1, 3)   Vo 5186, Br 185
E23124-25   Black-Eyed Susie (2, 3)   Vo 5179, Br 175, *CY 405, BR BL 59000,*
                COR MH 174, MCA 3013
E23126-27   Cluck Old Hen (1, 3)   Vo 5179, Br 175, *CY 405, BR BL 59000, COR*
                MH 174
E23128-29   Nine Pound Hammer (2, 3)   Br 177
E23130-31   Whoa! Mule (1, 3)   Br 179

New York, New York, 14 May 1927

As above
E23146-47   Echoes of the Chimes   Br 180
E23148-49   Boatin' Up the Sandy (1, 2, 3)   Br 182, *CY 525*
E23150-51   Johnson Boys (2)   Br 179, *CY 405*

[Brs issued as by Al Hopkins and His Buckle Busters; E23146-47 has vocal quartet by Al Hopkins, John Hopkins, Charlie Bowman, and Tony Alderman, piano by James O'Keefe]

New York, New York, 16 May 1927

As above
E23169-70   Hear Dem Bells (1, 2, 3)   Vo 5173, Br 184
E23171-72   Georgia Buck (3)   Vo 5182, Br 183
E23173-74   The Feller That Looked Like Me (1)   Br 184
E23175-76   C.C. & O. No. 558 (1, 2)   Br 177, *CY 405, VE 103*
E23177-78   Darling Nellie Gray (3)   Vo 5186, Br 185
E23179-80   She'll Be Coming 'Round the Mountain (2)   Vo 5240, Br 181
E23181-82   Ride That Mule (1, 2, 3)   Br 186

[Brs issued as by Al Hopkins and His Buckle Busters; E23171-72 includes vocal quartet; E23171-72 and E23177-78 include banjo by Charlie Bowman]

New York, New York, 17 May 1927

As above

E23183-84	Bug in the Taters (1, 3)	Br 182
E23185-86	Baby Your Time Ain't Long (2, 3)	Vo 5182, Br 183
E23187-88	Oh Where Is My Little Dog Gone (2)	Vo 5183, Br 187
E23189-90	Wasn't She Dandy (2, 3)	Vo 5183, Br 187
E23191-92	Roll on the Ground (1, 3)	Br 186
E23193-94	Daisies Won't Tell (2)	Vo 5178

[Brs issued as by Al Hopkins and His Buckle Busters; E23185-86 has banjo by Charlie Bowman; E23193-94 has guitar by Charlie Bowman]

Johnson City, Tennessee, 16 October 1928

Charlie Bowman and His Brothers: Charlie Bowman, fiddle; Elbert Bowman, guitar; Walter Bowman, banjo

W147208-2	Roll On Buddy	Co 15357, *CY 525*
W147209-2	Gonna Raise a Ruckus Tonight	Co 15357

New York, New York, 20 December 1928

Al Hopkins and His Buckle Busters: Frank Wilson, steel guitar; Al Hopkins, vocal; Walter Hughes, guitar; Elvis Alderman, fiddle (1); Ed Belcher, fiddle (2); John Hopkins, ukulele

E28916A and B	Lynchburg Town (1)	Br unissued
E28917A and B	Oh, Didn't He Ramble	Br unissued
E28918	Gideon's Band	Br 295
E28919	Old Dan Tucker (2)	Br 295
E28920	Old Uncle Ned (2)	Br 300
E28921	West Virginia Gals (2)	Br 318
E28922	Blue Bell (1)	Br 300
E28923	Carolina Moonshiner	Br 318
E28924	Polka Medley (Intro: Rocky Road to Dublin/Jenny Lind) (2)	Br 321
E28925	Marsovia Waltz	Br 321
E28926	Wild Hoss (1)	Br 335
E28927	Medley of Old Time Dance Tunes (Soldier's Joy/Turkey Buzzard/When You Go A-courting) (1)	Br 335, *CY 405, VE 106*

[E28921 includes only guitar and fiddle]

New York, New York, 20 February 1929
Charlie Bowman and His Brothers: Charlie Bowman, fiddle; Elbert Bowman, guitar; Walter Bowman, guitar; Frank Wilson, steel guitar

W147971-1 Polly Ann   Co 15372
W147972-2 Forky Deer   Co 15387, *CY 527*
W147973-1 Moonshiner and His Money   Co 15387, *CY 507, CO CS 9660*
W147975-2 Katy-did Waltz   Co 15372
[Co 15372 issued as by Frank Wilson and His Blue Ridge Mountain Trio]

Johnson City, Tennessee, 23 October 1929
Charlie Bowman: Charlie Bowman, fiddle; Fran Trappe, accordion

W149258- Wild Horse   Co unissued
W149259- Carolina Moonshine   Co unissued

Bibliography: Archie Green, "Hillbilly Music: Source and Symbol," *Journal of American Folklore* 78 (1965): 211-15; Joe Wilson, brochure notes to "The Hillbillies," CY 405.

Al Hopkins and His Buckle Busters (1924–1932)
See The Hillbillies.

James Horton and Family
A pseudonym on Superior for the E.R. Nance Family.

James Howard and Charles Peak (late 1920s)
According to the Victor files, Charles Peak was from Norton, Virginia, and James Howard lived in Harlan, Kentucky. This may be the same James Howard who recorded fiddle tunes for the Folksong Archive of the Library of Congress in the 1930s. Nothing more is known of these musicians.

Bristol, Tennessee, 30 October 1928
Howard and Peak, The Blind Musicians: James Howard, vocal/fiddle; Charles Peak, vocal/guitar

47246-2   I Cannot Be Your Sweetheart   Vi 40189
47247-2   Three Black Sheep   Vi 40189

Robert Howell
A pseudonym on Herwin for Holland Puckett.

David Hunt
A pseudonym on Champion for Willie Stoneman.

Henry Johnson
See Ezra Hill

Jordan and Rupert
A pseudonym on Supertone for Walter "Kid" Smith.

Jerry Jordan
A pseudonym on Supertone for Walter "Kid" Smith.

Luke Jordan (ca. 1920–ca. 1940s)
Little is known of Jordan's life beyond the most basic facts. He was born on January 28, 1892, possibly in Campbell or Appomattox County. By his late teens, Jordan had moved into Lynchburg, where he remained until his death on June 25, 1952.

Jordan is still remembered by black musicians in Lynchburg as a unique and forceful guitarist. Moreover, he had the reputation as a problem drinker and an expert angler who never held down a regular job. His "signature" songs were "Cocaine Blues" and "Church Bells Blues," which some local blues musicians still perform.

Charlotte, North Carolina, 16 August 1927
Luke Jordan: Luke Jordan, guitar/vocal

39819-1	Church Bells Blues	Vi unissued, *RCA INT 1175, RCA 731.046*
39819-2	Church Bells Blues	Vi 21076, *RBF 9*
39820-1	Pick Poor Robin Clean	Vi unissued, *RCA INT 1175, RCA 731.046*
39820-2	Pick Poor Robin Clean	Vi 20957, *RT 326*
39821-2	Cocaine Blues	Vi 21076, *STA 119, MA 2003, RT 326*
39822-1	Traveling Coon	Vi 20957, *RT 326, MA 2003*

New York, New York, 18 November 1929
As above
57703-1	My Gal's Done Quit Me	Vi 38564, *BRI 003, RT 318*
57704-3	Won't You Be Kind?	Vi 38564, *BRI 003*

New York, New York, 19 November 1929
As above
57705-	If I Call You Mama	Vi 23400

57706-2	Look Up, Look Down	Vi unissued
57707-	Tom Brown Sits in His Prison Cell	Vi 23400
57708-2	That's a Plenty	Vi unissued

Bibliography: Don Kent, "On the Trail of Luke Jordan," *Blues Unlimited* 66 (October 1969): 4-6; Kip Lornell (with Brett Sutton, Dell Upton, and Mike Mayo), brochure notes to "Western Piedmont Blues," BRI 003.

Jubilee Gospel Team
A pseudonym on Broadway for the Norfolk Jubilee Quartet.

Jubilee Male Quartet
A pseudonym on Joe Davis and Varsity for the Norfolk Jubilee Quartet.

Jubilee Quartet
A pseudonym on Paramount for the Norfolk Jubilee Quartet.

Kentucky Serenaders
A pseudonym on Supertone for Roy Harvey.

Bela Lam and His Greene County Singers (ca. 1920–ca. 1935)
Zandervon Obeliah "Bela" Lam was a Stanardsville (Greene County) farmer who came from a very musical background. During the 1920s he often performed music in the company of his wife, Rosa, their son, Alva, and Rosa's brother, John Paul Meadows. Because of their strong religious convictions the group primarily sang at church revivals, religious services, family gatherings, and fund-raising events throughout Paige, Greene, and Albemarle counties.

In 1927, Elkton, Virginia, furniture store owner and OKeh record distributor John Evans suggested that they travel to New York City to record. As part of their trip, Lam and his group also performed at a large theater in the city. Their recordings must have sold well, because they were later recalled for another session. The group continued to sing into at least the middle 1930s.

New York, New York, 7 July 1927
Bela Lam and His Greene County Singers: Bela Lam, banjo/tenor vocal; Alva Lam, guitar/lead tenor vocal; John Paul Meadows, bass vocal; Rosa Lam, alto vocal

81140-	Two Little Girls in Blue	OK unissued
81141-A	On the Resurrection Morning We Shall Rise	OK 45145
81142-A	Row Us over the Tide	OK 45126
81143-B	Poor Little Bennie	OK 45136, *LBC 13*

Bela Lam and his Greene County Singers, 1927, Greene County, Virginia. From left, Bela Lam, John Paul Meadows, Rosa Lam, Alva Lam. *Courtesy Blue Ridge Heritage Archive/J.R. Meadows*

Dr. Lloyd and Howard Maxey

81144-	Listen to the Mocking Bird	OK unissued
81145-B	When the Roll is Called up Yonder	OK 45228
81146-B	Follow Jesus	OK 45228
81147-B	Little Maud	OK 45177, *NWR 236*
81148-B	The Sweet Story of Old	OK 45145
81149-B	May, Dearest, May	OK 45136

New York, New York, 8 July 1927
As above
81150-A	See That My Grave Is Kept Clean	OK 45126
81151-A	Sweet Bye and Bye	OK 45177

Richmond, Virginia, 15 October 1929
As above
403124-B	Tell It Again	OK 45456
403125-A	If Tonight Should End the World	OK 45456
403126-	Glory Bye and Bye	OK 45407
403127-	Crown Him	OK 45407
403128-	I Had a Darling Little Girl	OK unissued
403129-	Watermelon Smiling on the Vine	OK unissued

[403128 and 403129 as by Bela Lam Family]

Le Orchestre Cartier

A pseudonym on Melotone for H.M. Barnes' Blue Ridge Ramblers.

Dr. Lloyd and Howard Maxey (ca. 1925–ca. 1938)

This duo was based in Ferrum, Virginia (Franklin County), when they recorded for OKeh Records. Maxey was born and raised in Franklin County and learned to play the fiddle from older relatives. He worked for the sheriff's department for many years before a bootlegging trial forced him to leave Franklin County in the early 1940s. Maxey moved to Bassett in Henry County where he made a living as a barber until his death from a heart attack on August 6, 1947. In addition to the OKeh session, Maxey was recorded by the Library of Congress in 1936.

William Kiddoo Lloyd was an Alabama-born medical doctor who settled in Ferrum in the mid-1920s following his internship in Norfolk. He began playing for square dances and was soon playing regularly with Maxey. Lloyd left Franklin County in the late 1930s to continue his medical career in nearby Montgomery County, where he died in an airplane crash on December 23, 1948.

Lloyd and Maxey heard about the 1927 OKeh session by word of mouth and on a whim they traveled seventy miles south by car to audition. Plied with liquor, they overcame their nervousness and OKeh approved them for a session. Carlton

Drewry, who accompanied them to Winston-Salem, wrote the comic narrative that is heard on "Girl I Left Behind Me."

Winston-Salem, North Carolina, 22 September 1927
Doctor Lloyd and Howard Maxey: Doctor Lloyd, guitar/vocal (1); Howard Maxey, fiddle

81379-B	Western Union	OK 45150
81380-B	Bright Sherman Valley (1)	OK unissued
81381-A	I'm Just Going Down to the Gate (1)	OK unissued
81382-	Darling's Black Mustache	OK unissued
81383-	Jordan is a Hard Road to Travel	OK unissued
81384-A	Girl I Left behind Me (1)	OK 45150

Bibliography: Kip Lornell, "Dr. Lloyd, Howard Maxey and OKeh Records," *Old Time Music* 43 (Winter 1986/87): 19-20.

Carl Martin (ca. 1916–1979)

Born in Big Stone Gap, Virginia, on April 15, 1906, Martin learned to play the fiddle and guitar from his father. He spent his childhood in Southwest Virginia before moving to Knoxville, Tennessee, in 1918. There he became involved with his half-brother Roland Martin's string band. By the time Martin arrived in Knoxville, he was an accomplished blues guitarist and fitted well into the band.

During the 1920s the Martins toured with medicine shows, busked on street corners, performed with all types of touring shows, and entertained at coal camps. Most of their traveling was in Virginia, West Virginia, Kentucky, Tennessee, and North Carolina. Playing with the string band exposed Martin to many forms of music—blues, hillbilly, popular tunes, and ragtime. And from his fellow musicians, Martin learned the fundamentals of playing the fiddle, string bass, and mandolin as well as improving his guitar technique.

In 1930 the group, which consisted of Carl and Roland Martin and fiddler Howard Armstrong, made one record for Brunswick. The trio was not pleased with the way the company handled the financial aspects of its arrangement, which put it off from recording again.

By late 1932 Martin and his friends had moved to Chicago and were making a steady living playing music in just about any situation—church services, weddings, dances, and beer joints were among their regular venues. About 1933, Spartanburg, South Carolina, guitarist Ted Bogan joined the band, forming a group that played together for many years.

Martin's bitter feelings about his bad experience with Brunswick seem to have waned quickly; he recorded several times as a featured artist between 1934 and 1936. He also appeared as an accompanist on many other recordings by such non-Virginia artists as Bumble Bee Slim, Mr. Freddie Spruell, and the State Street Boys.

Carl Martin

Except for a brief stint in the army, Martin played music as a full-time occupation until the middle 1950s, when the demand for his services diminished greatly. Martin remained in Chicago and in the middle 1960s he began playing and recording again, this time for Testament Records, at the urging of blues fans. In the early 1970s he was reunited with Ted Bogan and Howard Armstrong and once more toured across the country. This time the trio was performing and recording for a predominantly white audience. This revitalization of his career lasted until Martin's death on May 10, 1979, in Detroit.

Chicago, Illinois, 27 October 1934
Carl Martin: Carl Martin, guitar/vocal

80933-1	You Can Go Your Way	Bb 5745, *WO 123*
80934-1	Kid Man Blues	Bb 5745, *WO 123*

Chicago, Illinois, 8 January 1935
As above: add Roland Armstrong, string bass

C-877-1	Farewell to You, Baby	OK 8961, Vo 03003, *CON 002, YZ 1016, WO 123*
C-878-1	You Can't Play Me Cheap	Vo 03047, *CON 002, WO 123*
C-881-2	Badly Mistreated Man	OK 8961, Vo 03003, *CON 002, YZ 1016, WO 123*
C-882-2	Good Morning, Judge	Vo 03047, *CON 002, OJL 18, WO 123*

Chicago, Illinois, 27 July 1935
As above: omit Roland Armstrong

91427-1	Crow Jane	Bb 6139, *YZ 1013, WO 123*
91428-1	Old Time Blues	Bb 6139, *YZ 1013, BRI 008, WO 123*

Chicago, Illinois, 22 August 1935
As above
C-1101-A   That New Kind of Stuff   Vo 03496, *STA 107, WO 123*
[Reverse Vo 03496 by Casey Bill.]

Chicago, Illinois, 4 September 1935
As above: add possibly Willie B. James, guitar

90293-A	Joe Louis Blues	De 7114, *YZ 1016, WO 123*
90294-A	Let's Have a New Deal	De 7114, *BC 14, WO 123*

Chicago, Illinois, 24 March 1936
As above: add Chuck Segar, piano

90635-   I'm Gonna Have Fun (When I Get My Bonus)   Chm 50074, *WO 123*

Chicago, Illinois, 18 April 1936
As above: add unknown tenor saxophone and piano

90681-A   High Water Flood Blues   Chm 50074, *WO 123*

Bibliography: Pete Welding, brochure notes to "The Chicago String Band," TE 2220; ———, "Carl Martin 1906-1979," *Living Blues* 43 (Summer 1979): 28, 29, and 40. *See also* Tennessee Chocolate Drops.

John Martin
A pseudonym on Superior for Roy Harvey.

Troy Martin
See Elvin Bigger

Howard Maxey
See Dr. Lloyd

Midnight Four
A pseudonym on Herwin for the Norfolk Jazz Quartet.

Mobile Four
A pseudonym on Herwin for the Norfolk Jubilee Quartet.

Monarch Jazz/Jubilee Quartet of Norfolk (late 1920s)
Their name and aural evidence indicate that this vocal group is from the Hampton Roads region. It has been suggested that the singers were actually the Norfolk Jazz/Jubilee Quartet recording for OKeh under a pseudonym, but no substantiation has been found.

Richmond, Virginia, 15 October 1929
Monarch Jazz Quartet: four male voices

403130-B   What's the Matter Now?   OK 8736, *NW 290*
403131-B   He-Ha-Ha Shout   OK unissued
403132-B   Just Too Late   OK 8931
403133-A   Pleading Blues   OK 8931, *BRI 006*

Byrd Moore

Richmond, Virginia, 16 October 1929
As above
403130-C   What's the Matter Now?   OK unissued
403146-B   Four or Five Times   OK 8736
403147-B   Mean to Me   OK unissued

New York, New York, 12 November 1929
Monarch Jubilee Quartet of Norfolk: presumably as above

403252-B   When I Was a Moaner   OK 8778
403253-A   King Jesus, Stand by Me   OK 8797
403254-A   Somebody's Always Talking about Me   OK 8778

New York, New York, 14 November 1929
403262-A   When Death Shall Shake This Frame   OK 8797
403263-A   Somebody's Wrong   OK 8761
403264-B   I Ain't Got Nobody (And Nobody Cares for Me)   OK 8761
[OK 8761 issued as by the Monarch Jazz Quartet]

Byrd Moore (ca. 1910–ca. 1942)

Because he was a drifter and itinerant musician, the details of Byrd Moore's life remain unclear. Moore was possibly born in Blackwater, Virginia, as William B. Moore in April 1889, but moved throughout southwestern Virginia, southeastern Kentucky, and northeastern Tennessee during much of his life. He was most active as a guitarist, both as a sideman and group leader, during the 1920s and 1930s, playing with such diverse musicians as Scott Boatwright and Earl Johnson. In addition to playing music, Moore supported himself by working as a barber.

From recent research it appears that Moore lived in Whitesburg, Kentucky, where he married in the early 1920s. At about the same time he lived briefly with the family of Fiddlin' Powers and taught Carrie Belle Powers to play the guitar. By the middle 1920s he was performing regularly with banjo player Dock Boggs in and around Wise County.

Moore worked regularly and recorded with fiddler Melvin Robinette in 1929. About the same time he evidently spent some time in Monticello, Kentucky, with the old-time fiddle and banjo duo of Dick Burnett and Leonard Rutherford. Between 1928 and 1932 Moore often recorded as a sideman for musicians such as Clarence Greene and Jess Johnston, whom he apparently recruited for Gennett Records. Moore was also a member of Georgia fiddler Earl Johnson's fine string band that recorded for OKeh and Victor in 1928 and 1929.

During the early 1930s he lived in Esserville, Virginia, and was married to a local bootlegger. By the 1940s Moore was burdened by a difficult drinking

Byrd Moore's Hot Shots, 1929, probably Ashe County, North Carolina. From left, Byrd Moore, Clarence Greene, Tom Ashley. *Courtesy Clarence H. Greene*

problem and possibly diabetes. The late 1940s found him living in the Wise County Poorhouse without his music and in ill health. According to several unconfirmable reports, Moore died in the poorhouse in 1949.

Richmond, Indiana, ca. 22 June 1928
Byrd Moore: Byrd Moore, vocal/guitar; unknown banjo, (1)

13901-	Mamma Toot Your Whistle (1)	Ge 6586, Spt 9399
13902-	The Bully of the Town (1)	Ge 6763, Spt 9399
13903-A	All Night Long	Ge 6686, Cq 7259
13904-A and B	How I Got My Wife (1)	Ge rejected
13905-A	Way Down in Florida on a Bum (1)	Ge rejected
13906-	Harvey Logan	Ge 6549
13907-	Bed Bugs Makin' Their Last Go Round	Ge 6586, Cq 7259
13908-A	Hobo's Paradise (1)	Ge 6549, Spt 9184
13909-	Careless Lover (1)	Ge 6991
13910-A	On the Banks of the Old Tennessee (1)	Ge rejected

[Spt released as by Harry Carter; Cq released as by Oscar Carver; reverse Spt 9184 by H.K. Hutchison]

Richmond, Indiana, ca. 30 October 1928
As above
14400-	Snatch 'Em Back Blues	Ge 6763
14401-	Back Water Blues	Ge 6686

Richmond, Indiana, ca. 10 April 1929
Robinette and Moore: add Melvin Robinette, fiddle (1)/vocal (2); delete both vocals (3); speech by both men (4)

15020-	Birmingham Jail (1, 2)	Ge 6841, Chm 15750, Spt 9536, Spr 2640
15021-	Good Bye Sweetheart (1, 2)	Ge 7068, Spt 9536
15022-	When the Snowflakes Fall Again (1, 4)	Ge 6841, Chm 15732, Spt 9560
15027-	Mama Don't Allow No Hangin' Around (1)	Ge 6991
15028-	Flop Eared Mule (1, 3, 4)	Ge 6884, Spt 9500
15029-	Favorite Two Step (1, 3)	Ge 6957
15030-	That Old Tiger Rag (1, 3)	Ge 6957, Ch 427, Spr 2696

Richmond, Indiana, ca. 11 April 1929
As above
15036-	Last Days in Georgia (1, 3, 4)	Ge 6884, Spt 9500, Spr 2696, *CY 527*

[Ges issued as by Robinette and Moore; reverse Ge 7068 by Asa Martin and Doc Roberts; Chm 15732 as by Henry Johnson; Chm 15750 as by Ezra Hill and Henry Johnson (reverse of both by Rutherford and Foster); Spt 9500 and Spt 9536 issued as by Clark and Howell; Spt 9560 issued as by Harry Carter (reverse by Dick Parman); reverse Spr 2640 by Rutherford and Foster; Spr 2696 issued as by Jack Burdette and Bert Moss; Ch 427 issued as by Robinson and Evans (reverse by Louie Donaldson and Hoke Rice; Spt 9500 issued as "Flop Eared Mule"]

Johnson City, Tennessee, 23 October 1929
Byrd Moore and His Hot Shots: Clarence Greene, fiddle/vocal; Clarence Ashley, guitar/vocal; Byrd Moore, guitar/vocal

149240-1	Frankie Silvers	Co 15536, *OT 102*
149241-2	The Hills of Tennessee	Co 15536
149242-2	Careless Love	Co 15496, *CY 504*
149243-2	Three Men Went A-Hunting	Co 15496, *LBC 13, OT 101*

Richmond, Indiana, ca. 13 February 1930
Moore and Greene: Clarence Greene, fiddle/vocal (1); Byrd Moore, guitar/vocal (2); Allen D. Cole, fiddle (3); omit Greene (4)

16258-A	Lay Down Baby Blues	Ge rejected
16259-B	Cincinnati Rag	Chm 16357, Spr 2838
16260-A	Pig Angle	Chm 16357, Spr 2838
16261-	Pride of the Ball	Ge rejected
16262-A	In the Hills of Old Tennessee (1, 2)	Ge rejected
16263-A	West Virginia Sally Ann (3, 4)	Ge rejected

[Spr issued as by Moss and Long; 16262 as by Fiddlin' Greene and Byrd Moore; 16263 as by Byrd Moore and Allen D. Cole]

Richmond, Indiana, ca. 14 February 1930
As above

16264-A	Eagle Rock	Ge rejected
16265-A	The Lonesome Valley	Ge rejected
16267-A	Frankie Silver's Confession	Ge rejected
16269-A	Boatman's Dance (3, 4)	Ge rejected
16274-	The Up North Blues (4)	Ge rejected
16276-	Got the Guitar Blues (4)	Spr 2559

[Spr issued as by Bert Moss; 16264 may have either Greene or Cole on fiddle; 16274 may have Byrd Moore on banjo; 16276 has yodeling, probably by Moore]

Richmond, Indiana, ca. 17 September 1930
Byrd Moore and Jess Johnston: Jess Johnston, fiddle; Byrd Moore, guitar/vocal (1); omit Johnston (2)

William Moore

17087-A	Killin' Blues	Chm 16469, Spr 2539, *CY 548*
17089-A	My Trouble Blues	Chm 16469, Spr 2539
17091-	Jake Leg Blues (1, 2)	Spr 2559, *STA 110*
17092-A	Lovin' Blues (1, 2)	Ge rejected

[Spr 2539 issued as by Bert Moss and Joe Long; Spr 2559 issued as by Bert Moss; 17091 as by Byrd Moore]

Richmond, Indiana, ca. 10 October 1930
Johnston and Moore: Jess Johnston, guitar; Byrd Moore, guitar

17166-	Root Hog or Die	Ge rejected
17167-	It Might Have Been Worse	Ge rejected

Richmond, Indiana, ca. 25 August 1932
Byrd Moore and His Hot Shots: presumably Byrd Moore, guitar/vocal; Jess Johnston, fiddle or guitar; [?] McKinney, unknown instrument; [?] Henry, unknown instrument

18736-	Take a Circle around the Moon	Ge unissued
18737-	When I Walk into Your Parlor	Ge unissued
18738-	Spring Roses	Chm 16498
18739-	O Take Me Back	Chm 16498

See also Melvin Robinette.

William Moore (ca. 1915–ca. 1940)

Born in Tappahannock, Virginia, on March 3, 1893, William Moore played fiddle, piano, and guitar for local dances around Essex County. Many older local residents recall him, but how Moore came to record for the Paramount Record Company is unclear. Most people remember Moore as a barber who also farmed to supplement his income.

He worked in a Warsaw, Virginia, barbershop until the mid-1940s. Because of declining health, Moore moved to Warrenton, Virginia, in the late 1940s to live with his son. He died there of a heart attack on November 22, 1951, and is buried in a small Warrenton graveyard.

Chicago, Illinois, ca. January 1928
Bill Moore: Bill Moore, guitar/vocal/guitar solo with speech (1)

20309-1	One Way Gal	Pm 12648, *BRI 006, OJL 8, FL 103, MA 204*
20310-3	Ragtime Crazy (1)	Pm 12648, *RT 318, OJL 18, MA 204*
20312-2	Midnight Blues	Pm 12636, *RT 340, MA 204*
20313-1	Ragtime Millionaire	Pm12636, *YZ 1016, MA 204*
20314-3	Tillie Lee	Pm 12613, *MA 204*
20315-2	Barbershop Rag	Pm 12613, *BRI 006, YZ 1013, MA 204*

20323-1	Old Country Rock	Pm 12761, *OJL 2, MA 204*
20324-1	Raggin' the Blues	Pm 12761, *YZ 1013, MA 204*
	Silas Green from New Orleans	Pm unissued
	How the Sun Do Shine	Pm unissued
	Catfish Woman Blues	Pm unissued
	Chicken Feathers	Pm unissued
	Rough and Ready Blues	Pm unissued
	I Got Mine	Pm unissued
	Stranger Blues	Pm unissued
	Unfortunate Blues	Pm unissued

[Pm 12761 issued as by William Moore]

Bibliography: Kip Lornell, brochure notes to "Tidewater Blues," BRI 006; Paul Oliver, brochure notes to "Ragtime Blues Guitar," MA 204.

Bert Moss (and Joe Long)

A pseudonym on Superior for Byrd Moore (and Jess Johnston).

Moses and Long

A pseudonym on Superior for Byrd Moore and Clarence Greene.

Mountaineers

A pseudonym on Broadway for the Highlanders.

E.R. Nance Family (1928–1955)

The family of Earl Nance was deeply involved with performing religious music and teaching shape-note singing schools throughout north central North Carolina and south central Virginia. For most of the thirty years that the Nances were teaching, the family members were living in Yadkin County, North Carolina, between Booneville and Elkin.

For several months in 1931 the family lived in Iowa, where Earl had a brother. The Depression had hurt the farm economy in North Carolina and Nance hoped to find work in Iowa. The move did not work well and by the fall of 1931 the family had moved to Bassett in Henry County, Virginia, where they settled for several years while Nance taught shape-note singing in many local churches. After a few years in Stoneville, North Carolina, Earl Nance moved back to Yadkin County, where he remained until his death in 1955.

Teaching shape-note singing was a family enterprise that involved his wife, Maddie, and their children Earl Jr. and Helen. Both Maddie and Helen played keyboards and helped with the instruction. An instructional session took between two and ten days, though most often it was a weekly meeting that lasted

E.R. Nance Family

from one month to six weeks. Because teaching singing schools did not provide a full-time living, Earl Nance supplemented this income by working in textile mills or farming.

One other way that Nance tried to make extra income was by recording. Unfortunately, he attempted to launch his recording career at the worst possible time—in 1930 and 1931. In 1930 he brought the family up to New York City in order to audition for Art Satherley of the American Record Corporation. Satherley recorded many sides by the group, most of which remained unissued. In addition to the keyboard accompaniment of Helen and Maddie Nance, the family brought along two neighbors, Dewey and Sam Hill, who played harmonica, guitar, and autoharp. The Hill brothers also recorded some sides at the same session—these too remain unissued and are included here to maintain continuity.

The next session occurred when the family traveled to Iowa. Nance knew that Gennett Records was based in Richmond, Indiana, so he stopped in Richmond in April 1931 and successfully auditioned for Gennett's Champion label. These records came out during the depths of the Depression and sold poorly. The family also returned to New York City to make some recordings for the Brunswick Company. This time they brought two other neighbors with them, Byron Bryan and Sam Hallbrook, to provide string accompaniment. Once more, the records sold poorly.

Despite a failed recording career, the E.R. Nance family had a strong local impact because of its teaching and performing. The only family member still active in promoting shape-note singing is Helen Nance Church, who regularly teaches singing schools.

New York, New York, 28 April 1928
The Nance Singers: Earl Nance, bass voice; Maddie Nance, soprano voice; Rita Jolly, tenor voice; Valena Jolly, soprano voice; Helen Nance, alto voice/organ (1)/piano (2) Dewey Hill, vocal (3)/guitar (4)/harmonica (5); Sam Hill, autoharp (6)

9645-1	The King Needs Workers (1)	Pe 154
9646-	His Death Was Not in Vain (2)	ARC unissued
9647-	Lend Your Aid (2)	ARC unissued
9648-	Tell It with Joy (2)	ARC unissued
9649-	Little Darling Pal of Mine (3, 4, 5, 6)	ARC unissued
9650-	My Dream (3, 4, 5, 6)	ARC unissued
9651-	Old Hymns Are Best	ARC unissued

[9649 and 9650 are listed as by Hill Brothers and Helen Nance, and delete all other vocals except Helen Nance]

The Nance Family in 1925, Yadkin County, North Carolina. From left, Helen, Earl Jr., Maddie, and Earl. *Courtesy Helen Nance Church*

The Nance Family Singers in the ARC Studies, New York City, 1930. From left, Helen Nance, Valena Jolly, Rita Jolly, and Mrs. Maddie Nance (piano). *Courtesy Helen Nance Church*

E.R. Nance Family   123

New York, New York, 29 April 1930
As above
9652-   Sail Away Home (2)   ARC unissued
9653-   The Time Is Now (2)   ARC unissued
9654-   Happy Am I (2)   ARC unissued
9658-   The Place Prepared for Me (2)   ARC unissued
9659-   Hallelujah to the Lamb (3, 4, 5, 6)   ARC unissued
9660-   Looking to My Prayers (6)   ARC unissued
9661-2   On the Sea of Life (4)   Ba 0717, Ho 16108, Je 20018, Or 8018, Ro 5018
9662-   Watching You (2)   ARC unissued

[9659 deletes all vocals and is credited to the Hill Brothers; reverse of all issues of 9661-2 by Arthur Cornwell and William Cleary; 9660 through 9662 listed as by the E.R. Nance Singers]

New York, New York, 30 April 1930
As above
9663-   The Old Rugged Cross (1)   ARC unissued
9664-   The House upon a Rock (1)   ARC unissued
9665-   That Will Be a Happy Moment   ARC unissued
9666-   Is It Well with Your Soul? (1)   ARC unissued
9667-   I'd Like to Live There with You   ARC unissued
9675-   The Wild and Reckless Hobo (3, 4, 5, 6)   ARC unissued
9676-   Jack and Joe (3, 4, 5, 6)   ARC unissued
9677-   In Heaven (4)   ARC unissued

[The organ on 9664 may be by Maddie Nance; delete Earl Nance on 9667; 9675 and 9676 are credited to the Hill Brothers, delete all other vocals]

New York, New York, 2 May 1930
As above
9678-   When They Ring Those Golden Bells (1)   ARC unissued
9679-   What a Friend We Have in Jesus   ARC unissued
9685-2   If I Could Hear My Mother Pray Again (1)   Pe 154
9686-   Everybody's Happy There (1)   ARC unissued
9687-   When God's Singers Reach Heaven (1)   ARC unissued
9688-   The Speckled Peas   ARC unissued
9689-   The Barnyard Conference   ARC unissued

[The organ on 9678 may be by Rita Jolly; 9679 listed as by The Nance Female Quartet, which implies deleting Earl Nance; 9688 and 9689 are spoken comedy sketches without instrumental accompaniment]

New York, New York, 14 April 1931
Nance Family Singers with Traphill Twins: Helen Nance, alto voice; Earl Nance, bass voice; Maddie Nance, soprano voice; Byron Bryan, banjo; Sam Hallbrook, guitar

E-36575	Sweet Freedom	Br 565
E-36576	The Lawson Murder	Br 542
E-36577	Mother's Advice	Br 542
E-36578	I'm on My Way to Heaven	Br 565

Richmond, Indiana, ca. 20 April 1931
E.R. Nance "Booneville Singers:" Helen Nance, alto voice; Earl Nance, bass voice; Maddie Nance, soprano voice

17862-   The Lot in Canaan's Land   Ge test

Richmond, Indiana, ca. 26 August 1931
E.R. Nance Family with Clarence Dooley: As above, add Helen Nance, mandolin/piano (1); Clarence Dooley, guitar/vocal

17955-	Goodbye to My Stepstone	Chm 16316
17956-	A Mother's Advice	Chm 16316
17957-	The Lot in Canaan's Land	Chm 16410, Spr 2720
17958-	Sweet Freedom	Chm 16410, Spr 2813
17959-	I Am on My Way to Heaven	Chm 16330, Chm 45138, Spr 2750
17960-	The Time Is Now (1)	Ch 16418
17961-	All Will Be Well when the Night Is Past (1)	Ch 16369, Spr 2813

[Sprs issued as by James Horton and Family]

Richmond, Indiana, ca. 27 August 1931
As above

17962-	Somebody's Knocking at Your Door	Chm 16369, Spr 2750
17963-	I Want to Go—I Want to Go	Chm 16418
17964-	Do You Think I'll Make a Soldier (1)	Chm 16330, Chm 45138, Spr 2720

[17692 and 17693 delete all instrumental accompaniment; Sprs as by James Horton and Family]

See also Hill Brothers and Willie Simmons.

Nazareth Jubilee Singers
A pseudonym on Herwin for the Norfolk Jubilee Quartet.

J.P. Nester (ca. 1920–ca. late 1940s)
The banjo and fiddle duo of John Preston Nester and Norman Edmonds was from Hillsville in Carroll County, Virginia. For many years banjo player Nester,

born on November 26, 1876, and fiddler Edmonds played in Carroll County before deciding to try to record for a commercial company. In 1927 they crossed the rugged mountains to Bristol, Tennessee, where the Victor Company was holding auditions. Along with the Carter Family, Alfred Karnes, Jimmie Rodgers, and the Johnson Brothers, Nestor and Edmonds were successful. Despite their equal partnership, the Victor Company chose not to co-credit Norman Edmonds (born on February 9, 1899, in Wythe County, Virginia) on the record label itself.

Like many other early folk music recording artists, this duo never pursued a professional music career after their single session. Nestor and Edmonds returned to Hillsville and declined to record again when Victor returned to Bristol the following year. Both men remained in Carroll County and continued to play music for many years. Nester died on April 10, 1967. Norman Edmonds remained a vigorous fiddler, even recording an album for Davis Unlimited several years prior to his death on November 21, 1976.

Bristol, Tennessee, 1 August 1927
John Preston Nester: J.P. Nester, banjo/vocal; Norman Edmonds, fiddle

39744-2	Train on the Island	Vi 21707, *CY 535, FW FA 2953*
39745-1	Georgia	Vi unissued
39746-1	John My Lover	Vi unissued
39747-1	Black-Eyed Susan	Vi 21707, *CY 535, RCA LPV 552, CMF-001-L*

Bibliography: Stephen Davis and Richard Nobley, "Norman Edmonds," *Old Time Music* 7 (Summer 1973): 22-23.

Fred Newman
A pseudonym on Paramount for Roy Harvey.

Norfolk Jazz/Jubilee Quartet (ca. 1917–ca. 1942)
Prior to 1950, Tidewater was clearly the center for Afro-American gospel quartet singing in Virginia. Along with Birmingham, Alabama, Norfolk has been viewed as a stronghold for harmony singing. The Norfolk Jazz/Jubilee Quartet was one of the most popular community-based groups in Tidewater as well as the most prolifically recorded of the prewar quartets. Furthermore, their lengthy recording career documents the stylistic changes in popular and sacred Afro-American quartet singing in the United States over nearly a twenty-year period.

The group was formed during World War I by Len Williams (bass), Buddy Butts (tenor), Otto Tutson (second tenor), and Delrose Hollins (baritone). They were soon popular enough to appear on the vaudeville circuit as far west as

Chicago and north into New England. It was perhaps this visibility that attracted OKeh Records to contact them for a session in March 1921. During the Norfolk Jazz/Jubilee Quartet's earliest recording period its repertoire reflected its vaudeville orientation by stressing blues, "coon" songs, and other secular material.

In April of 1923 the Norfolk Jubilee and Jazz Quartet switched its allegiance to the Paramount Record Company, which was near the beginning of its legendary 12/13000 "race" series. This alliance lasted for six years and produced over forty releases. Interestingly, the Norfolk Jazz/Jubilee Quartet's association with Paramount yielded a high percentage of religious sides; perhaps the record company thought it could sell more sacred records. It is also possible that the group itself felt more drawn to the religious singing. In any event, the group continued to perform on the professional stage, traveling the East Coast on a full-time basis.

The Depression stopped the Norfolk Jazz/Jubilee Quartet's recording career as well as much of its travel. Instead the group concentrated on local programs and began singing at more churches. In 1937 Decca Records offered the quartet a chance to record, which brought the group to New York City. In New York the singers appeared on many radio programs and larger gospel shows with groups such as the Deep River Boys (alumni of Hampton Institute) and Norfolk's Golden Gate Quartet.

In 1940 the group's founder and prime moving force, Len Williams, collapsed on stage and died. His passing left the Norfolk Jazz/Jubilee Quartet without a strong leader. This factor, along with the tough years during World War II and perhaps other artistic and personal considerations, helped to dissolve the group in 1941. By that time two of its important singers, "Crip" Harris and Melvin Colden, had moved on to other groups.

New York, New York, March 1921
Norfolk Jazz Quartet: James Butts, tenor voice; Otto Tutson, lead voice; Delrose Hollins, baritone voice; Len Williams, bass voice

7808-A	Monday Morning Blues	OK 4345
7809-B	Jelly Roll Blues	OK 4318, Sun 4318
7810-B	Standing on the Corner	OK 4345
7812-B	Wide Wide World	OK 4366
7813-B	Preacher Man Blues	OK 4366
7814-B	Southern Jack	OK 4318, Sun 4318

New York, New York, July 1921
As above
70002-B	Cornfield Blues	OK 4380
70003-B	Big Fat Mamma	OK 4380
70004-B	Strut Miss Lizzie	OK 8007

Norfolk Jazz Quartet, 1940. From left, Len Williams (manager/bass), Melvin Colden (baritone), Isaiah Sessons (second tenor), Norman Harris (first tenor). *Courtesy Norfolk Journal and Guide*

A 1929 Paramount catalogue including a listing for a release by the Norfolk Jubilee Quartette. *Courtesy Dave Freeman (County Records).*

70005-B My Mammy   OK 8007
70006-C Blues That Drove Man to Ruin   OK 4391
70007-B I Hope I May Join the Band   OK 4400
70008-B Who Built the Ark?   OK 4400
70009-A Going Home Blues   OK 4391
[OK 4400 issued as by the Norfolk Jubilee Quartet]

New York, New York, September 1921
As above
70171-A Honey, Bless Your Heart   OK 8019
70172-B Wang Wang Blues   OK 8022
70173-B When I Walked Up I Was Sharp as a Tack   OK 8019
70174-B Get Hot   OK 8022
70176-A Every Ship Must Have a Harbor   OK 8034
70178-B I Could Learn to Love You   OK 8028
[Reverse of OK 8028 and OK 8034 by the Palmetto Jazz Quartet]

New York, New York, April 1923
As above: add J. "Buddy" Archer, tenor voice; delete James Butts

1365-2 Quartette Blues   Pm 12055
1365-2
  and 3 Sad Blues   Pm 12054
1366-1
  and 2 Stop Dat Band   Pm 12054
1367-1 Father Prepare Me   Pm 12035
1368-1 My Lord's Gonna Move This Wicked Race   Pm 12055
1370-2 Raise R-U-K-U-S Tonight   Pm 12032
1371-2
  and 3 Dixie Blues   Pm 10255
1374-1
  and 2 Ain't It a Shame   Pm 12032
[Pm 12032 issued as by the Norfolk Jazz Quartette; Pm 12035 issued as by the Norfolk Jubilee Quartet or as by the Jubilee Quartet]

New York, New York, July 1924
Norfolk Jubilee Quartet: as above

1803-1 Where Shall I Be   Pm 12234
1803-2 Where Shall I Be   Pm 12234, Bw 5074
1804-2 I'm a Pilgrim   Pm 12225, Bw 5000
1808-1 I'm Gonna Build Right on Dat Shore   Pm 12234
1808-2 I'm Gonna Build Right on Dat Shore   Pm 12234, Bw 5074
1809-1
  and 2 Crying Holy unto the Lord   Pm 12217, Pm 13146, Bw 5077

Norfolk Jazz/Jubilee Quartet

1810-1
and 2   Roll Jordan Roll   Pm 12233
1811-1
and 2   I'm Going to Meet My Mother   Pm 12233
1812-1   Swing Low Sweet Chariot   Pm 12225, Bw 5000
1813-1   Eziekel Saw de Wheel [sic]   Pm 12217, Pm 13146
1813-2   Eziekel Saw de Wheel [sic]   Pm 12217, Bw 5077
1814-2   Pleading Blues   Pm 12218
1817-1
and 2   Jelly Roll's First Cousin   Pm 12218

[Pm 12225, Pm 12233, Pm 12234 issued as by the Norfolk Jubilee Quartette; Pm 13146 and later copies of Pm 12217 also issued as by the Norfolk Jubilee Quartette; Pm 12218 as by the Norfolk Jazz Quartette; Bw 5000 (1804-2) issued as by the Jubilee Gospel Singers; Bw 5000 (1812-1), Bw 5074, Bw 5077 issued as by the Virginia Jubilee Singers; Bw 5077 (1813-2) issued as "Ezekiel Saw de Wheel"]

New York, New York, August 1924

As above
1846-   There Will Be Glory   Pm unissued
1847-   I'm Gonna Open My Mouth to the Lord   Pm unissued

New York, New York, March 1925

As above
2048-1
and -2   What You Going to Do when the Worlds on Fire   Pm 12266
2049-2   When I Was a Moaner   Pm 12266
2050-1   Throw out the Lifeline   Pm 12267, Sil 3575
2051-2   Get on Board, Little Children, Get on Board   Pm 12268, He 92009
2052-3   Every Time I Feel the Spirit   Pm 12268
2053-3   I'm Gonna Make Heaven My Home   Pm 12267, Sil 3575
2056-2   Somebody's Always Talking about Me   Pm 12301, Bw 5002
2057-2   Sit Down Sit Down I Can't Sit Down   Pm 12031, Bw 5002

[Bw 5002 issued as by the Virginia Jubilee Singers; He 92009 issued as by the Southland Jubilee Singers—not to be confused with the Southland Singers listed in this volume; Sil 3575 issued as by the Midnight Four; reverse of He 92009 by the Wiseman Sextet]

New York, New York, January 1926

As above
2394-1
and 2   Pharoah's Army Got Drowned   Pm 12342
2395-2   Great Jehovah   Pm 12342
2396-1   I'm Gonna Do All I Can for My Lord   Pm 12356
2396-2   I'm Gonna Do All I Can for My Lord   He 92030
2397-1   Jesus Lay Your Head in the Window   Pm 12356

2397-2   Jesus Lay Your Head in the Window   He 92030
2398-1   Revival Day   Pm 12371
2399-1
 and 2   Do You Want to Be a Lover of the Lord   Pm 12421, Bw 5036
2401-1
 and 2   See the Sign of Judgement   Pm 12371

[Bw 5036 issued as by the Virginia Jubilee Singers; He 92030 issued as by the Mobile Four]

New York, New York, October 1926

As above
2713-4   Oh the Shoes That My Lord Gave Me   Pm 12421, Bw 5036
2714-1   I Want to Cross over to See My Lord   Pm 12694, Pm 13145, He 93026, Chm 50020
2717-3   If Anybody Asks You Who I Am   Pm 12468, Pm 13147, Bw 5082
2718-3   Let the Church Roll On   Pm 12468, Pm 13147, Bw 5082
2719-3   Queen St. Rag   Pm 12453
2721-3   Louisiana Bo Bo   Pm 12453

[Bw 5036, Bw 5082 issued as by the Virginia Jubilee Singers; He 93026 issued as by the Georgia Sacred Singers; Pm 12453 issued as by the Norfolk Jazz Quartet; Reverse of Pm 13145, Chm 50020 by Carroll Clark]

New York, New York, February 1927

As above
2811-2   Swing Low, Sweet Chariot   Pm 12445, He 93003
2812-2   Down by the Riverside   Pm 12445, He 93003
2814-1   I'm Nearer My Home   Pm 12694, He 93026
2815-1   Daniel in the Lions' Den   Pm 12499, Bw 5051
2816-2   The Old Account Was Settled Long Ago   Pm 12499, Bw 5051
2817-1   I Will Guide Thee   Pm 12515
2818-1
 and 2   Shepard Where Is Your Little Lamb [sic]   Pm 12515

[Bw 5051 as by the Virginia Jubilee Singers; He 93003 as by the Nazareth Jubilee Quartet; He 93026 as by the Georgia Sacred Singers]

New York, New York, September 1927

As above
2871-1   King Jesus Stand by Me   Pm 13148
2871-2   King Jesus Stand by Me   Pm 12589
2872-2   My Lord's Gonna Move This Wicked Race   Pm 12035
2873-1
 and 2   Father Prepare Me   Pm 12035
2875-2   Ride On, King Jesus   Pm 12669, Pm 13149
2877-1   Our Father   Pm 12669, Pm 13149

Norfolk Jazz/Jubilee Quartet

2880-1	I Have Anchored My Soul	Pm 12589, Pm 13148
2881-1	Crying Holy unto the Lord	Pm 12217
2882-2	Ezekiel Saw de Wheel	Pm 12217
2883-1	Where Shall I Be	Pm 12234
2884-2	I'm Gonna Build Right on Dat Shore	Pm 12234
2885-	His Eye Is on the Sparrow	Pm unissued
2886-2	I Wouldn't Mind Dying If Dying Was All	Pm 12630, Pm 13154, Bw 5048, Chm 50006, He 93028
2887-1	His Eye Is on the Sparrow	Pm 12630, Bw 5048, He 93028

[Bw 5048, He 93028 issued as by the Georgia Sacred Singers]

New York, New York, October 1927

As above

2900-3	How It Is with Me	Pm 12785
2901-1	Wonder Where Is the Gamblin' Man	Pm 12715, Pm 13150, Cr 3328, Va 6011, *HEG 310*
2902-1 and 2	He Just Hung His Head and Died	Pm 12734, Pm 13155, Bw 5047, He 93025, Chm 50005, *HEG 310*
2903-1	Sinner You Can't Hide	Pm 12749
2904-2	When the Moon Goes Down	Pm 12890, Bw 5049, He 92037
2905-2	Lord I Don' Care Where They Bury My Body	Pm 12734, Pm 13155, Bw 5047, He 93025, Chm 50005, *HEG 310*
2906-1 and 2	I Want to Know Will He Welcome Me There	Pm 12785
2907-1	I'm Going Through	Pm 12749
2908-2	You're Goin' to Need That Pure Religion	Pm 12715, Pm 13150, Cr 3328, Va 6008, JD 7000

[Bw 5047, Bw 5049, He 92037 issued as by the Georgia Sacred Singers; JD and Va as by the Jubilee Male Quartet; Va 6011 issued as by the Down South Boys; reverse of Va 6008, JD 7000 by the Famous Blue Jay Singers; Va 6011 by Black Billy Sunday]

Probably New York, New York, February 1929

As above: add unknown piano (1); Norman "Crip" Harris; delete J. "Buddy" Archer

6100-3	Way Down in Egypt land [sic] (1)	Pm 12818, Pm 13151
6101-1	I Heard the Voice of Jesus Say	Pm 12993
6102-2	I'm Pressing on to That City	Pm 12993
6104-2	Tell Me What You Say	Pm 12929
6105-2	Oh What a Beautiful City	Pm 12929
6106-1	There Will Be Glory	Pm 12957
6107-2	I'm Gonna Open My Mouth unto the Lord (1)	Pm 12957, Chm 50006
6108-2	Moanin' in the Land Will Soon Be Over	Pm 12890, Bw 5049, He 92037, *HEG 310*

6109-1	I'm Gonna Serve God Till I Die	Pm 12818
6109-2	I'm Gonna Serve God Till I Die	Pm 13151, Pm 13154
6111-2	Please Give Me Some of That (1)	Pm 12844
6112-1	Oh Whats the Matter Now [sic] (1)	Pm 12844

[Pm 12844 issued as by the Norfolk Jazz Quartet; Bw 5049 and He 92037 issued as by the Georgia Sacred Singers. An alternative issue of He 92037 by Katherine Baker also exists.]

New York, New York, 14 July 1937
As above: Raymond Smith, tenor voice; Melvin Colden, baritone voice; Len Williams, bass voice; Norman "Crip" Harris, tenor voice and lead; unknown tiple (1)

62376-A	You Got to Live So God Can Use You	De 7359, *HEG 310*
62377-A	Way Down in Egypt Land	De 7421, *HEG 310*
62378-A	Didn't It Rain	De 7359, *HEG 310*
62379-A	Believe in Jesus	De 7533, *HEG 310*
62380-A	My Feet Been Taken out the Mirey Clay	De 7421
62381-A	King Jesus Stand by Me	De 7572
62382-A	Tell That Broad (You Came Too Late) (1)	De 7333
62383-B	Swinging That Blues (Ever Had the Blues) (1)	De 7333
62390-A	Ha Ha Shout (1)	De 7383
62391-A	What's the Matter Now? (1)	De 7383

[De 7333, De 7383 issued as by the Norfolk Jazz Quartet]

New York, New York, 15 July 1937
As above

62392-A	I Can't Stay Away	De 7595
62393-A	Pure Religion	De 7336, *HEG 310*
62394-A	Where's That Gambling Man Gone?	De 7582, *HEG 310*
62395-A	My Lord's Gonna Move This Wicked Race	De 7336
62396-A	Free at Last	De 7402, *HEG 310*
62397-A	Sit Down, Sit Down, I Can't Sit Down	De 7402

New York, New York, 16 July 1937
As above

62414-A	Stand by Me	De 7559
62415-A	He's Mine, Yes He's Mine	De 7559
62416-	Just Dream of You (1)	De 7349
62417-	Shim Sham Shimmie at the Cricket's Ball (1)	De 7349

[De 7349 issued as by the Norfolk Jazz Quartet; De 7559 issued as by the Norfolk Jubilee Singers]

New York, New York, 19 July 1937
As above

62423-A	Beedle De Beedle De Bop Bop (Adi Aedi Idio) (1)	De 7443, *HEG 310*

62424-A   Suntan Baby Brown (Suntan Lady) (1)   De 7443, *MCA 144.003*
[De 7443 as by the Norfolk Jazz Quartet]

Charlotte, North Carolina, 5 June 1938
As above
64032-A   Stand by the Bedside of a Neighbor   De 7472, De 48004, *HEG 310*
64033-A   Job   De 7481
64034-A   Great Change   De 7595, *HEG 310*
64035-A   Come On! Let's Go to Heaven   De 7572
64036-A   Jesus Is Making Up My Dying Bed   De 7481, *HEG 310*
64037-A   Jonah in the Belly of the Whale   De 7472, De 48004, *HEG 310, MCA 510187, MCA VIM 5*
64038-A   When the Train Comes Along   De 7533, *HEG 310*
64039-A   No Hiding Place   De 7582, *HEG 310*

New York, New York, 23 August 1939
As above
66182-A   You Better Run   De 7758
66183-A   Shine for Jesus   De 7635
66184-A   Dig My Jelly Roll   De 7662
66185-A   Moaning the Blues   De 7662
66186-A   I'd Feel Much Better   De 7808, *BRI 006*
66187-A   This Old World Is in Bad Condition   De 7635
[De 7662, De 7808 issued as by the Virginia Four; De 7758 issued as by the Norfolk Jubilee Singers]

New York, New York, 19 April 1940
As above
67595-A   The Death Train Is Coming   De 7758
67596-A   Queen Street Rag   De 7808
[De 7758 issued as by the Norfolk Jubilee Singers; De 7808 issued as by the Virginia Four]

Bibliography: Ray Funk, brochure notes to "The Norfolk Jubilee Quartet," HEG 310; Vaughn Webb, brochure notes to "Hampton Roads Quartet Tradition," BRI 009.

Norris Brothers
A pseudonym on Supertone for Walter "Kid" Smith.

Odus and Woodrow
See Southern Melody Boys

Old South Quartette (ca. 1895–ca. 1930)

Little is known about the history of this black vocal ensemble from Richmond, Virginia, before it came under the direction of Polk Miller—a local white musician and entrepreneur. From 1893 until 1899 Miller toured the East Coast performing music and telling stories in Afro-American dialect. In 1899 he added the Old South Quartette to his performances.

During the first twelve years of this century, Polk Miller and the Old South Quartette, which was probably a community group "discovered" by Miller in Richmond, performed for wealthy white audiences in the Northeast and Midwest. Their act even took them to Carnegie Hall in New York City. In 1910 they were among the first black folk groups to make commercial recordings when they made seven cylinders for the Edison Company.

In 1912 Polk Miller was forced to exclude the Old South Quartette from his act by racist public pressure. Miller died in October 1913, but the quartet had been taken over by another, as yet unknown, management. They continued to tour into the late 1920s, playing vaudeville houses and theaters and still performing their varied repertoire of spirituals, comedy songs, and "plantation" melodies. During this same period they broadcast over WRVA in Richmond. Finally in 1928 they recorded for the QRS company.

Probably Richmond, Virginia, ca. 13 November 1990
Polk Miller and His Old South Quartette: James L. Stamper, bass voice; Randell Graves, tenor voice and lead; unknown tenor voice; unknown baritone voice; Polk Miller, lead vocal (1), banjo (2), guitar (3)

        The Bonnie Blue Flag (1, 3)   Ed 2175
        Laughing Song (2)   Ed 2176
        What a Time (2)   Ed 2177
        The Watermelon Party (2)   Ed 2178
        Rise and Shine (1, 2)   Ed 10332
        The Old Time Religion (1)   Ed 10333
        Jerusalem Mournin'   Ed 10334

[The first four Ed selections are amberol-type cylinders, which generally play for about four minutes. Ed 10332–34 have a shorter playing time and are issued by Polk Miller's Old South Quartette.]

Long Island City, New York, ca. August 1928
Old South Quartette: unknown male vocal quartet with guitar; unknown banjo (1)

157-A	Oh What He's Done for Me (1)	QRS 7025
159-	Watermillion Party [sic]	QRS 7029
162-A	Oysters and Wine at 2 A.M.	Bw 5031
164-A	Pussy Cat Rag	QRS 7006, Bw 5031

"OLD SOUTH QUARTETTE"

Old South Quartette, circa 1904. *Blue Ridge Heritage Archive/Kip Lornell*

166-A	When de Corn Pone's Hot	QRS 7029
168-	No Hiding Place Down Here	QRS 7025
	Oysters and Wine at 2 A.M.	QRS 7006

Bibliography: Doug Seroff, "Polk Miller and the Old South Quartette," *JEMF Quarterly* 18 (Fall/Winter 1982): 147-150; Doug Seroff, "Polk Miller and the Old South Quartette," 78 Quarterly, No. 3 (1988): 27-41; Jim Walsh, "Polk Miller and His Old South Quartet," *Hobbies* (January 1960).

Palmetto Jazz Quartet (early 1920's)

Nothing of substance is known of this quartet. A few of the Norfolk gospel singers from the 1920s recall the group, and one of its songs, "Norfolk Religion," calls attention to their possible origins. Their sound resembles that of other Hampton Roads groups.

New York, New York, ca. early September 1921
Palmetto Jazz Quartet: four male voices

70143-B	Base Ball Blues	OK 8023	
70145-A	Sweet Mamma (Papa's Getting Mad)	OK 8016
70149-B	Norfolk Religion	OK 8034	
70150-A	Home Again Blues	OK 8023	
70155-A	Old Pal Why Don't You Answer Me	OK 8016
70156-A	"U" Need Some Loving	OK 8028	
70165-A	My Jazz Gal	OK 8011	

[Reverse of OK 8011 by Tim Brymn; reverse of OK 8028 and OK 8034 by the Norfolk Jazz Quartet]

Red Patterson's Piedmont Log Rollers (1926–1933)

Like several other early hillbilly artists closely associated with Virginia, Patterson was born just south of Eden, North Carolina, about 1900. Patterson spent his childhood on the family tobacco farm before moving into Eden in about 1914 to work in the textile mills. It was at about this time that he began playing the piano and banjo and within a few years was playing for dances with musicians such as Charlie Poole.

By the mid-1920s the promise of slightly more lucrative textile mill work brought Patterson to Fieldale (Henry County). Before long he was playing regularly in a string band that included two brothers from nearby Stuart, Virginia, Lee (guitar) and Dick Nolan (tenor banjo), and fiddler player Percey Setliff. For many months Red Patterson's Piedmont Log Rollers entertained local citizens by playing for company functions and square dances.

The key to the group's recording was Kelly Harrell, a veteran of several OKeh

Red Patterson's Piedmont Log Rollers, 1927, probably Henry County, Virginia. From left, Percy Setliff, Dick Nolan, Lee Nolan, Red Patterson. *Courtesy Kinney Rorrer*

and Victor recording sessions and a Fieldale textile worker. At Harrell's urging Red Patterson and his group traveled south to Charlotte, North Carolina, with Harrell and his Virginia String Band to record eight selections for Victor. Harrell's band included vocalist Henry Norton of Danville, who also performed on the Patterson sides. The Piedmont Log Roller sides sold well locally, but their sales were not sufficient to encourage Victor to recall them for another session.

The Depression and the marriages of several of the musicians eventually broke up the band. By the late 1930s Patterson was still interested in music, but no longer played regularly. During his later years, Patterson returned to North Carolina, living on a farm he bought in Alamance County, where he died in February 1969.

Charlotte, North Carolina, 12 August 1927
Red Patterson's Piedmont Log Rollers: Percey Setliff, fiddle; Red Patterson, banjo and lead vocal; Dick Nolan, tenor banjo; Lee Nolan, guitar; Henry Norton, tenor vocal (1)

39797-2	My Sweetheart Is a Shy Little Fairy (1)	Vi 21187
39398-2	Don't Forget Me, Little Darling	Vi 21187
39799-3	Down on the Banks of the Ohio	Vi 35874, *RCA LPV 548*
39802-2	The White Rose	Vi 21132
39803-2	The Battleship Maine	Vi 20936
39804-2	Poor Little Joe	Vi 35874
39805-2	The Sweet Sunny South	Vi 21132, *CY 502*
39806-2	I'll Never Get Drunk Anymore	Vi 20936

[39806 has a group vocal by all five; Vi 35874 is a 12" disc issued as by Piedmont Log Rollers]

Bibliography: Kinney Rorrer, "Red Patterson and the Piedmont Log Rollers," *Old Time Music* 34 (Summer/Autumn 1980): 5-6.

Charles Peak
See James Howard.

Dave Pearson
See Spangler & Pearson

Norman Phelps' Virginia Rounders (ca. 1934–ca. 1938)
Little is known of this group. Their fiddler, Earl Phelps, was born in South Norfolk, Virginia. It is presumed that the other Phelpses in the band are brothers and were also from Tidewater Virginia. In addition to recording for Decca, members of the Virginia Rounders appeared as musicians in "B" western

Norman Phelps' Virginia Rounders

movies made in the late 1930s. Willie Phelps also recorded for several small labels following World War II.

New York, New York, 24 February 1936
Norman Phelps' Virginia Rounders: probably Earl Phelps, fiddle; Ken Card, tenor banjo; Willie Phelps, guitar; Norman Phelps, bass; unidentified vocal; vocal chorus (1); omit vocal (2)

60548-A	Lulu's Back in Town	De 5193
60549-A	Roll Along Prairie Moon	De 5192
60550-A	You Gotta See Mama Every Night	De 5212
60551-	I'm Gonna Sit Right Down and Write Myself a Letter	De 5193
60552-	It's Tight Like That	De 5191, *MCA VIM 4015*
60553-	Skunk in the Collard Patch (2)	De 5252
60554-	Bear's Gap	De 5307
60555-	Black Eyed Susan Brown	De 5268
60556-B	Sweet Violets	De 5191
60557-A	Talkin' 'bout You	De 5237
60561-A	Minnie the Mermaid	De 5286
60562-A	The Rose in Her Hair	De 5192
60563-	Margie	De 5245
60564-	I Like Mountain Music	De 5252
60565-	Nobody's Business But My Own (1)	De 5237
60569-	Since You Left Me All Alone	De unissued
60570-	Swing Low, Sweet Chariot	De 5245
60571-	My Mother	De 5204
60572-	Nobody's Darlin' But Mine	De 5024
60573-A	Mother and Dad	De 5220, Me 45209, Min 14077
60574-	Please Take Me Back to My Darling	De 5220, Me 45209, Min 14077
60575-A	Honeysuckle Rose	De 5307, *MCA VIM 4015*
60576-	When I Wore Daddy's Brown Derby	De 5286
60577-	Bye Bye Blues	De 5268
60578-	Atlanta Blues	De 5212

[60573 and 60574 as by Earl and Willie Phelps, with vocal duet]

New York, New York, 8 May 1936
As above

61094-A	I Like Bananas	De 5224
61095-A	The Terrible Tupelo Storm	De 5223
61096-A	The Moose River Mire Song (The Glitter of Gold)	De 5223
61097-A	My Baby's Hot	De 5224
61098-A	On a Road That Winds Down to the Sea	De 5225, Br 1100
61099-A	A Beautiful Lady in Blue	De 5225, Br 1100

[De 5223 issued as by Willie Phelps: with the Virginia Rounders]

Bibliography: Ken Griffis, "The Ray Whitley Story," *JEMF Quarterly* 6, no. 18 (Summer 1970): 67. (This article contains a brief mention of Earl Phelps.)

Pine Mountain Ramblers

A pseudonym on Champion for the Sweet Brothers.

Pipers Gap Ramblers (ca. 1916–ca. 1940)

This group was formed in about 1916 by two sets of brothers from the Coal Creek section of Carroll County—Ike and Haston Lowe, who played fiddle and banjo, and Josh and Walter Hanks on guitar and tambourine. They often played for community dances in Pipers Gap and other small settlements in southeastern Carroll County.

In September 1927, the band decided to try its hand at making records by traveling to Winston-Salem, North Carolina, where OKeh was auditioning groups. The Pipers Gap Ramblers passed the test and recorded six sides, of which two were released. After the recording session they continued to play music in and around Galax. By the 1940s such old-time bands were becoming passé in Carroll County, and the Pipers Gap Ramblers disbanded.

Winston-Salem, North Carolina, 26 September 1927

Pipers Gap Ramblers: Ike Lowe, fiddle; Haston Lowe, banjo; Josh Hanks, guitar/vocal; Walter Hanks, tambourine/vocal

81621-	Cold Icy Floor	OK unissued
81622-	Judgement Morning	OK unissued
81623-A	I Ain't Nobody's Darling	OK 45185, *CY 535, HE V*
81624-A	Yankee Doodle	OK 45185, *CY 535, HE V*
81625-	Katie Kline	OK unissued
81626-	I Won't Never Get Drunk No More	OK unissued

Bibliography: Wayne Martin, brochure notes to "Round the Heart of Old Galax: Vol. 3," Cy 535; Bobby Patterson, brochure notes to "Old Time Tunes From Coal Creek," HE V.

Plainsmen (and Rufus Hall)

A pseudonym on Broadway for Roy Harvey.

Charlie Poole (ca. 1912–1931)

Although he was born in Randolph County, North Carolina, on March 22, 1892, and raised in neighboring Alamance County, Charlie Poole is often associated with Virginia. He was a rambling man who, after turning to music full-time in the 1920s, rarely stayed in one place very long. Between 1925 and 1931 Poole traveled frequently and was as often found in West Virginia or Virginia as in his home base of Spray (now Eden), North Carolina.

Charlie Poole in the middle 1920s, probably in Spray, North Carolina.
Courtesy Kinney Rorrer

His roots, though, lie in the mill towns of north central North Carolina. He was playing banjo by the age of eight and was strongly influenced by the classical-style banjo recordings of Fred Van Epps as well as by local musicians. His early adult life was spent working in textile mills and playing music.

The local textile mills employed many people, including fine unrecorded string band musicians like Will Heffinger, Will Woodlieff, Daner Johnson, and Dan Carter. Mills were a hotbed of musical activity and Charlie Poole was a vital part of this scene from 1918 onward. Within this milieu Poole formed a band with Posey Rorer (fiddle) and Norman Woodlieff (guitar) that took the train to New York City to record for Columbia in 1925.

The stunning success of Poole's first recordings only led to an increase in his wanderlust, as the group was easily able to secure more out-of-town jobs that led them to the coalfields of West Virginia. It was on a trip to Bluefield, West Virginia, that Poole met guitarist Roy Harvey, a contemporary who was his musical peer and who soon joined the North Carolina Ramblers.

Throughout the late 1920s and into the early 1930s, Charlie Poole and the North Carolina Ramblers maintained a loose, easy-going lifestyle. They played music for innumerable dances and other social functions, drank plenty of bootleg liquor, and traveled extensively. The group itself went through several changes in personnel as Lonnie Austin replaced Posey Rorer on the fiddle and Roy Harvey took over the guitarist's seat from Norman Woodlieff. Their recordings for Columbia were augmented by 1929 sessions for Paramount and Brunswick that were issued under the respective pseudonyms of The Highlanders and the Allegheny Highlanders.

The Depression cut into Poole's recording activities, but did not diminish his live performances or his drinking. By the winter of 1930-31, however, the economic situation had grown so serious that Poole was forced to take a third-shift mill job. He was struggling with alcohol and the grim reality of not being able to make a full-time living from music, a difficult juncture for a man so used to a free-wheeling life style. Poole's death came on May 21, 1931, and, in fact, was attributed to a heart attack that was no doubt brought on by his hard living. Even today Poole is fondly remembered and qualifies as a "folk legend" in south central Virginia.

New York, New York, 27 July 1925
Charlie Poole accompanied by the North Carolina Ramblers: Charlie Poole, banjo/vocal; Posey Rorer, fiddle; Norman Woodlieff, guitar

140786-1	The Girl I Left in Sunny Tennessee	Co 15043, *CY 540*
140787-1	I'm the Man That Rode the Mule 'round the World	Co 15043, *CY 540*
140788-2	Can I Sleep in Your Barn Tonight Mister	Co 15038, *CY 509*
140789-1	Don't Let Your Deal Go Down Blues	Co 15038, *CY 505*

Charlie Poole, on cover of the monthly *Columbia Records* in 1927. *Courtesy of Dave Freeman (County Records)*

New York, New York, 16 September 1926
North Carolina Ramblers: Posey Rorer, fiddle; Charlie Poole, banjo; Roy Harvey, guitar

142627-1	Flyin' Clouds	Co 15106, VT 2488, Cl 5428, *CY 540*
142631-1	Wild Horses	Co 15279, *CY 509*
142632-1	Forks of Sandy	Co 15106, *HI 8005*
142633-2	Mountain Reel	Co 15279, *CY 505*

[VT and Cl issued as by Smoky Blue Highballers; reverse, under the same credit, by the Blue Ridge Highballers]

New York, New York, 17 September 1926
Charlie Poole with the North Carolina Ramblers: add Charlie Poole, vocal

142637-1	Good-Bye Booze	Co 15138, *CY 516*
142638-1	Monkey on a String	Co 15099, *CY 509*

New York, New York, 18 September 1926
As above

142645-2	Leaving Home	Co 15116, *CY 505*
142646-1	Budded Rose	Co 15138, *CY 516*

New York, New York, 20 September 1926
As above

142657-3	There'll Come a Time	Co 15116, VT 2492, Cl 5432, *CY 509*
142658-2	White House Blues	Co 15099, *CBS CS 9660, CY 505, FW FA 2951*
142659-1 and 2	The Highwayman	Co 15160, *CY 516*
142660-1	Hungry Hash House	Co 15160, VT 2492, Cl 5432, *CY 506, OT 100*

[VT and Cl issued as by Pete Harrison's Bayou Boys]

New York, New York, 25 July 1927
As above

144509-1	If I Lose, I Don't Care	Co 15215, *CY 509*
144510-	On the Battle Fields of Belgium	Co unissued
144511-1	You Ain't Talking to Me	Co 15193, *CY 540, HI 8005*
144512-2	Coon from Tennessee	Co 15215, *CBS CS52796, CY 540*
144513-	When I Left My Good Old Home	Co unissued
144514-3	The Letter That Never Came	Co 15179, *CY 505*
144515-1	Take a Drink on Me	Co 15193, *CY 505*
144516-1 and 2	Falling by the Wayside	Co 15179, *CY 540*

New York, New York, 27 July 1927
Charlie Poole: Charlie Poole, banjo; Lucy Terry, piano

Charlie Poole (banjo), Posey Rorer (fiddle), and Clarence Foust (guitar), circa 1923. *Courtesy Kinney Rorer*

144517-	Down in Georgia	Co unissued
144518-1	Sunset March	Co 15184, *ARB 201, PU 3002*
144519-	Teasin' Fritz	Co unissued
144521-2	Don't Let Your Deal Go Down Medley	Co 15184, *ARB 201, PU 3002*

New York, New York, 23 July 1928
Charlie Poole with the North Carolina Ramblers: Lonnie Austin, fiddle; Charlie Poole, banjo/vocal; Roy Harvey, guitar

146767-2	A Young Boy Left His Home One Day	Co 15584, *HI 8005*
146768-2	My Wife Went Away and Left Me	Co 15584, *CY 516*
146769-2	I Cannot Call Her Mother	Co 15307
146770-2	I Once Loved a Sailor	Co 15385, *HI 8005*
146771-2	Husband and Wife Were Angry One Night	Co 15342, *HI 8005*
146772-1	Hangman, Hangman, Slack the Rope	Co 15385
146773-1	Ramblin' Blues	Co 15286, *CY 505*
146774-2	Took My Gal A–Walkin'	Co 15672, *CY 505*
146775-1	What Is Home without Babies	Co 15307, *HI 8005*
146776-2	Jealous Mary	Co 15342, *CY 540*
146778-1	Old and Only in the Way	Co 15672, *CY 516*
146779-2	Shootin' Creek	Co 15286, *CY 501, CY 505*

New York, New York, 6 May 1929
As above

148469-3	Bill Mason	Co 15407, *CY 509, CBS CS 9660*
148470-1	Goodbye Mary Dear	Co 15456, *CY 516*
148471-1	Leaving Dear Old Ireland	Co 15425, *CY 516*
148472-1	Baltimore Fire	Co 15509, *CY 509*

New York, New York, 7 May 1929
As above

148474-1	The Wayward Boy	Co 15456
148475-2	Sweet Sunny South	Co 15425, *CY 505*
148476-2	He Rambled	Co 15407, *CY 505*
148477-1	The Mother's Plea for Her Son	Co 15509

New York, New York, 9 May 1929
The Highlanders: Charlie Poole, banjo/vocal (1); Odell Smith, fiddle; Lonnie Austin, fiddle; Lucy Terry, piano; Roy Harvey, guitar/vocal (2)

2902-1	Under the Double Eagle	Pm 3184, Bw 8152, *ARB 201, PU 3002*
2910-2	Richmond Square	Pm 3184, Bw 8152, *ARB 201, PU 3002*
2911-2	Flop Eared Mule	Pm 3171, *ARB 201, PU 3002*
2912-1	Lynchburg Town	Pm 3171, *ARB 201, PU 3002*
2913-2	San Antonio (2)	Pm 3177, Pm 3267, Bw 8288

Charlie Poole 147

2914-2	What Is Home without Babies (2)	Pm 3177, Pm 3267, Bw 8288
2915-1	Tennessee Blues (1)	Pm 3200, Bw 8146, QRS 9016, *ARB 201, PU 3002*
2916-1	May I Sleep in Your Barn Tonight Mister	Pm 3200, Bw 8146, QRS 9016, *ARB 201, PU 3002*

[Matrix numbers 2913 and 2914 issued as by Fred Newman; Bw 8146 as by the Tennessee Mountaineers; Bw 8152 as by the Mountaineers, QRS as by Chumber's Breakdown Gang; Speech by all group members on 2910-11]

New York, New York, 11 May 1929

Allegheny Highlanders: Odell Smith, fiddle/speech; Lonnie Austin, fiddle/speech; Lucy Terry, piano; Charlie Poole, banjo/speech/vocal (1); Roy Harvey, guitar/speech/vocal (2)

E-29798	A Trip to New York—Part I	Br 324, *ARB 201, PU 3002*
E-29799	A Trip to New York—Part II (1)	Br 324, *ARB 201, PU 3002*
E-29800	A Trip to New York—Part III	Br 325, *ARB 201, PU 3002*
E-29801	A Trip to New York—Part IV (2)	Br 325, *ARB 201, PU 3002*

New York, New York, 23 January 1930

Charlie Poole with the North Carolina Ramblers: Charlie Poole, banjo/vocal; Roy Harvey, guitar; Odell Smith, fiddle

149900-1	Sweet Sixteen	Co 15519, *CY 505*
149901-2	My Gypsy Girl	Co 15519, *CY 509, FSSMLP KB 3796*
149902-1	The Only Girl I Ever Loved	Co 15711, *HI 8005*
149903-	I Left My German Home	Co unissued
149904-2	Write a Letter to My Mother	Co 15711, *CY 516*
149905-	When I'm Far Away	Co unissued
149906-1	If the River Was Whiskey	Co 15545, *CY 505, OT 100*
149907-1	It's Moving Day	Co 15545, *CY 509*
149908-2	Southern Medley	Co 15615, *CY 540*
149909-3	Honeysuckle	Co 15615, *CY 540*

[No fiddle on matrix 149908; no vocal, but speech by Poole and Harvey on 149908 or by Smith and Harvey on 149909; Co 15615 as by Charlie Poole and Roy Harvey]

New York, New York, 9 September 1930

As above

150773-1	Good-bye Sweet Liza Jane	Co 15601, *CY 516*
150774-2	Look Before You Leap	Co 15601, *CY 516*
150775-2	One Moonlight Night	Co 15688, *CY 509*
150776-	Little Doctor Fell in the Well	Co unissued
150777-2	Just Keep Waiting till the Good Times Come	Co 15636, *CY 505, HI 8005*
150778-2	Mother's Last Farewell Kiss	Co unissued, *CY 540, HI 8005*
150799-2	Milwaukee Blues	Co 15688, *CY 504, CY 516, NW 236*

150780-2   Where the Whippoorwill Is Whispering Good-night   Co 15636, *HI 8005*
[No banjo on 150778 and 150780]

Bibliography: Kinney Rorrer, *Rambling Blues: The Life and Songs of Charlie Poole* (London: Old Time Music, 1982).

See also Roy Harvey and Posey Rorer.

Fiddlin' Powers Family (1918–1930)
James Cowan Powers, born in October 1877, in Russell County, Virginia, learned to play the fiddle from his older brother, "Uncle Billy" Powers, during the 1890s. He married Matilda Lambert about 1901; in 1916 she contracted tuberculosis and died within a year. Just before the close of World War I, when his youngest child, Ada, was eight years old, Powers decided to forgo his career in farming, carpentry, and leather working and move into music full-time. Along with Ada (ukulele), Powers included Carrie (guitar), Orpha (mandolin), and Charles (banjo and guitar) in his family band that played throughout southwestern Virginia and was often heard competing in fiddle contests.

As the band's popularity grew, so did its performance radius and by 1920 it was playing in the four states within 150 miles of Russell County, Virginia—Kentucky, West Virginia, Tennessee, and North Carolina. The Fiddlin' Powers Family show lasted about one hour and included specialty acts such as a banjo solo, vocal duets, and trick fiddling. This format was similar to that of the contemporary vaudeville shows.

In 1924 the Powers Family encountered Fiddlin' John Carson, Georgia's pioneering hillbilly recording artist, at a contest in Johnson City, Tennessee. They were highly impressed by the reception given to Carson and decided that they should pursue a recording career. That summer they traveled to New York City to audition for the Victor Company. Victor liked their music and was looking for a rival to John Carson's strong-selling OKeh records. The Powers recordings were the first selections to document the family strings band tradition that pervaded the South.

The recordings were successful and helped to expand the group's bookings. They also performed over radio station WOPI in Bristol, which further bolstered their popularity. Their radio work led to other bookings with higher fees, but the Powerses continued to perform throughout their established five-state area.

It is unclear why the Powers Family did not record for Victor again, but in 1925 they recorded ten selections for the Edison Company. This session was followed in 1927 by a final recording opportunity offered by OKeh, which had set up a temporary studio in Winston-Salem, North Carolina.

By this time, the Powers Family band was breaking up because the children

The Fiddlin' Powers Family in a formal New York City portrait from circa 1926. Charlie Powers (guitar), Cowan Powers (fiddle), Ada Powers (ukelele), Orpha Powers (mandolin). *Courtesy Barry Poss (Sugar Hill Records)*

were growing up and marrying. By 1930 each of the children had married, effectively ending the family band. Fiddlin' Powers himself continued to play for many years before he died of a heart attack about 1953.

New York, New York, 11 August 1924
The Powers Family: Fiddlin' Cowan Powers, fiddle; Orpha Powers, mandolin; Charlie Powers, banjo; Ada Powers, ukulele

        Way Down in Georgia   Vi test

Camden, New Jersey, 18 August 1924
Fiddlin' Powers and Family: add Charlie Powers, vocal (1); Carson Robison, guitar/vocal (2)

30578-1 and -2	Brown's Dream	Vi unissued
30579-1 and -2	Old Swinnie	Vi unissued
3580-1 and -2	Three Forks of Kentucky River	Vi unissued
30581-	The Little Old Log Cabin in the Lane (2)	Vi 19448
30582-2	Old Joe Clark (2)	Vi 19434
30583-1	Sour Wood Mountains (1)	Vi 19448

Camden, New Jersey, 19 August 1924
As above

30584-1 and -2	Cumberland Gap	Vi unissued
30585-1 and -2	Back Creek Girls	Vi unissued
30588-1 and -2	Billy in the Low Ground	Vi unissued
30589-1 and -2	Birdie	Vi unissued
30590-2	Patty on the Turnpike	Vi 19450, *CY 525*
30591- and -2	Sally Goodin	Vi unissued
30592-2	Callahan's Reel	Vi 19450
30595-1 and -2	Rocky Road to Dinah's House	Vi unissued
30596-2	Sugar in the Gourd	Vi 19449
30597-1	Cripple Creek	Vi 19449
30598-2	Ida Red (2)	Vi 19434

Holland Puckett

East Orange, New Jersey, 2 October 1925
As above: delete Carson Robison; add possibly Carrie Bell Powers, guitar

10612	Old Joe Clark	Ed 51662, Ed 5076
10613	Sour Wood Mountains (1)	Ed 51789, Ed 5123

East Orange, New Jersey, 3 October 1925
As above
10614	Ida Red	Ed 51662, Ed 5094
10615	Pretty Fair Miss (1)	Ed unissued
10616	Cripple Creek (1)	Ed 51789, Ed 5219

East Orange, New Jersey, 6 October 1925
As above
10620	Cluck Old Hen (1)	Ed 52083, Ed 5246
10621	Rocky Road to Dinah's House (1)	Ed 5421

East Orange, New Jersey, 7 October 1925
As above
10622	Little Old Log Cabin in the Lane	Ed unissued
10623	Sugar in the Gourd (1)	Ed 52083, Ed 5134
10624	Wild and Reckless Hobo (1)	Ed 5131

Winston-Salem, North Carolina, 28 September 1927
As above: add John L. "Steamboat" Porter, harmonica; Carrie Bell Powers, guitar

81639-	Shady Tree	OK unissued
81640-B	Did You Ever See the Devil, Uncle Joe?	OK 45268
81641-B	Old Molly Hare	OK 45268
81642-	Charlie Karo	OK unissued
81643-A	Old Virginia Reel—Part 1	Ok 45154
81644-A	Old Virginia Reel—Part 2	OK 45154

Bibliography: Roy Sturgill, "Fiddlin' Cowan Powers and Family—Pioneer Recording Artists of Country Music," *Bulletin of the Historical Society of Southwest Virginia* (1984): 54-65; Charles Wolfe, "Fiddlin' Powers and His Family," *Old Time Music* 42 (Winter 1985/86): 7-10.

Holland Puckett (early 1920s–1934)

Born on July 15, 1899, on a farm in The Hollows, Virginia, in Patrick County, Holland Puckett lived between Ararat, Virginia, and nearby Mount Airy, North Carolina. He was closely associated with such important Surry County musicians as Ben Jarrell and Da Costa Woltz. It was with Woltz and his band that Puckett traveled to Richmond, Indiana, where he first recorded.

Holland Puckett, 1927, as shown on a page of a Gennett catalogue.
Courtesy Mrs. Eula Marshall

Puckett was a dapper man who worked as a bookkeeper for one of Mount Airy's many tobacco warehouses. Music was his hobby and he often played with other musicians in Patrick County. According to musicians who knew him, Puckett picked the banjo in addition to singing and playing the guitar and harmonica. Nothing more is known of his life, except that he died on July 28, 1934. Puckett's death allegedly was caused by a knife wound inflicted during a fight over a poker game.

Richmond, Indiana. ca. April 1927
Holland Puckett: Holland Puckett, vocal/guitar/harmonica (1)

12771-A	Put On Your Old Gray Bonnett (1)	Ge 6144, Chm 15299, Ch 270, Ch 329, He 75554
12772-	Weeping Willow Tree (1)	Ge 6144, Chm 15334, Sil 8158, Spt 9243, Ch 270, Ch 330
12772-A	Weeping Willow Tree (1)	Be 1179
12784-	He Lives on High	Ge 6206, Ch 15333, Sil 5075, Sil 8176, Spt 9263
12785-	A Mother's Advice	Ge 6163, Chm 15299, Ch 330, He 75556
12786-	The Dying Cowboy	Ge 6271, Chm 15428, Sil 5065, Sil 25065, Sil 8152, Spt 9253, He 75557
12789-	Chas. A. Brooks	Ge 6163, He 75556

[Chms issued as by Harvey Watson; reverse Chm 15333 by Ben Jarrell; reverse Chm 154334 by David Miller; reverse Chm 15428 by Bradley Kincaid; Spt issued as by Harvey Watson, except Spt 9253 issued as by Si Puckett; reverse Spt 9243 by John McGhee; reverse Spt 9263 by Ben Jarrell; Chs issued as by Harvey Watson; Be issued as by Riley Wilcox; Hes issued as by Robert Howell; reverse He 75554 by Da Costa Woltz Southern Broadcasters; reverse He 75557 by David Miller]

Richmond, Indiana, ca. May 1927
As above

12814-	Drunken Hiccoughs	Ge 6189, Chm 15356, Ch 328
12815-A	The Broken Engagement	Ge 6189, He 75562
12815-B	The Broken Engagement	Be 1179
12816-	The Bright Sherman Valley	Ge 6433, Sil 5064, Sil 25064, Sil 8153, Spt 9254, Ch 329, He 75562
12817-	I'll Remember You Love in My Prayers	Ge 6206, He 75559
12818-	The Keyhole in the Door	Ge 6271, Sil 5064, Sil 25064, Sil 8153, Spt 9254, Ch 328
12819-	Little Birdie (1)	He 75563
12820-	Come and Kiss Me, Baby Darling	Ge 6433, Sil 5065, Sil 25065, Sil 8152, Spt 9253, He 75563

[Chm issued as by Harvey Watson; reverse Chms by John Hammond; Spts issued as by Si Puckett; Chs issued as by Harvey Watson; Be issued as by Riley Wilcox; Hes issued as by Robert Howell; reverse of He 75559 by Ben Jarrell]

Richmond, Indiana, ca. 11 May 1928
As above
13804-A	The Jail Bird	Ge rejected
13805-A	The Old Cottage Home	Ge 6532, Spt 9342
13806-A	Sadie Ray	Ge rejected
13807-A and B	The Scolding Wife	Ge rejected
13808-A	Too Late, Too Late	Ge rejected
13809-	The Maple on the Hill (1)	Ge 6532, Spt 9186
13810-	Faded Bunch of Roses (1)	Ge 6720, Spt 9186
13811-A	Leaf by Leaf the Roses Fall	Ge rejected
13812-A	Old Virginia Rambler	Ge rejected
13813-A	Little Bessie	Ge 6720, Spt 9324
13814-A	Red White and Blue	Ge rejected

[Spt 9186 issued as by Si Puckett]

Si Puckett

A pseudonym on Supertone and Silvertone for Holland Puckett.

James Ragan (and Oliver Beck)

A pseudonym on Challenge for Roy Harvey.

Railroad Boys

A pseudonym on Superior for Roy Harvey.

Jack Reedy and His Walker Mountain Stringband (late 1920s)

Jack Reedy was born in Smyth County, Virginia, about the turn of the century. He learned to play the banjo in his teens and was involved with music all of his life, though he often worked full-time at furniture factories.

The years between 1925 and 1936 marked his most intense musical activity. During this time Reedy toured and recorded with the Blue Ridge Ramblers and the Hillbillies and often performed in Virginia and West Virginia with Frank and Ed Blevins. He also developed a finger-picked banjo style that was a precursor to three-finger picking heard in bluegrass bands fifteen years later. Between 1933 and 1936 he played at the White Top Folk Festivals in Washington County, often with the Blevinses.

In the late 1930s Reedy did radio work in Bristol, Tennessee, and Bluefield, West Virginia. He tried to make a full-time living with his music, but never made the difficult transition. Reedy was still playing music when he died of a heart attack in Bluefield, Virginia, in 1940.

Ashland, Kentucky, ca. 15 February 1928
Jack Reedy and His Walker Mountain String Band: Jack Reedy, banjo; Fred Roe, fiddle; Henry Roe, guitar

        Ground Hog   Br 221, *CY 504*
        Chinese Breakdown   Br 221

See also H.M. Barnes' Blue Ridge Ramblers, Frank Blevins, and Hillbillies

Fred Richards (ca. 1925–ca. 1935)

Fred Richards was a charter member of the Four Virginians and also recorded as a solo artist for Columbia and the American Record Corp. He was almost certainly living in or around Pittsylvania County in the middle 1920s when he performed with the Four Virginians. The details of his life, however, remain totally obscure.

Johnson City, Tennessee, 23 October 1929
Fred Richards: Fred Richards, guitar/vocal

149246-2	My Katie	Co 15483
149247-2	Danville Blues	Co 15483
149248-	Women Rule the World	Co unissued
149249-	Old Pal	Co unissued

New York, New York, 23 May 1933
As above

13378-	Freight Wreck of No. 52	ARC unissued
13379-	Carolina Sunshine	ARC unissued
13380-	Hobo's Yodel	ARC unissued
13381-	Watching the Moon	ARC unissued

See also Four Virginians.

Richmond Starlight (Jazz) Quartette (late 1920s)

Virtually nothing is known about this vocal group. It performed in and around Richmond, Virginia, throughout the late 1920s and possibly had a career on the professional vaudeville stage. Like many of the commercially recorded black quartets from Hampton Roads and Richmond, the Richmond Starlight Quartette easily mixed secular and sacred singing.

Long Island City, New York, ca. December 1928
Richmond Starlight Quartette: male vocal quartet

197-A	Won't Be Worried No More	QRS 7056
198-	Oh You Better Mind	QRS 7056

Richmond Starlight Quartette as they appeared in a 1929 QRS Record catalogue. *Courtesy Doug Seroff*

Richmond's Harmonizing Four

Long Island City, New York, ca. December 1928
Richmond Jazz Quartette: as above

207-	Monkey Man Blues	QRS 7028
211-A	Gone Jazz Crazy	QRS 7028

Richmond, Virginia, 18 October 1929
Richmond Starlight Quartette: as above

403187-B	Jazz Crazy Blues	OK unissued
403188-B	Gone Pretty Mama	OK unissued
403189-B	Mary, Don't You Weep	OK unissued
403190-B	Mother, You'll Surely Be Late	OK unissued

Richmond's Harmonizing Four (ca. 1928–present)

One of America's oldest continuous gospel groups, the Harmonizing Four of Richmond, has been performing since the late 1920s. Formed as a community group, it quickly attracted a local following. By the late 1930s the group had branched out to perform full-time, usually working the circuit between Richmond, Virginia, and New York City. This region contained many transplanted Virginians who had moved to Washington, D.C., Baltimore, Philadelphia, and northern New Jersey in search of work.

Just prior to the recording ban in 1943, the group finally got the chance to record for Decca. This was to be the first of many recordings spanning the next forty years; by now the group has recorded hundreds of selections for Gotham, Vee Jay, and many local labels.

The group gained a national reputation during the most intense period of interest in quartet singing from 1945 through 1955. They were led by Joe Williams, who joined the Harmonizing Four several years after its formation, until his death in the fall of 1988. The Harmonizing Four still perform in the Middle Atlantic states, though not as actively as in the past.

New York, New York, 5 June 1943
Richmond's Harmonizing Four: Joe Williams, lead voice (1); Thomas Johnson, lead voice (2); John Scott, lead voice (3); Levi Hansley, bass voice; Vance Joyner, baritone voice; Lonnie Smith, tenor voice

71383-A	I Done Done What You Told Me to Do (1, 2)	De 7909
71384-	Every Time I Feel the Spirit (1, 2)	De 48108
71385-	Who'll Be a Witness for My Lord (1, 2)	De 48108
71386-A	Great Camp Meeting in the Promised Land (1, 2)	De 48121
71387-	What a Time (1, 2)	De unissued
71388-	There's a Fire Down Yonder (1, 2)	De unissued

Richmond's Harmonizing Four, 1943, Richmond, Virginia. From left, Lonnie Smith, Vance Joyner, Levi Hansley, Joe Williams, Thomas Johnson. *Courtesy Blue Ridge Heritage Archive/Lonnie Smith*

71389-A Keep Inchin' Along (1, 2)   De 48121
71390-A When I've Done the Best I Can (Then My Savior Will Carry Me Home) (2, 3)   De 7909

[More than one lead voice is heard on these selections, which is accomplished by "lead switching" between the vocalists. Some copies of De 7909 have a 71383-AA matrix number; the meaning of the second A is unclear.]

Bibliography: Vaughan Webb, brochure notes to "Richmond- Petersburg Quartet Tradition," BRI 011.

Riley's Mountaineers

A pseudonym on Gennett and Supertone for Frank Jenkins' Pilot Mountaineers—see Ernest V. Stoneman.

Roanoke Jug Band (1926–1933)

Formed primarily by employees of the American Viscose Company plant in Vinton, Virginia, the Roanoke Jug Band was a string band that played throughout south central Virginia. The group never used a jug among their many instruments; it was included in their name for its novelty effect. The Roanoke Jug Band vied in fiddle contests, performed at local schoolhouses for dances, and broadcast over Roanoke radio station WDBJ.

It was through their radio work that the Roanoke Jug Band received the opportunity to record for OKeh Records in 1929. Other station performers, among them its house pianist, Herndon Slicer, were also invited to Richmond to audition. The Roanoke Jug Band did well and each of its four sides was issued by OKeh.

The band continued to play well into the Depression. Marriages and the pressure of family forced most of its members to drop out of music, though they all continued to live in or near Roanoke. Clyde Dooley died of a heart attack about 1938. Billy Altizer continued to lead another string band that played over WDBJ until his death in 1939. Banjo player Walter Keith also died of a heart attack about 1947. In July 1984 Ray Barger passed away. Mahlon Overstreet and Richard Mitchell continue to live in Roanoke.

Richmond, Virginia, 18 October 1929
Roanoke Jug Band: Billy Altizer, fiddle/vocal (1); Walter Keith, banjo; Richard Mitchell, mandolin; Ray Barger, guitar; Mahlon Overstreet, guitar

403177-A Johnny Lover (1)   OK 45423, *CY 531*
403178-A Stone Mountain Rag   OK 45423 *BRI 010*
403179-A Triangle Blues   OK 45393
403180-B Home Brew Rag (1)   OK 45393

Roanoke Jug Band in 1929. From left (standing), Mahlon Overstreet, Clyde Dooley, Ray Barger, and Walter E. Keith; (seated) Billy Altizer and Richard Mitchell. *Courtesy Blue Ridge Heritage Archive*

Bibliography: Kip Lornell, " 'The Jug Didn't Mean a Thing'—The Roanoke Jug Band," *Old Time Music* 41 (Spring 1985): 15-16.

Melvin Robinette (ca. 1920–early 1930s)

A fiddler who learned from his father at the age of sixteen, Melvin Robinette spent the next nine years of his life playing music almost full time. He was born on April 10, 1905, just east of Coeburn, Virginia, in Wise County. In addition to his father, Robinette was influenced by Fiddlin' Cowan Powers, another local fiddler and pioneering recording artist. Robinette also liked the black blues music he heard on recordings and incorporated some of this phrasing into his own playing.

He began entering fiddle contests in 1924 and did quite well. One of his regular bands consisted of a Scott County family, the Boatwrights, with whom he played for several years. This group, in fact, unsuccessfully auditioned for Victor when the company set up a portable recording studio in Bristol in October 1927. The problem seems to have been a matter of internal disagreements regarding the band's repertoire rather than a lack of talent.

In any event, Robinette's fiddle playing was finally documented shortly thereafter when he joined with vocalist and guitarist Byrd Moore. Moore was already a veteran of several sessions and had strong contacts with the Gennett Company of Richmond, Indiana. The duo practiced hard for the session and in early April 1929 they drove up to Indiana and recorded eight tunes for Gennett.

After his recording debut, Robinette stayed in music professionally for another year or so. He joined the Boatwrights and together with Dock Boggs, a banjo player from Norton, Virginia, they toured southwestern Virginia with a music and comedy act. They stayed on the road for many months, making a living playing coal camps and small theaters.

In the end it was the incessant traveling and grueling competition and the animosity of fiddlers' conventions that drove him from the full-time music circuit. He made carpentry his livelihood and moved to several places around the country to ply his trade. Today he is retired and living in Tullahoma, Tennessee.

Richmond, Indiana, 10 April 1929

Robinette and Moore: Melvin Robinette, fiddle/speech (1)/vocal (2); Byrd Moore, guitar/speech (3)/vocal (4)

15020-	Birmingham Jail (2, 4)	Ge 6481, Chm 15750, Spt 9536, Spr 2640
15021-	Goodbye Sweetheart (2, 4)	Ge 7086, Spt 9536
15022-	When the Snowflakes Fall Again (2, 4)	Ge 6841, Chm 15732, Spt 9560
15027-	Mama Don't Allow No Hanging Around (4)	Ge 6991
15028-	Flop Eared Mule (1, 3)	Ge 6884, Spt 9500

15029-	Favorite Two Step	Ge 6957
15030-	That Tiger Rag	Ge 6957, Spr 2696, Ch 427

Richmond, Indiana, 11 April 1929
As above
15036   Last Days in Georgia   Ge 6884, Spt 9500, Spr 2696, *CY 527*

[15022 and 15027 issued on Ge as by Byrd Moore only; reverse Ge 6991 by Byrd Moore alone; reverse of Ge 7068 by Martin and Roberts; Chm 15732 issued as by Henry Johnson, reverse by Rutherford and Foster; Chm 15750 issued as by Ezra Hill and Henry Johnson, reverse by Rutherford and Foster; Spts as by Clark and Howell, reverse by Dick Parham; Spr 2696 as by Jack Burdette and Bert Moss; reverse Spr 2640 by Rutherford and Foster; Ch 427 as by Robinson and Evans, reverse by Hoke Rice and Louie Donaldson; Spt 9500 (15028) issued as "Flop Eared Mule"]

Bibliography: Charles K. Wolfe and Tony Russell, "Melvin Robinette," *Old Time Music* 19 (Winter 1975/6): 4-7.
See also Byrd Moore.

Robinson and Evans
A pseudonym on Challenge for Byrd Moore and Melvin Robinette.

Posey Rorer (ca. 1900–1936)
Born in Franklin County, Virginia, September 22, 1891, Posey Wilson Rorer lived for his first thirty years with severely clubbed feet. Rorer began playing banjo before the age of ten, but by the time he had turned twelve the fiddle had become his main instrument. In search of lucrative work, Rorer moved to the coalfields of southern West Virginia in 1917, where he remained for almost three years. He returned to Franklin County because of the 1919 flu epidemic, and Charlie Poole came with him.

During the early 1920s, Rorer often played with Poole in Franklin, Henry, Patrick, and Floyd counties. Another source of their financial support was making bootleg liquor. One of the first things that Rorer did with his money was to pay for an operation that helped to improve his club feet.

By 1925 Charlie Poole was leading his North Carolina Ramblers to regional fame and had gained a Columbia Record Company contract. Posey Rorer was one of the group's mainstays until 1928 when they split up over disagreements related to record royalties and their diverging approaches to music. From then on Rorer performed with other local musicians, though he continued to be interested in a recording career of his own. In addition to recording with the North Carolina Ramblers Rorer appeared on sessions led by Buster Carter and Preston Young, Walter "Kid" Smith, and several others.

Until 1933 Rorer made his living from playing music and making records.

Posey Rorer brought this group to New York City in order to record for Edison Records. Posey Rorer (fiddle), Matt Simmons (guitar), Frank Miller (seated), circa 1929. *Courtesy Blue Ridge Heritage Archive*

Finally the Depression became too strongly entrenched for him to continue his career as a fiddler. Rorer scraped by for several years as a woodcutter and early in 1936 began work for the Works Progress Administration. On June 6, 1936, he died of a heart attack.

New York, New York, 18 September 1926
North Carolina Ramblers led by Posey Rorer: Posey Rorer, fiddle; Charlie Poole, banjo; Roy Harvey, guitar

142641-1	Too Young to Marry	Co 15127
142642-1	Ragtime Annie	Co 15127, *CY 509*
142643-	Little Dog Waltz	Co unissued
142644-1	A Kiss Waltz	Co unissued, *CY 540, HI 8005*

New York, New York, 24 September 1928
Posey Rorer and the North Carolina Ramblers: Posey Rorer, fiddle; Matt Simmons, guitar/lead vocal; Frank Miller, tenor vocal

18749-B	If I Could Hear My Mother Pray Again	Ed unissued
18750-B	Beautiful Beckoning Hands	Ed 5617
18751-B	He's Coming Back Again	Ed unissued
18752-A and B	We'll Understand It Better By and By	Ed rejected
18753-B	Wild and Reckless Hobo	Ed 11009

New York, New York, 25 September 1928
As above

18754-B	Blue Eyed Eller	Ed unissued
18755-B	Sweet Sunny South Take Me Home	Ed unissued
18756-B	I'll Meet Mother after All	Ed 52414, Ed N-20005
18757-B	Did You Mean Those Words You Said	Ed unissued

New York, New York, 26 September 1928
As above

18760-B	As We Sat Beneath the Maple on the Hill	Ed 5615, Ed 52414, Ed N-20005, *CT 6001*
18761-B	The Drunkard's Dream	Ed unissued
18762-B	Down in the Georgia Jail	Ed 5613

[Ed 5613, Ed 5615, and Ed 5617 are cylinders; Ed 52414 is a thick disc; Ed 11009 was probably never issued]

Bibliography: Kinney Rorer, *Rambling Blues: The Life and Songs of Charlie Poole* (London: Old Time Music, 1982).

See also Roy Harvey, and Charlie Poole.

George Runnels (and Howard Hall or Ed Sawyer)
A pseudonym on Champion for Roy Harvey.

Salem Highballers (1926–ca. 1932)
Henry McCray came from quite a musical family. His father was a fiddler, and his uncles played fiddles, banjos, and guitars. McCray taught his sons to play music and during the early 1920s they provided entertainment for their neighbors in the Catawba section west of Salem, Virginia. In the middle 1920s McCray moved into the town of Salem and about 1926 began playing over the new radio station in Roanoke, WDBJ.

Between 1925 and 1930 the McCray Family often broadcast over WDBJ, gaining a wide local following. In 1929 they joined other station musicians, most notably the Roanoke Jug Band, in a trip to Richmond to record for the OKeh company. The company released only one record by the McCray Family, which bore the enigmatic credit, The Salem Highballers, a name never used by the family in their local performances.

The band continued to play around Roanoke County into the early 1930s. It got together less often as the boys married and had less time for music. The group's guiding force and founder, Henry McCray, died about 1950 when he was about 80 years of age. The last surviving member of the group, Carl McCray, passed away in the spring of 1984.

Richmond, Virginia, 18 October 1929
Carl McCray: Carl McCray, guitar/vocal

403171-A	When Grape Juice Turns to Wine	OK unissued
403172-A	Where Is My Mother?	OK unissued

Richmond, Virginia, 18 October 1929
Salem Highballers: Henry McCray, fiddle; Fred McCray, guitar; Robert McCray, banjo; Carl McCray, guitar

403173-A	Salem #1	OK unissued
403174-A	Snow Bird on the Ash Bank	OK 45455
403175-A	Dinah, Old Lady	OK unissued
403176-B	Going on to Town	OK 45455

Dillard Sanders
A pseudonym on Silvertone and Supertone for G.B. Grayson and Henry Whitter.

Uncle Jim Seany

A pseudonym on Champion for Ernest V. Stoneman.

Shelor Family (ca. 1920–ca. 1930)

This group, also billed as "Dad Blackard's Moonshiners" by the Victor Company, hailed from Meadows of Dan in Patrick County. Its leader was Joe "Dad" Blackard, who was born in Stuart, Virginia, in 1859. The English folksong collector Cecil Sharpe visited Meadows of Dan in August 1918 and collected at least five songs from Joe Blackard. In addition to being a banjo player and ballad singer, he also regularly taught shape-note singing schools.

In 1910 he bought a piano for his ten-year-old daughter Clarice, who soon learned to play many of the same old-time tunes as her father. In 1919 she married a local man, Jesse Shelor (born in 1894), a fiddler who often played for dances and other community events. Shelor often performed in a family band that included his older brother, Pyrhus (born circa 1890), also a fiddler.

Between 1906 and 1914, the Shelor family lived at times in Danville, Virginia, and Spray, North Carolina, where the textile mills provided many jobs. It was there that the two brothers met Charley La Prade, a famed local fiddler who later recorded for Columbia and Paramount. Pyrhus and Jesse learned many tunes from La Prade as well as from a Patrick County fiddler named Wallace Spangler. Some of these tunes were recorded by Jesse and Clarice Shelor in later years.

During the 1920s Joe Blackard, Clarice Blackard Shelor, Jesse Shelor, and Pyrhus Shelor often got together to play music for dances, school closings, and other social functions in Meadows of Dan. Following their recording session for Victor the group continued to play for several years until both Joe Blackard and Pyrhus Shelor became ill and died. Jesse and Clarice continued to make music locally and were recorded several times in the 1960s and 1970s.

Bristol, Tennessee, 3 August 1927

The Shelor Family: Joe Blackard, banjo/vocal; Clarice Shelor, piano/vocal; Jesse Shelor, fiddle; Pyrhus Shelor, fiddle

39761-3	Big Bend Gal	Vi 20865, *RCA LPV 552*
39762-2	Suzanna Gal	Vi 21130
39763-3	Sandy River Belle	Vi 21130, *CY 504*, *CMF 011-L*
39764-2	Billy Grimes, the Rover	Vi 20865, *NW 236*, *CMF 011-L*

[Vi 21130 issued as by Dad Blackard's Moonshiners]

Bibliography: Tom Carter, "The Blackard-Shelor Story: Biography of a Hillbilly Stringband," *Old Time Music* 24 (Spring 1977): 4-7.

Silver Leaf Quartette of Norfolk, late 1940s. From left, William Boush, Melvin Smith, Luther Daniels (seated), William Winfield. *Courtesy Blue Ridge Heritage Archive/Melvin Smith*

Silver Leaf Quartette of Norfolk (1919–1979)

Founded when quartets were beginning to reach a zenith of popularity in Norfolk, the Silver Leaf Quartette proved to be one of the most enduring vocal ensembles. The group began as a community quartet in the Berkley section of Norfolk, singing in local churches. The Silver Leaf Quartette quickly gained a legion of fans and was soon singing throughout Tidewater.

By 1928 the group's touring was regularly taking it to the urban centers of the Northeast, most often New York City. Its New York appearances were a cause for celebration in Norfolk and accounts of its triumphs were regularly featured in the *Norfolk Journal and Guide,* Tidewater's black newspaper. In addition to appearing in local churches, the Silver Leaf Quartette was also singing over radio stations that covered greater New York. In 1927 the singers began semiannual spring tours of northern cities that continued for about six years.

A major break came in the summer of 1928 when the OKeh company approached the Silver Leaf Quartette about recording some of its most popular numbers. The group eagerly agreed and went into the studios in mid-June, starting an affiliation that endured for nearly three years.

Over the summer of 1929 the Silver Leaf Quartette fulfilled an extended tour in New York City that included 21 straight nights at the Metropolitan Baptist Church. Though their recording career ended in March 1931, the quartet continued to tour until the outbreak of World War II. Their itinerary took them into Canada, west to North Dakota, and south into Florida.

In 1947 the Silver Leaf Quartette began an extensive booking at Virginia Beach's exclusive Cavalier Hotel, where they were billed as the Cavalier Singers. By this time two of the original or early members from the 1920s—William Thatch and William Boush—had dropped out of the quartet. Through the late 1950s, however, quartet singing was so popular that the group remained together for local engagements.

By 1960 the Silver Leaf Quartette was singing only occasionally. The singers continued to perform at special programs and held their own anniversaries. The group permanently retired about 1979 when bass singer Luther Daniels died. His passing was followed in 1985 by the death of Melvin Smith, who had joined the Silver Leaf Quartette in 1924 and had managed the group for nearly four decades.

New York, New York, 16 June 1928
Silver Leaf Quartette of Norfolk: Melvin Smith, first tenor and lead; William Thatch, falsetto voice; William Boush, baritone voice; Ellis McPherson, bass voice

400795-A   I Can Tell the World   OK 8594
400796-B   I Am a Pilgrim   OK 8594, ARC 6-12-63, Vo 04395

Silver Leaf Quartette of Norfolk

New York, New York, 22 October 1928
As above: add Professor Robert Wilson, organ (1)

401255-A	I'm Going Through with Jesus (1)	OK 8628
401256-B	When Jesus Comes	OK 8655, Ve 7086, Cl 6060, Di 5113
401257-A	Our Father	OK 8644, Ve 7068, Cl 6042, Di 5040, ARC 6-12-62
401258-B	My Soul Is a Witness for My Lord	OK 8655, Ve 7078, Cl 6052, Di 5040

[Ve, Cl, and Di issued as by the Gold Palm Quartet]

New York, New York, 23 October 1928
As above
401259-B   Sleep On, Mother (1)   OK 8644, Ve 7068, Cl 6042, Di 5113
401260-A   Hope I'll Join the Band (1)   OK 8628
401261-A   You Better Leave That Liar Alone   OK 8667, Ve 7078, Cl 6052, Di 5175
401262-B   That's What's the Matter with the Church Today   OK 8667, Ve 7086, Cl 6060, Di 5175

[Ve, Cl, and Di issued as by the Gold Palm Quartet]

New York, New York, 27 February 1930
As above: delete Professor Robert Wilson

403782-B   Jesus Is Mine   OK 8814, ARC 6-12-61
403783-A   The Beautiful Lamp   OK 8783, ARC 6-12-61
403784-B   Saviour Let Me Press Thy Hand   OK 8793
403785-B   The Ship Is at the Landing   OK 8777, ARC 6-12-62
403786-B   One Happy Time   OK 8793

New York, New York, 28 February 1930
As above
403787-B   There Will Be Glory   OK 8803
403788-B   Lover of the Lord   OK 8783, ARC 6-12-60

New York, New York, 5 March 1930
As above: add unknown piano (1)

403826-B   Will the Circle Be Unbroken   OK 8777, ARC 6-12-63, Vo 04395
403827-C   Lord I'm Troubled   OK 8814, ARC 6-12-60
403828-B   Sittin' in the Circle with the Saints (1)   OK 8803

New York, New York, 18 March 1931
As above: delete unknown piano; omit Ellis McPherson, add Luther Daniels, bass voice

404887-A	The Lord Is Walking with Me	OK 8874
404888-B	God Promised to Provide for Me	OK 8914
404889-B	Jesus Is All and All	OK 8874
404890-A	Daniel Saw the Stone	OK 8914
404891-B	We'll Anchor By and By	OK unissued
404892-B	Oh! Glory Glory	OK unissued

Bibliography: Vaughan Webb, brochure notes to "Hampton Roads Quartet Tradition," BRI 009.

Willie Simmons
See Hill Brothers.

Walter "Kid" Smith (ca. 1920–ca. 1969)

Born on August 12, 1895 in Carroll County, Virginia, Smith spent his youth in Greenbriar County, West Virginia. He worked as a sawyer and a boxer and learned the rudiments of guitar playing. But Smith was primarily a vocalist who specialized in the sacred and minstrel show songs that he learned from his father.

By the middle 1920s, Smith had moved to Rockingham County, North Carolina, and began to sing with local musicians such as Posey Rorer, Will Woodlieff, Lewis McDaniel, and Buster Carter. By the late 1920s some Spray-based musicians had recorded, and it was through their connections that Smith gained his first recording opportunity. Between 1929 and 1931 he recorded nearly three dozen sides in the company of his North Carolina and south central Virginia friends.

Throughout the 1930s Smith earned his living through music. His family became musically involved in his career, too, often accompanying him on guitar and ukulele. Together the Smith Family played on many radio programs and live performance dates in North Carolina and Virginia. Another regular outlet for their talents was the medicine show and tent show circuit that provided so many entertainers with steady, albeit often seasonal, work. In 1936 Smith and his family participated in their final recording session for the American Record Corp.

Following World War II Smith stayed on the road with tent shows and also continued his radio work. He traveled more extensively during this era, getting as far west as Montana and south to Texas. As recently as 1966 Smith still had a regular radio program over WPHL in Winchester, Virginia. Smith and his wife retired from music in 1969 and settled in Fredericksburg, Virginia. In about September 1977, Smith passed away.

VICTOR AND COLUMBIA ARTISTS
KID SMITH AND FAMILY WITH HIS CAROLINA BUDDIES

"OUR LATEST RELEASE"
COLUMBIA---No. 15652-D.
VICTOR---No. 23576-A

Walter Smith and Family as they appeared on a 1931 advertisement. From left: Thelma Smith, Odell Smith (no relation), Dorothy Smith, Walter Smith, and Norman Woodlieff. *Courtesy Dave Freeman (County Records)*

Walter Smith Family, circa 1932. Walter Smith and his wife (rear), Thelma, Dorothy, and possibly Lorene (front). *Courtesy Kinney Rorrer*

Richmond, Indiana, 20 March 1929
Walter Smith: Walter Smith, vocal; Posey Rorer, fiddle; Norman Woodlieff, guitar/solo vocal (1); Smith and Woodlieff, vocal duet (2)

14933-	Brace Up and Be a Man She Said (1)	Ge unissued
14934-	I'll Remember You Love in My Prayers (2)	Chm 15812, Spt 9389, Cq 7277
14935-A	I Ain't Gonna Grieve My Lord Anymore (2)	Chm 15812, Spt 9389, Cq 7277
14936-	It Won't Be Long until My Grave Is Made (2)	Ge 6858, Chm 15730, Spt 9494, Chm 45072, *CY 508*
14937-	The Old School House Play Ground (2)	Ge 6809, Chm 15855, Ch 431
14938-	I'd Rather Be with Rosy Nell (2)	Ge 6858, Ch 431
14939-	I Long to Kiss You All the Time (2)	Ge unissued
14940-	The Bald-Headed End of a Broom	Ge 6887, Chm 15772, Spt 9454
14941-	It's Sad to Leave You Sweetheart (2)	Ge 6809, Chm 15730, Spt 9389, Cq 7277, Chm 45072
14942-	Old Johnny Bucker Won't Do	Ge 6825, Spt 9407
14943-	The Cat's Got the Measles, The Dog's Got the Whoopin' Cough	Ge 6825, Chm 15772, Spt 9407
14944-	Why Did You Prove Untrue (1)	Ge unissued
14945-	I Fell in Love with a Married Man (1)	Ge 6824, Ch 428
14946-	Brace Up and Be a Man She Said (1)	Ge 6824, Ch 428

[Chms issued as by Jim Taylor and Bill Shelby; Spts issued as by Jerry Jordon or Jordon and Rupert, except Spt 9389, which was issued as by Norris Brothers; Chs issued as by Conley and Logan; reverse Ge 6887 and Spt 9454 by Carson Robison; reverse Chm 15855 by Patterson and Caplinger]

New York, New York, 25 March 1930
Carolina Buddies: Walter Smith, vocal; Posey Rorer, fiddle; Buster Carter, banjo; Lewis McDaniel, guitar, McDaniel and Smith, vocal duets (1)

150114-2	The Murder of the Lawson Family (1)	Co 15537, *CO CS966, BF 15521*
150115-1	In a Cottage by the Sea (1)	Co 15537, *BF 15521*
150116-1	The Story That the Crow Told Me	Co 15641, *BF 15521*
150117-1	My Sweetheart Is a Shy Little Miss	Co 15641, *BF 15521*

[150117 contains a speech by Carter]

New York, New York, 27 March 1930
Kid Williams: as above; omit vocals (2); Lewis McDaniel, solo guitar/vocal (3)

9515-2	Green Mountain Polka (2)	Pe 143
9516-2	Long Eared Mule (2)	Je 20003, Or 8003, Ro 5003

Walter "Kid" Smith

9517-1	Please Daddy Come Home (1)	Je 20003, Or 8005, Pe 152, Ro 5005
9524-	My Happy Home I Left in Carolina (1) Je 20000, Or 8005, Pe 145, Ro 5005	
9525-	My Father Don't Love Me (3)	Je 20004, Or 8004, Ro 5004
9526-	The Hard Luck Soldier (3)	ARC unissued
9527-	I Want to Be Called Pet and Sweetheart (1)	Pe 152
9528-	Don't Be Angry with Me Sweetheart	ARC unissued

New York, New York, 28 March 1930

As above

9529-2	Sandy River Belle (2)	Je 20003, Or 8003, Pe 142, Ro 5003
9530-	Old Virginia Breakdown (2)	ARC unissued
9531-1 and -2	I Know I'll Meet Mother After All (1) Je 20017, Or 8017, Pe 145, Ro 5017	
9532-2	Mother, Kiss Your Darling (1) Ba 32095, Je 20017, Or 8017, Ro 5017, Ho 16106, Cq 7744	
9535-	Aggravating Mother-in-law	Je 20006, Or 8006, Pe 146, Ro 5006
9536-	Love Is a Funny Thing Pe 146	
9537-	North Carolina Blues (3)	Je 20006, Or 8006, Pe 144, Ro 5004
9538-1	Down among the Budding Roses Je 20004, Or 8004, Pe 144, Ro 5004	

[9537 and 9538 issued as by Roy Martin or Roy Martin and His Guitar; some copies of Ro 5017 issued as by Kid Smith and Bill Morgan, acc: Dixie Ramblers; reverse of Ba 32095, Ho 16106, and Cq 7744 unknown; Pe 143 issued as by Dixie Ramblers]

New York, New York, 5 May 1930

Kid Williams: Walter Smith, vocal; Patt Patterson, steel guitar; Lois Dexter, tenor banjo; Lewis McDaniel, guitar/vocal (1); Lewis McDaniel, solo guitar/vocal (2)

9705-1	Birmingham Jail (1) Je 20020, Or 8020, Pe 160, Ro 5020, Cq 7739, Ba 32096	
9706-1	The Prisoner and the Rose	Je 20020, Or 8020, Ro 5020, Ba 32096
9707-1	When He Died He Got a Home in Hell Je 20028, Or 8028, Ro 5028, Cq 7739	
9708-2	I'm Glad I Counted the Cost	Je 20028, Or 8028, Ro 5028, Ho 16094
9709-	Swinging in the Lane with Nell (1)	ARC unissued
9710-	The Drunkard's Child ARC unissued	

New York, New York, 6 May 1930

As above

9711-	Behind the Hen House (2)	ARC unissued
9712-	Whisper Your Mother's Name (2)	ARC unissued
9713-	Desert Blues (2) ARC unissued	

9714-   May I Sleep in Your Barn Tonight Mister (2)   Pe 160
9715-   Bye and Bye You Will Forget Me (1)   ARC unissued

[9711-9714 listed as by Roy Martin or Roy Martin and His Guitar; unknown harmonica on 9708]

New York, New York, 12 May 1930

Lewis McDaniel-Gid Smith: omit Patterson and Dexter (3)

62220-1	I've Loved You So True (1)	Vi 23505, *BF 15521*
62221-2	It's Hard to Leave You Sweetheart (1, 3)	Vi 40287, *OT 102, BF 15521*
62222-2	I Went to See My Sweetheart (2, 3)	Vi 23505, *BF 15521*
62223-2	One More Kiss Before I Go (2, 3)	TT 1560, *BF 15521*
62224-2	We'll Talk about One Another (1, 3)	Vi 40287, *BF 15521*
62225-2	My Father Doesn't Love Me (2, 3)	TT 1560, *BF 15521*

[Unknown harmonica on 62223; yodeling on TT 1560]

New York, New York, 24 February 1931

Carolina Buddies: Walter Smith, vocal; Norman Woodlieff, guitar/vocal duet (1); Odell Smith, fiddle; Norman Woodlieff, solo vocal (2)

151340-2	Work Don't Bother Me (1)	Co 15663, *BF 15521*
151341-2	He Went In Like a Lion (But Came Out Like a Lamb) (2)	Co 15663, *BF 15521*
151342-	No No Positively No	Co unissued
151343-	How I Love Pretty Little Liza	Co unissued
151344-	My Evolution Gal	Co 15770, *BF 15521*
151345-2	Otto Wood the Bandit	Co 15652, *BF 15521*
151346-2	Broken Hearted Lover (1)	Co 15652, *BF 15521*
151347-	Mistreated Blues	Co 15770, *BF 15521*

New York, New York, ca. early March 1931

Virginia Dandies: as above

1218-2	There's a Mother Old and Gray Who Needs Me Now (2)	Cr 3103, Pm 3280, Ho 32025
1220-2A	There's a Beautiful City Called Heaven (1)	Cr 3145
1221-1B	God's Getting Worried	Cr 3145
1222-2	'Mid the Green Fields of Virginia (1)	Cr 3103, Pm 3305, Ho 23025
1224-1 and -2	The Cabin with the Roses (1)	Pm 3305, *CT 6001*
	Rosy Nell (1) Cr unissued	
	That Beautiful City of Gold (1) Cr unissued	
	Sweet Estelle (2) Cr unissued	
	I'll Meet Her When the Sun Goes Down Cr unissued	

Walter "Kid" Smith

> What Whiskey Will Do (2)   Cr unissued
> Shady Grove   Cr unissued

[Cr 3103 issued as by Jake Woodfield; Pm 3280 issued as by Jake Woodlieff; Ho issue credit unknown]

Charlotte, North Carolina, 19 May 1931
Kid Smith and Family: Walter Smith, vocal; Odell Smith, fiddle; Thelma Smith, guitar/vocal; Dorothy Smith, ukulele/vocal; Norman Woodlieff, guitar/vocal

| 69313-1 | Whisper Softly, Mother's Dying | Vi 23576 |
| 69314-2 | Little Bessie   Vi 23576 | |

New York, New York, 1 December 1936
As above: omit Odell Smith and Norman Woodlieff

20346-	You Give Me Your Love (and I'll Give You Mine)	ARC 7-03-51
20347-	Whisper Softly, Mother's Dying ARC unissued	
20348-	Come Up Here My Little Bessie ARC unissued	
20349-	Homestead in the Wildwood ARC unissued	

New York, New York, 2 December 1936
As above
20352-	Lying Daddy Blues ARC 7-04-76
20353-	Mama Cat Blues ARC 7-04-76
20354-1	Mississippi Freight Train Blues ARC 7-03-52, Cq 8788
20355-2	Ten I Served and Ten to Serve ARC 7-04-52, Cq 8787
20356-	It Won't Be Long till My Grave Is Made ARC unissued

[20355 has only one female voice]

New York, New York, 5 December 1936
As above
20369-	I'm Not Angry with You Darling ARC 7-03-51
20370-	Don't Wait till I'm Laid 'neath the Clay ARC unissued
20371-2	Mama You're a Mess ARC 7-03-52, Cq 8788

New York, New York, 8 December 1936
As above
20349-4   Homestead in the Wildwood   ARC 7-04-52, Cq 8787

Bibliography: Norm Cohen, "Walter 'Kid' Smith," *JEMF Quarterly* 9, Part 3, no. 32 (Autumn 1973): 128-32; Kinney Rorrer, *Rambling Blues: The Life and Songs of Charlie Poole* (London: Old Time Music, 1982); Tony Russell, "Alias Walter Smith," *Old Time Music* 17 (Summer 1975): 12-18.

Smoky Blue Ramblers
A pseudonym on Velvet Tone and Clarion for the Blue Ridge Highballers and for Charlie Poole.

Smoky Mountain Ramblers
A pseudonym on Supertone for H.M. Barnes' Blue Ridge Ramblers.

Smyth County Ramblers (late 1920s)
Because of the unusual spelling of this group's name (which in the eastern United States is unique to Smyth County, Virginia) and its geographical proximity to the field recording location, it is presumed that this group was from Virginia. The group's fiddle player, Jack Pierce, also performed and recorded with the Grant Brothers as a member of the Tenneva Ramblers.

Bristol, Tennessee, 27 October 1927
Smyth County Ramblers: Jack Pierce, fiddle/vocal (1); Weldon Reedy, banjo; Malcolm Worley, guitar/vocal (2); Carol Cruise, guitar/vocal (3)

47229-2	My Name is Ticklish Reuben (1, 2)	Vi 40144
47230-2	Way Down in Alabama (1, 3)	Vi 40144

See also Grant Brothers.

Southern Melody Boys (1934–1938)
The core of the Southern Melody Boys consisted of banjo player Joseph Odus Maggard, born on January 31, 1915, in Perry County, Kentucky, and Woodrow Wilson Roberts, a guitarist born in Wise County, Virginia, on December 21, 1912. They joined together to play for dances and to perform over Bristol radio station WOPI. Initially this duo performed with fiddler Pat Hill, but midway through their career Joe McConnell joined them on fiddle.

Their broadcasting enabled them to book engagements in theaters and schools throughout southwestern Virginia and northeastern Tennessee. During their four years together the Southern Melody Boys operated as full-time musicians with their primary income being derived from personal appearances.

The aural documentation of the Southern Melody Boys took place late in their career. The duo apparently auditioned for Victor and was asked down to Charlotte to record for Bluebird during Victor's annual winter field recording session. This was followed by a brief session for Decca; none of the Southern Melody Boys' records sold well.

The group broke up during the summer of 1938 when Maggard married and settled down to raise a family. He has had a variety of trades over the years; since

Woodrow Roberts (guitar) and Odus Maggard (banjo) toured and recorded as the "Southern Melody Boys" in the middle 1930s. *Courtesy George Edens*

1951, though, most of his time has been spent barbering in Kingsport, Tennessee. Roberts has supported himself as a construction worker, is self-employed, and lives in Clinton, Tennessee.

Charlotte, North Carolina, February 1937
Southern Melody Boys: Odus Maggard, banjo/lead vocal/solo vocal (1); Woodrow Roberts, guitar/tenor vocal

> Tribulation Days   Bb 6883, MW 7222, MW 7349, *RO 1033*
> If You See My Savior   Bb 6883, MW 7222
> Down in Baltimore   Bb 7057, MW 7225
> Wind the Little Ball of Yarn (1)   Bb 7057, MW 7227
> Carry Me over the Tide   MW 7223
> Dividing Line   MW 7223
> I'll Remember You, Love, in My Prayer   MW 7224
> Sweet Locust Blossoms   MW 7224
> When the Autumn Leaves Fall   MW 7225
> Lonely and Sad   MW 7226
> Back in California (1)   MW 7226
> Lonesome Scenes of Winter (1)   MW 7227

[Reverse of MW 7349 unknown]

Charlotte, North Carolina, June 1938
Odus and Woodrow: as above

64116-A	When the Spring Roses Are Blooming	De 5570
64117-A	I Been Here a Long Long Time	De 5603
64118-A	Waiting for the Boatman	De 5570
64119-A	I Told the Stars about You	De 5603

Bibliography: George Edens, "Southern Melody Boys," *Old Time Music* 13 (Spring 1974): 13-16.

Southland Jubilee Singers

A pseudonym on Herwin for the Norfolk Jubilee Quartet.

Southland Jubilee Singers (ca. 1917–ca. 1934)

The Southland Jubilee Singers were founded as a male/female, piano-accompanied gospel group. By 1921 the members were performing as a "double" quartet, consisting of four men and four women. According to a contemporary report in the *Norfolk Journal and Guide,* only the male members of the double quartet went to New York to record early in 1921.

The group performed throughout the 1920s, frequently being billed as the

From left: Dave Pearson, Babe Spangler, and Scott Peck, circa 1928, Richmond, Virginia. *Courtesy Dave Freeman (County Records)*

Old Southland Jubilee Singers or the Old Southland Sextet. They toured extensively across the United States and during their act often performed as soloists, duos, and other combinations. The number of members varied between eight and ten, and they often included a pianist as an accompanist.

The *Norfolk Journal and Guide* (eastern Virginia's black newspaper) reports on this group suggest they participated in making a movie in January of 1929. In addition to singing in churches, the Southland Jubilees often performed for white audiences as part of stage shows. The group seems to have broken up in the mid-1930s.

New York, New York, ca. January 1921
Southland Jubilee Singers: Hamilton James, tenor voice; Jonas Anderson, tenor voice; Jerry Anderson, bass voice; Frank Horace, bass voice

7685-B	My Lord's Writing All the Time	OK 4390
7686-B	Shout All over God's Heaven	OK 4390
7689-B	Little David Play on Your Harp	OK 4271, Ph 4271
7690-C	Great Camp Meeting	OK 4271, Ph 4271

New York, New York, ca. 11 September 1924
As above: male voices presumably as above, add Eugene C. Burke, piano; add several unknown female voices

| 72804-B | My Lord's Gonna Move This Wicked Race | OK 8170 |

[Reverse OK 8170 by Elkins-Payne Jubilee Singers; Southland Jubilee Singers was also used as a pseudonym for Bryant's Jubilee Quartette on Chm and the Wiseman Quartet and Norfolk Jubilee Quartet on He; other selections from the January 1921 date may have also come out on Ph and Sun]

Bibliography: Vaughan Webb, brochure notes for "Hampton Roads Quartet Tradition," BRI 009.

Spangler and Pearson (late 1920s)

Because of his radio broadcasts over WRVA between 1926 and 1931 John Wallace "Babe" Spangler was one of his era's most influential fiddlers. Born in Meadows of Dan in Patrick County, Virginia, on November 15, 1882, Babe learned his art from his father, Wallace W. Spangler, who was one of the region's premier fiddle players. By the time Babe Spangler moved to Richmond, Virginia, in 1906 he was a fluid, graceful musician playing many older, traditional tunes.

Spangler's first job was as a guard at the state penitentiary, a position he held for many years until an increasingly serious hereditary eye condition markedly impaired his sight. He turned his entrepreneurial skills to the grocery and lumber business, and gradually to music. In 1925 WRVA signed on the air and by about 1927 Spangler was one of the station's musical stars.

He led a string band and was known as the "Old Virginia Fiddler." His broadcasts were featured on the live radio program, the Corn Cob Pipe Show, which was heard nightly at 11:00 P.M. WRVA was a clear- channel station, and its signal reached all of the eastern United States with Spangler's blend of traditional fiddle tunes, sentimental songs, and popular instrumentals.

In October 1929 Spangler and one of his Corn Cob Pipe associates, guitarist Dave Pearson, were invited to record for the OKeh Company, which had set up its portable equipment in Richmond. Although Spangler's records did not gain wide sales, he remained a regular on WRVA until 1938. During the interim he and his brother, Trump, played at many musical events, including the Whitetop Folk Festival in 1934.

After 1938 Spangler continued to play fiddle professionally for a few years, but gradually got out of the music business. Though he often came back to Meadows of Dan to visit relatives, Spangler continued to live in Richmond. He played the fiddle for his own enjoyment until his death in 1970.

Richmond, Virginia, 14 October 1929
Spangler and Pearson: Babe Spangler, fiddle; Dave Pearson, guitar

403120-B	Climbing Up the Golden Stairs	OK unissued
403121-A	Golden Slippers	OK unissued
403122-A	Midnight Serenade	OK 45387, *CY 201*
403123-A	Patrick County Blues	OK 45387, *CY 201*

Bibliography: Tom Carter and Barry Poss, brochure notes for "The Old Virginia Fiddlers: Rare Recordings 1948-49," Cy 201; Larry Shumway and Tom Carter, "The History and Performance Style of J.W. 'Babe' Spangler, The Old Virginia Fiddler," *JEMF Quarterly* 14, no. 52 (Winter 1978): 198-208.

Sparkling Four Quartette (ca. 1922–ca. 1930)

According to the OKeh Record Company files, the Sparkling Four were managed by Alexander A. Thorogood, 1007 Bute Street, Norfolk, Virginia. Contemporary newspaper accounts suggest that the group engaged in many quartet contests in Hampton Roads between 1922 and 1927. It is likely that the Sparkling Four Quartette was a community group, probably based in Norfolk. How long the group remained together beyond its final recording session is unclear.

Long Island City, New York, August 1928
Sparkling Four Quartette: Walter Cason, bass voice; Dick Bell, tenor voice; Joe Key, lead voice; "Spark," baritone voice

105-	Shepherd, Feed My Sheep	QRS 7011
107-A	Keep On to Gallalee [sic]	QRS 7011
	Great Change	QRS 7000
	I Cannot Drift	QRS 7000
	Wait Till I Get On My Robe	QRS 7010
	Who'll Join the Union	QRS 7010

Richmond, Virginia, 13 October 1929
Sparkling Four: presumably as above

403100-B	Good News	OK unissued
403101-B	Hallelujah (Who'll Join the Union)	OK unissued
403102-A	They Won't Believe in Me	OK 8741
403103-A	Hold the Wind	OK 8741

Bibliography: Vaughan Webb, brochure notes to "Hampton Roads Quartet Tradition," BRI 009.

Stone Mountain Entertainers
A pseudonym on Broadway for Roy Harvey.

Ernest Stoneman (early 1920s–1968)
Ernest V. Stoneman was one of the pioneering country music recording artists. Born near Galax, Virginia (Carroll County), on May 14, 1893, he was a carpenter, coal miner, and mill worker in addition to his career in music. Stoneman's early life was spent in rural Carroll County, where he informally learned to play the harmonica, guitar, and banjo from some of the local musicians. It was during his youth that Stoneman also acquired many of the ballads and religious songs that he later recorded.

One of the very first country musicians to record was Henry Whitter, a native of Fries, Virginia, whom Stoneman knew quite well. After hearing Whitter's 1924 OKeh recordings, Stoneman was inspired to try to break into the fledgling hillbilly record business. After saving his money for several months, he traveled to New York City and sufficiently impressed the OKeh executives that they offered him a recording opportunity.

Unlike the records of many of his peers from south central and south western Virginia, Stoneman's recordings sold relatively well, and he was called back to the studios many times. In fact, he made a living playing music and recorded many sacred and secular selections between 1924 and 1934. Even after his recording career declined, Stoneman remained in the music business.

But by the early 1930s he recognized that the textile-based economy of Carroll County had been permanently damaged and moved his large family to

LATEST AMBEROL EDISON RECORDS

5463 — Slavonic Rhapsody
  Sodja's Band

5343 — Ain't She Sweet?
  Song — Johnny Marvin

5357 — Once I Had A Fortune
  Singing, Fiddle, Banjo and Guitar
  Ernest V. Stoneman and The Dixie
  Mountaineers

5353 — The More We Are Together
  Fox Trot — B. A. Rolfe and his Palais d'Or
  Orchestra
  Vocal Refrain by the Orchestra

5358 — Bells of Hawaii
  Singing with Hawaiian Accompaniment
  Aloha-Land Serenaders

5337 — The Crepe On The Old Cabin Door
  Singing, Harmonica and Guitar
  Vernon Dalhart

5364 — Jean McNeil
  Comic Song — Harry Lauder

5362 — Lindbergh The Eagle Of The U. S. A.
  Vernon Dalhart

5365 — Saved By Grace
  Sacred Song — Edison Mixed Quartet

5360 — Hallelujah
  Fox Trot — Golden Gate Orchestra
  Vocal Refrain by Arthur Fields

5352 — The Mocking Bird
  Fiddle with Piano Accompaniment
  John Baltzell
  Champion Old Time Fiddler

5359 — The Doll Dance
  Fox Trot — B. A. Rolfe and his Palais d'Or
  Orchestra

5355 — The Fatal Wedding
  Singing, Harmonica and Guitar
  Ernest V. Stoneman
  The Blue Ridge Mountaineer

5354 — Rosy Cheeks
  Fox Trot — Oreste and his Queensland
  Orchestra
  Vocal Refrain by J. Donald Parker

5356 — Lucky Lindy
  Vernon Dalhart

THOMAS A. EDISON, INC.
ORANGE, N. J.
"A Product of the Edison Laboratories"

Edison Catalogue advertising Stoneman releases

Washington, D.C., in search of better job opportunities. Between the depths of the Depression and the early 1940s, Stoneman and his family retained their musical ties. His children gradually became more involved in music and they often broadcast over local radio stations. Stoneman's steadiest source of income, however, remained his carpentry skills.

After World War II, his musical career began to ascend. The children became part of his band and two of them, Roni and Scotty, went on to establish themselves professionally. "Pop" once more found himself in demand as a professional musician, both for recordings and personal appearances.

Stoneman's musical and recording career prospered even more during the "folk boom" of the 1960s, which rekindled interest in American folk music. He received recognition from the commercial interests in country music when in 1967 the Stoneman Family was named the "Vocal Group of the Year" by the Country Music Association. He basked in this newfound interest in his music until his death 14 June 1968.

New York, New York, ca. 4 September 1924
Ernest V. Stoneman: Ernest V. Stoneman, vocal/harmonica/autoharp

S 72787-A	The Face That Never Returned	OK unissued
S 72788-A	The Titanic	OK unissued

New York, New York, ca. 8 January 1925
As above
S 72787-B	The Face That Never Returned	OK 40288
S 72788-B	The Titanic	OK 40288
S 73089-A	Freckled Face Mary Jane	OK 40312
S 73090-A	Me and My Wife	OK 40312

New York, New York, 27 May 1925
As above: add Emmett Lundy, fiddle (1)

S 73371-	Uncle Sam and the Kaiser	OK 40430
S 73372-A	Jack and Joe	OK 40408
S 73373-A	Sinful to Flirt	OK 40384
S 73374-	Dixie Parody	OK 40430
S 73375-A	Dying Girl's Farewell	OK 40384, *RO 1008*
S 73376-A	The Lighting Express	OK 40408
S 73377-A	Piney Woods Girl (1)	OK 40405, *CY 535*
S 73378-A	The Long Eared Mule (1)	OK 40405

[OK 40405 issued as by Ernest V. Stoneman and Emmett Lundy]

Ernest Stoneman

Asheville, North Carolina, 27 August 1925
As above
9284-	The Sailor's Song	OK 45015
9285-A	Blue Ridge Mountain Blues	OK 45009
9286-A	All I've Got's Gone	OK 45009
9287-	The Fancy Ball	OK 45015
9288-	The Kicking Mule	OK 45036
9289-A	The Wreck on the C & O	OK 7011
9290-A	John Hardy	OK 7011

[OK 7011 is a 12" disc; no harmonica on 9284]

Asheville, North Carolina, April 1926
Ernest Stoneman, vocal/harmonica (1)/autoharp (2)/guitar (3)

S 74102-B	The Religious Critic (1, 2)	OK 45051
S 74103-A	When My Wife Will Return to Me (3)	OK 45051
S 74104-A	Asleep at the Switch (1, 2)	OK 45044
S 74105-A	The Orphan Girl (1, 2)	OK 45044
S 74108-B	Kitty Wells (1, 3)	OK 45048
S 74109-A	The Texas Ranger (1, 3)	OK 45054
S 74110-B	In the Shadow of the Pines (1, 2)	OK 45048
S 74111-A	Don't Let Your Deal Go Down (3)	OK 45054

New York, New York, 21 June 1926
Ernest V. Stoneman, the Blue Ridge Mountaineer: vocal/guitar/autoharp

11053-B	Bad Companions	Ed 51788	
16169-	Bad Companions	Ed 5201	
11054-A	When the Work's All Done This Fall	Ed 51788	
16180-	When the Work's All Done This Fall	5188	
11055-A	Wreck of the C & O	Ed 51823	
16181-	Wreck of the C & O	Ed 5198	
11056-A	Wild Bill Jones	Ed 51869	
16182-	Wild Bill Jones	Ed 5196	
11057-A	John Henry	Ed 51869	
16176-	John Henry	Ed 5194	

[For these and all subsequent Ed releases the 50000 series are discs, and the 5000 series are cylinders]

New York, New York, 22 June 1926

11058-A	Sinking of the Titanic	Ed 51823
16178-	Sinking of the Titanic	Ed 5200
11059-A	Watermelon Hanging on the Vine	Ed 51864

Bolen Frost(?) (banjo), Hattie Stoneman (fiddle), Irma Frost (mandolin), unidentified man with book, Ernest Stoneman (guitar). *Courtesy Blue Ridge Heritage Archive*

Ernest Stoneman 187

16183-   Watermelon Hanging on the Vine   Ed 5191
11060-C   The Old Hickory Cane   Ed 51864
161??   The Old Hickory Cane   Ed 5241
[11058-A and 16178 issued as by the Blue Ridge Mountaineer]

New York, New York, 23 June 1926
As above:
11063-   My Little German Home across the Sea   Ed 51909
11064-   Bury Me Beneath the Willow   Ed 51909
16184-   Bury Me Beneath the Willow   Ed 5187

New York, New York, ca. August 1926
As above: add Joe Samuels ("Fiddler Joe"), fiddle (4)

S 74300-A   Silver Bell (4)   OK 45060
S 74301-A   May I Sleep in Your Barn Tonight, Mister (4)   OK 45059
S 74302-A   My Pretty Snow Dear (4)   OK 45060
S 74303-   Are You Angry with Me, Darling? (4)   OK 45065
S 74304-A   The Old Hickory Cane   OK 45059, *CY 533*
S 74305-   He's Going to Have a Hot Time By and By   OK 45062
S 74306-   The Old Go Hungry Hash House   OK 45062
S 74307-   Katie Kline   OK 45065
[S 74300 through S 74303 issued as by Ernest V. Stoneman and Fiddler Joe]

New York, New York, 28 August 1926
Ernest Stoneman: delete Fiddler Joe and add Hattie Stoneman, fiddle

X 233-A   May I Sleep in Your Barn Tonight Mister?   Ge 3368, Ch 153, Ch 312, He 75530, *OH 173*
X 234-A
and -B   The Girl I Left Behind in Sunny Tennessee   Ge 3368, Ch 151, He 75529, *OH 173*
X 235-A   Silver Bell   Ge 3369, Ch 153, He 75529
X 236-A   Pretty Snow Dear   Ge 3369, Ch 152, He 75530
X 237-A   Katy Cline   Ge 3381, Ch 151, He 75528
X 238-A   Barney McCoy   Ge 3381, Ch 152, Ch 309, He 75528
[X 237 deletes fiddle and adds unknown banjo, possibly Bolen Frost]

New York, New York, 21 September 1926
Ernest V. Stoneman and His Dixie Mountaineers: vocal group, Ernest V. Stoneman, Kahle Brewer, Walter Mooney, Tom Leonard, Hattie Stoneman; Irma Frost, organ; Kahle Brewer, fiddle; Ernest V. Stoneman, guitar/harmonica

BVE36198-2 Going Down the Valley   Vi 20531, *CY 508*
BVE36199-2 The Sinless Summer   Vi 20531, *RO 1008*

BVE36500-2 In the Golden Bye and Bye   Vi 20223, *OH 173*
BVE65001-2 I Will Meet You in the Morning   Vi 20223, *OH 173*
BVE36502-1 The Great Reaping Day   Vi 20532, *OH 173*
BVE36503-1 I Love to Walk With Jesus   Vi 20224, *OH 173*
BVE36504-2 Hallelujah Side   Vi 20224, *RO 1008*
[No harmonica on BVE36198 through BVE36502]

New York, New York, 24 September 1926

As above: delete vocal group (1)

BVE36507-1 I'll Be Satisfied   Vi 20533, *OH 173*
BVE36508-1 West Virginia Highway (2)   Vi 20237
BVE36509-2 Peek-a-boo Waltz (1)   Vi 20540, *OH 172*
BVE36510-2 When the Redeemed Are Gathered In   Vi 20532, *OH 172*
BVE36511-1 I Would Not Be Denied   VR 20532
BVE36512-2 Going up Cripple Creek (1)   Vi 20294, *RO 1008*
BVE36513-2 Sourwood Mountain (1)   Vi 20235, *CAM LPM 6015*
BVD36514-2 Little Old Log Cabin in the Lane (1)   Vi 20235, MW 8305
[BVE36508-1 and BVE36509-2 issued as by Ernest V. Stoneman and Kahle Brewer; unknown banjo and no harmonica on BVE36507-1 through BVE36511-1; organ only on BVE36507-1, BVE36510-2, and BVE36511-1]

New York, New York, 25 September 1926

As above: Ernest V. Stoneman, guitar/harmonica/vocal; unknown banjo

BVE36515-2 Ida Red   Vi 20302
BVE36516-2 Sugar in the Gourd   Vi 20294, *CY 507*
BVE36517-2 Old Joe Clark   Vi 20302, *RO 1008*
BVE36518-2 All Go Hungry Hash House   Vi 20237, *RO 1008*
[BVE36518-2 deletes harmonica and issued as by Ernest V. Stoneman]

New York, New York, 24 January 1927

Ernest V. Stoneman and the Dixie Mountaineers: Ernest V. Stoneman, vocal/guitar/harmonica; Kahle Brewer, fiddle; Bolen Frost, banjo; George Stoneman, banjo

11460-A		
and -C	Bright Sherman Valley	Ed 51951
	Bright Sherman Valley	Ed 5383
114610-A		
and -C	Once I Had a Fortune	Ed 51935, *HI 8004*
	Once I Had a Fortune	Ed 5357

Ernest Stoneman   189

New York, New York, 25 January 1927
As above:
11462-B   The Long Eared Mule   Ed 52056
11463-C   Hop Light Ladies   Ed 52056, *HI 8004*
11464-B,C   Two Little Orphans—Our Mama's In Heaven   Ed 51935
16294-   Two Little Orphans—Our Mama's in Heaven   Ed 5338
11465-A,C   Kitty Wells   Ed 51944, *HI 8004*
16295-   Kitty Wells   Ed 5341
[Ed 52056 issued as by the Dixie Mountaineers and deletes the vocal]

New York, New York, 27 January 1927
Ernest V. Stoneman Trio: Ernest V. Stoneman, vocal/guitar; Kahle Brewer, fiddle; George Stoneman or Bolen Frost, banjo

W 80344-   The Wreck of the Old 97   OK unissued, *LBC 9*
W 80345-   Little Log Cabin in the Lane   OK unissued
W 80346-   Flop Eared Mule   OK unissued
W 80347-A   Lonesome Road Blues   OK 45094
W 80348-A   Round Town Gal   OK 45094
W 80439-   Old Joe Clark   OK unissued

New York, New York, 28 January 1927
Ernest V. Stoneman and the Dixie Mountaineers: Ernest V. Stoneman, vocal/guitar/ harmonica (1); Kahle Brewer, fiddle; unknown banjo (2)

11481-C   Hand Me Down My Walking Cane (1, 2)   Ed 51938
16253-   Hand Me Down My Walking Cane (1, 2)   Ed 5297, *OH 172*
11482-B   Tell Mother I Will Meet Her (1)   Ed 51938
16256-   Tell Mother I Will Meet Her (1)   Ed 5382

New York, New York, 29 January 1927
As above
11483-A   We Courted in the Rain   Ed 51994
16268-   We Courted in the Rain   Ed 5308
11484-C   The Bully of the Town   Ed 51951
16266-   The Bully of the Town   Ed 5314
[Fiddle deleted on 11484-C and 16266; "We Courted in the Rain" issued as by Ernest V. Stoneman and the Blue Ridge Mountaineers]

New York, New York, 29 January 1927
Ernest V. Stoneman: Ernest V. Stoneman, vocal/guitar/harmonica (1); probably Kahle Brewer, fiddle

W 80360-B   The Fatal Wedding   OK 45084
W 80361-A   The Fate of Talmadge Osborne (1)   OK 45084, *BRI 004*

New York, New York, 5 February 1927

As above: unknown banjo replaces harmonica (1)

GEX 493-A The Poor Tramp Has to Live   Ge 6044, Chm 15233, Ch 324, Ch 398, Ch 244, Sil 5001, Sil 8155, Sil 25001, Spt 9255, He 75535
GEX 494-A Sweet Bunch of Violets   GE 6065, He 75541, Chm 15233, Sil 5004, Sil 25004, *CY 533*
GEX 495-A Kenny Wagner's Surrender   Ge 6044, Chm 15222, He 75535, Sil 5004, Sil 25004, *HI 8003, OH 173*
GEX 496-A When the Roses Bloom Again   Ge 6065, Chm 15222, Ch 244, Spt 9255, Sil 5001, Sil 8155, Sil 25001, He 75541, *OH 173*
GEX 497-A Long Eared Mule (1)   Ge 6052, Sil 5003, Sil 25003
GEX 498-A Round Town Gals (1)   Ge 6052, Sil 5003, Sil 25003, Chm 15248

[Ch 324 and Ch 398 issued as by Uncle Jim Seany; Ch 244 issued as by Uncle Ben Hawkins; Chm 15222 and Chm 15233 issued as by Uncle Jim Seany; Chm 15248 issued as by Uncle Ben Hawkins and His Gang; Sil and Spt issued as by Uncle Ben Hawkins or Uncle Ben Hawkins and His Gang, except Sil 25003 issued as by Logan City Trio; Ge issued as by Ernest V. Stoneman and his Graysen (*sic*) County Boys]

New York, New York, 10 May 1927

The Dixie Mountaineers: unknown fiddle; Ernest V. Stoneman, vocal/harmonica/guitar; Mrs. Ernest Stoneman, vocal

11690-C	Fate of Talmadge Osborne	Ed 52026
16318-	Fate of Talmadge Osborne	Ed 5369
11691-A	The Orphan Girl	Ed 52077
16319-	The Orphan Girl	Ed 5367
11692-	Pass Around the Bottle	Ed unissued
11693-C	The Fatal Wedding	Ed 52026
?????	The Fatal Wedding	Ed 5355

["The Fatal Wedding" issued as by Ernest V. Stoneman and Mrs. Stoneman]

New York, New York, ca. early May 1927

Ernest V. Stoneman: Ernest V. Stoneman, vocal/guitar/harmonica; unknown fiddle (1); unknown banjo (2)

7222-1   Hand Me Down My Walking Cane (1)   Ba 1993, Do 3964, Re 8324, Or 916, Ho 16490
7223-1   Pass Around the Bottle   Ba 2157, Do 3985, Re 8346, Ho 16490, Or 916, Ch 665, Cq 7064, Cq 7755, Pm 3021, Bw 8054
7224-1   When the Roses Bloom Again (2)   Ba 1993, Do 3964, Re 8324, Ho 16498, Or 946
7225-1   Bully of the Town   Ba 2157, Do 3984, Re 8347, Ho 16500, Or 947, Ch 665, Cq 7755, Pa 32279, Pe 12358, Spt 32279, Ca 8217, Ro 597, Li 2822

[All Or and Ho issued as by Sim Harris]

Ernest Stoneman 191

New York, New York, May 1927
Ernest V. Stoneman: Ernest V. Stoneman, vocal/harmonica/guitar

7286-	The Old Hickory Cane	Pa 32271, Pe 12350, Do 0187, Re 8369, *CY 533*
7287-A	The Fatal Wedding	Ca 8220, Ro 600, Li 2825
7287-B	The Fatal Wedding	Pa 32278, Pe 12357, Ch 666, Ba 2158, Do 3984, Re 8347, Ho 16498, Or 946
????-	Pass Around the Bottle	Pa 32278, Pe 12357, Ca 8217, Ro 597, Li 2882
7288-	Sinful to Flirt	Pa 32271, Pe 12350, Ch 666, Cq 7064, Ca 8220, Ro 600, Li 2825, Ba 2158, Do 3985, Re 8346, Ho 16500, Or 947

New York, New York, 12 May 1927
Mr. and Mrs. Stoneman: Ernest V. Stoneman, harmonica/guitar/vocal; Mrs. Hattie Stoneman, fiddle (1)/vocal

W 81075-B When the Silvery Colorado Wends Its Way   OK unissued
W 81078-   Two Little Orphans   OK unissued
W 81079-A
  and -B   The Road to Washington (1)   OK 45125, *OH 173*
W 81080-B The Mountaineer's Courtship   OK 45125, *FW FA 2953, OH 173*

New York, New York, 19 May 1927
Ernest V. Stoneman: Ernest Stoneman, guitar/harmonica/vocal

BVE38763-2 The Poor Tramp   Vi 20672, *RO 1008*
BVE38764-2 The Fate of Talmadge Osborne   Vi 20672, *OH 173*
BVE38765-2 The Old Hickory Cane   Vi 20799
BVE38766-2 Till the Snowflakes Fall Again   Vi 20799, *OH 172*

New York, New York, 21 May 1927
As above
BVE38918-1 The Story of the Mississippi Flood   Vi 20761, *OH 173*
BVE38919-2 Joe Hoover's Mississippi Flood Song   Vi unissued
[Reverse Vi 20671 is by Ernest Rodgers]

Bristol, Tennessee, 25 July 1927
Ernest V. Stoneman and his Dixie Mountaineers: Ernest V. Stoneman, vocal/guitar/harmonica (1); Kahle Brewer, fiddle/vocal (2); Walter Mooney, vocal (3); Irma Frost, organ (4)/vocal (5); Eck Dunford, fiddle; vocal group, probably composed of Ernest Stoneman, Kahle Brewer, Edna Brewer, Hattie Stoneman, and Irma Frost (6)

BVE 39700-1 The Dying Girl's Farewell (2, 3)   Vi 21129, *RO 1008*
BVE39701-3 Tell Mother I Will Meet Her (2, 3)   Vi 21129, *CY 533, CMF 011-L*

BVE39702-2 The Mountaineers Courtship (1, 5)   Vi 20880, *CMF 011-L*
BVE39703- Midnight on the Stormy Deep (1, 5)   Vi unissued, *CMF 011-L*
BVE39704-3 Sweeping through the Gates (4, 6)   Vi 20844, *RO 1008*
BVE39705-2 I Know My Name Is There (4, 6)   Vi 21186, *RO 1008, LBC 1*
BVE39706-2 Are You Washed in the Blood? (4, 6)   Vi 20844, MW 8136, *RO 1008, CMF 011-L*
BVE39707-2 No More Goodbyes (4, 6)   Vi 21186, *CY 533*
BVE39708-2 The Resurrection (4, 6)   Vi 21071, *OH 172, CMF 011-L*
BVE39709-2 I Am Resolved (4, 6)   Vi 21071
[Vi 21129 issued as by Ernest Stoneman, K. Brewer, M. Mooney; BVE39702-2 issued as by Ernest Stoneman, Irma Frost, Eck Dunford; BVE39703 listed as by Ernest Stoneman and Irma Frost; BVE39703 has guitar by Eck Dunford; reverse MW 8136 unknown]

Bristol, Tennessee, 27 July 1927
Uncle Eck Dunford: Mrs. Hattie Stoneman, fiddle/vocal (1); Uncle Eck Dunford, vocal/guitar; Iver Edwards, ukulele/harmonica

BVE39716-1 The Whip-poor-will Song (1)   Vi 20880, *OH 173*
BVE39717-2 What Will I Do, for My Money's All Gone (1)   Vi 21578
BVE39718-2 Skip to My Lou, My Darling   Vi 20938, *OH 172, CMF 011-L*
BVE39719-1 Barney McCoy (1)   Vi 20938
[BVE39717-1 and Vi 20938 issue as by Uncle Eck Dunford; BVE39717-1 issued as by Uncle Eck Dunford and Hattie Stoneman]

Bristol, Tennessee, 27 July 1927
Blue Ridge Cornshuckers: Kahle Brewer, fiddle; George Stoneman, banjo; Ernest V. Stoneman, vocal (1)/guitar, Jews harp and kazoo; Bolen Frost, banjo; Eck Dunford, guitar (2)/vocal (3); Iver Edwards, harmonica and ukelele

BVE39720-2 Old Time Corn Shuckin' Part 1(1)   Vi 20835, *CMF 011-L*
BVE39721-4 Old Time Corn Shuckin' Part 2 (2, 3)   Vi 20835, *CMF 011-L*

New York, New York, 12 September 1927
The Dixie Mountaineers: unknown personnel and instrumentation

11882-	The Little Black Moustache	Ed rejected
11883-	Puttin' on the Style	Ed rejected
11884-	All Go Hungry Hash House	Ed rejected
11885-	Sally Goodwin	Ed rejected

New York, New York, 13 September 1927
As above
11886-   When the Redeemed Are Gathered In   Ed rejected
11887-   He Was Nailed to the Cross for Us   Ed rejected

New York, New York, 15 September 1927
Ernest V. Stoneman: Ernest Stoneman, guitar/harmonica/vocal

BVE39182-2 Josephus and Bohunkus   Vi unissued

Atlanta, Georgia, 22 October 1927
Uncle Eck Dunford: Eck Dunford, narrative vocal; Ernest V. Stoneman, banjo

BVE40334-1   Sleeping Late   Vi 21224
BVE40335-1   My First Bicycle Ride   Vi 21131, *OH 172*
BVE40336-1   The Taffy Pulling Party   Vi 21244
BVE40337-2   The Savingest Man on Earth   Vi 21131, *RO 1008*

Atlanta, Georgia, 22 February 1928
Ernest V. Stoneman and His Blue Ridge Cornshuckers: Ernest V. Stoneman, vocal/guitar; probably Eck Dunford, fiddle/vocal (1); George Stoneman or Bolen Frost, banjo (2); unknown harmonica, probably Ernest V. Stoneman (3); Irma Frost, vocal (4); George Stoneman, vocal (5)/guitar solo (6)

BVE41932-2   Possum Trot School Exhibition, Part 1 (2)   Vi 21264, *CY 512*
BVE41933-2   Possum Trot School Exhibition, Part 2 (2)   Vi 21264, *CY 512*
BVE41934-2   A Serenade in the Mountains (2)   Vi 21518, *CY 512*
BVE41935-1   A Serenade in the Mountains (2)   Vi 21518, *CY 512*
BVE41936-   Claude Allen (2, 4)   Vi unissued
BVE41937-1   The Two Little Orphans (2)   Vi 21648, *CY 533*
BVE41938-   Once I Had a Fortune (2, 3)   Vi unissued
BVE41939-1   The Raging Sea, How It Roars (2, 3)   Vi 21648, *BRI 002, FSSM 3796*
BVE41940-   Uncle Joe (1, 2)   Vi unissued
BVE41941-1   Sweet Summer Has Gone Away (2, 5)   Vi 21578, *OH 173*
BVE41942-   Tell Me Where My Eva's Gone (2, 5)   Vi unissued
BVE41943-   Old Uncle Jessie (1, 2)   Vi unissued
BVE41944-   Stonewall Jackson (6)   Vi unissued

[BVE41936 listed as by Ernest V. Stoneman and Irma Frost; BVE41938 listed as by Ernest V. Stoneman; BVE41940 and BVE41943 listed as by Uncle Eck Dunford; BVE41941-2 and BVE41942 listed as by Uncle Eck Dunford and George Stoneman; BVE41944 listed as by George Stoneman]

New York, New York, 24 April 1928
The Dixie Mountaineers: Ernest Stoneman, vocal/guitar/harmonica; unknown fiddle, banjo, and vocal chorus

18433-A   He Was Nailed to the Cross for Me   Ed 52290
18434-B   When the Redeemed Are Gathered In   Ed 52290
?????   When the Redeemed Are Gathered In   Ed 5527

18435-A	All Go Hungry Hash House	Ed 52350
16448-	All Go Hungry Hash House	Ed 5528
18435-A	There'll Come a Time	Ed 52369, Ed 5636
18437-A	Sally Goodwin	Ed 52350
16449-	Sally Goodwin	Ed 5529
N214B	Sally Goodwin	Ed 0000
18438-	Careless Love	Ed 52386
16450-	Careless Love	Ed 5530

[18437 deletes the harmonica; Ed 0000 was a special lateral cut development disc]

New York, New York, 25 April 1928
As above

18440-B	The East Bound Train	Ed 52299, *HI 8004*
?????	The East Bound Train	Ed 5548
18441-B	The Unlucky Road to Washington	Ed 52299, *HI 8004*
16470-	The Unlucky Road to Washington	Ed 5545
18442-B	The Old Maid and the Burglar	Ed 52369, *HI 8004*
16451-	The Old Maid and the Burglar	Ed 5531
18443-A	Down on the Banks of the Ohio	Ed 52312, *OH 172*
18444-B	We Parted at the River	Ed 52312
?????	We Parted at the River	Ed 5635
18445-A	It's Sinful to Flirt	Ed 52386, *HI 8004*
?????	It's Sinful to Flirt	Ed 5547

New York, New York, May 1928
Ernest V. Stoneman: Ernest Stoneman, vocal/guitar/harmonica

108203-	In the Shadow of the Pine	Pa 32380, Pe 12459

Richmond, Indiana, 5 July 1928
Ernest Stoneman, Willie Stoneman, and the Sweet Brothers: exact personnel is unknown; however, the following instrumental line-up is correct: guitar, banjo, fiddle (1); guitar and banjo (2); guitar and fiddle (3)

GE14005-A Katy Lee (2)   Ge 6565, Chm 15565
GE14006-A My Mother and My Sweetheart (3)   Ge 6655
GE14007-A Prisoner's Lament (3)   Ge 6567, Chm 15565, Spt 9184, Spt 9305
GE14008- Once I Knew a Little Girl (3)   Ge rejected
GE14009-A Somebody's Waiting for Me (1)   Ge 6620, Spt 9323, Chm 15586
GE14010-A Falling by the Wayside (1)   Ge 6655, Spt 9185, Chm 15586
GE14011-A Sugar Hill (1)   Ge 6687

[Ge 6565 issued as by Willie Stoneman (GE14005) and the Sweet Brothers (GE14006); Chm 15565 issued as by Dave Hunt (GE14005) and John Clark (GE14007); Ge 6567 issued as by Herbert Sweet (GE14007); Spt 9184, Spt 9185, and Spt 9305 issued as by Sam Caldwell; Ge 6620 issued as by the Sweet Brothers; Chm 15586 issued as by the

Ernest Stoneman

Clark Brothers; Spt 9323 issued as by the Caldwell Brothers; Ge 6687 issued as by the Virginia Mountain Boomers]

Richmond, Indiana, 6 July 1928
Willie Stoneman: as above

GE14012-A Wake Up in the Morning (2)   Ge 6565, Chm 15610, Spt 9083
[Chm 15610 issued as by Dave Hunt (GE14012)]

Richmond, Indiana, 9 July 1928
Ernest Stoneman, Willie Stoneman, and the Sweet Brothers: as above

GE14015-A New River Train (1)   Ge 6619, Spt 9400, *HI 8001, CY 533*
GE14016-A John Hardy (1)   Ge 6619, *HI 8001, CY 533*
GE14017-A Say, Darling, Say (1)   Ge 6733, Spt 9400, *HI 9001, CY 535*
GE14018-A I'm Gonna Marry That Pretty Little Girl (1)   Ge destroyed, *HI 8001, CY 535*

[Ge 6619 and Ge 6733 issued as by Justin Winfield; Spt 9400 issued as by Uncle Ben Hawkins; according to the Gennett ledgers GE14018 was destroyed on June 26, 1929; however, a test pressing survived]

Richmond, Indiana, 10 July 1928
As above
GE14019-A Cousin Sally Brown   Ge 6687
GE14020-A Bluff Hollow Sobs   Ge destroyed
GE14021-A I Got a Bulldog (1)   Ge 6620, *HI 8001, CY 535*
GE14022-A East Tennessee Polka (1)   Ge 6567, Spt 9406
GE14023-A Rambling Reckless Hobo   Ge 6567, Spt 9305, Chm 15610

[Ge 6687, Ge 6567, and Spt 9305 issued as by the Virginia Mountain Boomers; Chm 15610 issued as by the Pine Mountain Ramblers (GE 14023; reverse of Spt 9406 unknown]
[The following pseudonyms seem to have been used in the sessions above: Ernest Stoneman and the Sweet Brothers-Justin Winfield and Uncle Ben Hawkins; Willie Stoneman-David Hunt; Herbert Sweet-John Clark, Sam Caldwell, Clark Brothers; Sweet Brothers-Caldwell Brothers, Clark Brothers; Virginia Mountain Boomers, who probably consist of some combination of the Stonemans and the Sweet Brothers-Pine Mountain Ramblers]

Bristol, Tennessee, 30 October 1928
The Stoneman Family: Ernest V. Stoneman, vocal (1)/guitar and harmonica (2); Eck Dunford, vocal (3)/fiddle (4)/guitar (5); Bolen Frost, banjo; Hattie Stoneman, vocal (6)/mandolin (7)/fiddle (8)

BVE47248-   Beautiful Isle o'er the Sea (1, 2, 3, 4, 6)   Vi unissued
BVE47249-   Willie, We Have Missed You (1, 2, 4)   Vi unissued

BVE47252-   The Fate of Shelly and Smith (1, 2, 3, 4, 6)   Vi unissued
BVE47253-2 The Broken-Hearted Lover (1, 2, 3, 4, 6)   Vi 40030, *OH 172*
BVE47254-2 Angeline the Baker (2, 3, 5, 7)   Vi 40060
[BVE47254-2 issued as by Uncle Eck Dunford]

Bristol, Tennessee, 31 October 1928
As above
BVE47255-1 Old Shoes and Leggins (2, 3, 4, 7)   Vi 40060, *FW FA 2951*
BVE47256-   Minnie Brown (1, 2, 3, 8)   Vi unissued
BVE47257-1 We Parted by the Riverside (1, 2, 4)   Vi 40030, *OH 172*
BVE47258-2 Down to Jordan and Be Saved (1, 2, 3, 4)   Vi 40078
BVE47259-2 There's a Light Up in Galilee (1, 2, 3, 4, 6)   Vi 40078, *CY 533*
BVE47260-2 Going up the Mountain after Liquor Part 1 (1, 3, 4)   Vi 40116
BVE47261-2 Going up the Mountain after Liquor Part 2 (1, 3, 4)   Vi 40116
BVE47262-2 The Spanish Merchant's Daughter (1, 2, 4, 6)   Vi 40206, *FW FA 2953*
BVE47263-   Twilight Is Stealing over the Sea (1, 2, 3, 4, 6)   Vi unissued
[Vi 40078 deletes banjo; BVE47255 issued as by Uncle Eck Dunford; Vi 40078 issued as by Ernest V. Stoneman's Dixie Mountaineers]

Bristol, Tennessee, 1 November 1928
As above
BVE47264-2 Too Late (1, 2, 4, 5, 6)   Vi 40206
BVE47265-   I Should Like to Marry (1, 2, 4, 5, 6)   Vi unissued

New York, New York, 21 November 1928
Ernest Stoneman and His Dixie Mountaineers: exact personnel uncertain, but presumed to be Ernest Stoneman, vocal/guitar/harmonica; Bolen Frost, banjo; Eck Dunford, fiddle

18881-B	Goodbye Dear Old Stepstone	Ed 52489, *OH 172*
18882-B	Fallen by the Wayside	Ed 52461, *OH 172*
	Fallen by the Wayside	Ed 5686
18883-B	All I've Got's Gone	Ed 52489
18884-	My Mother and My Sweetheart	Ed rejected
18885-	Remember the Poor Tramp Has to Live	Ed rejected
18886-B	The Prisoner's Lament	Ed 52461
	The Prisoner's Lament	Ed 5673

New York, New York, 22 November 1928
As above
18887-	Midnight on the Stormy Deep	Ed unissued
	Midnight on the Stormy Deep	Ed 5536
18888-	The Pretty Mohea	Ed rejected
18891-A	I Remember Calvary	Ed 52479, *OH 172*

Edison catalogue, 1927.
Courtesy of Kinney Rorrer

Frank Jenkins (banjo), Oscar Jenkins (fiddle) and Ernest V. Stoneman (guitar) played together in the late 1920s and recorded for Gennett.
Courtesy Dave Freeman (County Records)

	I Remember Calvary	Ed 5676
N586-A	I Remember Calvary	Ed N-20004
18892-A	He Is Coming after Me	Ed 52479, *OH 172*
N587-A	He Is Coming after Me	Ed N-20004

[Ed N-20004 was a laterally cut disc]

Chicago, Illinois, August 1929

Oscar Jenkins' Mountaineers: Ernest V. Stoneman, guitar/vocal; Oscar Jenkins, banjo; Frank Jenkins, fiddle

| 21381-2 | Burial of Wild Bill | Pm 3240, Bw 8249, *CY 522* |
| 21382-1 | The Railway Flagman's Sweetheart | Pm 3240, Bw 8249 |

Richmond, Indiana, 12 September 1929

Frank Jenkins' Pilot Mountaineers: as above

GE15589-A	The Railroad Flagman's Sweetheart	Cq 7269
GE15590-A	The Murder of Nellie Brown	Cq rejected
GE15591-A	When the Snowflakes Fall Again	Cq 7270
GE15592-A	The Burial of Wild Bill	Cq 7270
GE15593-A	I Will Be All Smiles Tonight	Cq rejected
GE15594-A	In the Year of Jubilo	Cq rejected
GE15595-A	A Message from Home Sweet Home	Cq 7269
GE15596-A	Sunny Home in Dixie	Ge 7034, Spt 9677
Ge15597-A	Old Dad	Ge 7034, Spt 9677

[Cq issued as by Alex Gordon; Ge and Spt issued as by Riley's Mountaineers]

New York, New York, 8 January 1934

Ernest Stoneman and Eddie Stoneman: Ernest V. Stoneman, vocal/guitar/harmonica; Eddie Stoneman, banjo/autoharp/vocal

14545-	Good-bye Dear Old Stepstone	ARC unissued
14546-	The Railroad Flagman's Sweetheart	ARC unissued
14547-	After the Roses Have Faded Away	ARC unissued
14548-	Meet Me by the Seaside	ARC unissued
14549-	Six Months Is a Long Time	ARC unissued
14550-	My Own Sweetheart	Vo 02901, *OH 172*
14551-	I'm Alone, All Alone	ARC unissued
14552-1	There's Somebody Waiting for Me	Vo 02632
14553-2	Nine Pound Hammer	Vo 02665

New York, New York, 9 January 1934

As above

| 14554-1 | Broke Down Section Hand | Vo 02655 |
| 14555-1 | Texas Ranger | Vo 02632 |

14556-	Prisoner's Advice	ARC unissued
14557-2	All I Got's Gone	Vo 02901, *OH 172*
14560-	Golden Bye and Bye	ARC unissued
14561-	Hallelujah Side	ARC unissued

[14554 through 14557 listed or issued as by Ernest Stoneman]

New York, New York, 10 January 1934
As above

14562-	I'll Live On	ARC unissued
14563-	Reaping Days	ARC unissued
14564-	The Sweetest Way Home	ARC unissued

Bibliography: Norm Cohen, Eugene Earle, and Graham Wickham, "The Early Recording Career of Ernest V. 'Pop' Stoneman: A Bio-Discography," *JEMF Special Series #1*, 1968; Norm Cohen and Eugene Earle, "An Ernest Stoneman Discography," *JEMFQ* 16, no. 57 (Spring 1980): 36-49; Tony Russell, brochure notes to "Ernest V. Stoneman and the Blue Ridge Corn Shuckers," Rounder 1008; Ivan Tribe, brochure notes to "Ernest V. Stoneman Vol. II: With Family and Friends," OH 173.

See also Uncle Eck Dunford, Sweet Brothers, and Crockett and Fields Ward.

Willie Stoneman

See Ernest V. Stoneman.

Sweet Brothers (late 1920s)

Herbert and Earl Sweet were born in Washington County, Virginia, but apparently resided in Grayson County for many years. They were living near Damascus when they met Ernest Stoneman about 1926. In 1928 this outstanding violin and banjo duo accompanied Stoneman to Richmond, Indiana, to record for Gennett Records.

The trio apparently stayed together for about one year before splitting up because of the distance between Damascus and Galax. It is uncertain what happened to the Sweet Brothers, though they are reported to have moved to Pennsylvania. Because of their close association with Ernest V. Stoneman, the few recordings issued under their name are listed under Stoneman's entry

Bibliography: Wayne Martin, brochure notes to "Round the Heart of Old Galax: Volume 1," CY 533.

See also Ernest V. Stoneman.

Tartar and Gay (1924–ca. 1935)

Stephen Tarter and Harry Gay played music in the rough coal camps in southwestern Virginia and southern West Virginia during their partnership. They also performed for both black and white dances throughout northeastern Tennessee. Tarter was the principal vocalist, and he played the fiddle, mandolin, and piano in addition to the guitar. Harry Gay played second guitar and occasionally sang.

Stephen Tarter was born near Knoxville, Tennessee, about 1895. He was a talented watch repairman in addition to being a musician. Tarter met Gay, born in Gate City, Virginia, November 23, 1904, in Johnson City, and they played together for over a decade. Near the middle of their tenure together, Tarter and Gay successfully auditioned for Victor Records when Victor came to Bristol, Tennessee, in the fall of 1928.

Following this session the men continued their busy, but not full-time, music making until Stephen Tarter's death from a heart attack about 1935. Harry Gay all but gave up music following the sudden death of his friend. He continued to live around Johnson City until his own death in 1983.

Bristol, Tennessee, 2 November 1928
Tarter and Gay: Stephen Tarter, guitar/vocal; Harry Gay, guitar

| 47279-3 | Brownie Blues | Vi 38017, *YA 1013, BRI 008, MA 204* |
| 47280-3 | Unknown Blues | Vi 38017, *YA 1013, MA 204* |

Bibliography: Kip Lornell, "Tarter and Gay," *Living Blues* 27 (1976): 18; Kip Lornell and Roddy Moore, "Tarter and Gay Revisited," *Juke Blues* 8 (Spring 1987): 21.

Jim Taylor and Bill Shelby

A pseudonym on Champion for Walter "Kid" Smith.

Tennessee Chocolate Drops (1928–1933)

This Afro-American string band was a loose group that traveled throughout the coalfields of southwest Virginia, eastern Kentucky, and southern West Virginia. In addition to playing in the coal camps, they participated in medicine shows and performed at theaters. Each of the musicians—Howard Armstrong, Roland Martin, and Carl Martin—was a versatile musician capable of playing several instruments.

The group disbanded about 1933, but its members continued to play music separately. In the early 1970s Armstrong and Carl Martin were reunited with another former partner, Ted Bogan. Known as Martin, Bogan, and Armstrong, they toured and recorded for Flying Fish and Rounder. Despite Martin's death in 1979, Bogan and Armstrong continue to perform their eclectic repertoire.

Billy Vest

Knoxville, Tennessee, 3 April 1930
Tennessee Chocolate Drops: Howard Armstrong, fiddle; Roland Martin, guitar; Carl Martin, bass

K-8066	Knox County Stomp	Vo 1517, Vo 5472, *WO 123*
K-8067	Vine Street Drag	Vo 1517, Vo 5472, *WO 123*

[Vo 5472 issued as by the Tennessee Trio]

Bibliography: Kip Lornell and Roddy Moore, "On Tour with a Black String Band in the 1930's: Howard Armstrong and Carl Martin Reminisce," *Goldenseal* 2, no. 4 (1976): 9-12, 48-51; Pete Welding, "Carl Martin 1906-1979," *Living Blues* 43 (Summer 1979): 28, 29, 40.

See also Carl Martin.

Tennessee Mountaineers
A pseudonym on Broadway for the Highlanders.

Tenneva Ramblers
See the Grant Brothers.

Greyson Thomas and Will Lotty
A pseudonym on Champion for G.B. Grayson and Henry Whitter.

Three Kentucky Serenaders
A psuedonym on Supertone and Silvertone for Roy Harvey.

Billy Vest (c. 1925–c. 1955)
William A. "Billy" Vest was born in Afton, Virginia, (Albermarle County) on August 8, 1910. In his late teens Vest fell under the spell of Jimmie Rodgers, "The Blue Yodeller." Rodgers' records served as his musical model; by 1929 Vest was billing himself as the "Strolling Yodeller." During the late 1920s he was performing at the movie theater in nearby Crozet, Virginia, and was broadcasting over WRVA in Richmond.

His brief recording career was unfortunately initiated in 1931 during the depths of the Depression, which virtually doomed an unknown like Vest. Nevertheless, he continued with his musical career for at least another twenty years. Throughout the 1930s and 1940s he roamed the country broadcasting over radio stations and performing at small clubs.

About 1935, while on a tour in Saskatchewan, Canada, he met and married his wife, Josephine. He remained in Saskatchewan for nearly a year performing

Billy Vest, circa 1932, possibly in Saskatchewan, Canada. *Courtesy Blue Ridge Heritage Archive/Clivis Harris*

and broadcasting over CKCK in Regina. By the end of the decade he was back in Albermarle County performing with his brother Bob in a group, "The Old Virginia Nighthawks." He was playing with his group and as a solo artist, and was among the first performers on Charlottesville's first radio station, WCHV.

The 1940s saw him touring the southwestern United States. For a while he worked as an "advance man," playing at small movie theaters to promote an upcoming Hoot Gibson western film. He also occasionally broadcast over the CBS radio network and appeared in several of Gene Autry's "B" westerns. By the end of the 1940s Vest and his wife were living in Dallas, where he was part of the "Big D Jamboree."

During the early 1950s Vest was fighting a losing battle with a number of respiratory diseases. By 1955 he was forced to give up music and had retired in order to live near his birthplace in Afton. Vest remained in Albermarle County until his death on July 20, 1985.

New York, New York, 17 April 1931
Billy Vest "The Strolling Yodeller": Billy Vest, vocal/guitar

151521-	Billy's Blue Yodel	Co 15692
151522-	She Died Like a Rose	Co 15692
151523-	The Club Had a Meeting	Co unissued
151524-	Little Girl's Plea	Co unissued
151525-	A Crown of Soft Brown Hair	Co unissued
151526-	Oh! Sir I Was Only Flirting	Co unissued
151527	She'll Never Find Another Daddy Like Me	Co 15669
151528	I Loved You Better Than You Knew	Co 15669

Richmond, Indiana, 6 June 1931
Billy Vest: Billy Vest, vocal/guitar; Kyle Roop, guitar; Aubry Smith, fiddle

N17813   Weeping Willow Tree   Ge test

New York, New York, 11 April 1933
Billy Vest: Billy Vest, vocal/guitar

13224	The Big City Jail Cq 8235, Or 8231, Ro 5231, Ba 32762, Me 12691, Pe 19211, Vo 5494
13225	When It's Honeysuckle Time ARC unissued
13226	The Last Goodbye Cq 8236
13227	Dark Eyes Plea ARC unissued
13228	Frankie & Johnnie #2 Cq 8235, Or 8231, Ro 5231, Ba 32762, Me 12691, Pe 19211
13229	The Tramp's Last Ride Cq 8236, Vo 5494

[Vo 5494 issued as by Jack Harper]

Virginia Female Jubilee Singers (early 1920s)

Aurally, this group is similar to other black gospel groups from Tidewater. Several other groups from eastern Virginia, the Norfolk Jazz/Jubilee Quartet, the Palmetto Jazz/Jubilee Quartet, and the Excelsior Quartet, were also affiliated with OKeh Records at the same time.

New York, New York, ca. 7 September 1921
Virginia Female Jubilee Singers: four female voices

70146-B	O Mary, Don't You Weep, Don't You Mourn	OK 4430
70147-B	Revival Day	OK 4558
70148-A	The Old Ark's A-Movering	OK 4482

New York, New York, ca. 13 September 1921
As above

70157-B	Lover of the Lord	OK 4430, *JEMF 108*
70158-C	King Jesus Is A Listening	OK 4451
70161-A and -B	When Jesus Christ Was Born	OK 4437
70162-A	I've Been a Sinner All My Life	OK 4482
70164-A	Wait Until I Get on the Road Oh Yes! Oh Yes!	OK 4451
70166-B	Go Down Moses Way Down in Egypt Land	OK 4437
70181-A	My Time Ain't Long	OK 4558

Virginia Four (late 1920s)

Despite the fact that nothing of substance is known of this group, they are included because of their name and their aural similarity to other Hampton Roads vocal groups.

New York, New York, 2 December 1929
Virginia Four: four male voices; Loren L. Watson, piano (1)

57730-1	Since I Been Born (1)	Vi 38569
57731-	It'll Soon Be Over With	Vi 23376, Bb 5724
57732-	Don't Leave Me Behind	Vi 23376, Bb 5724
57733-1	Comin' Down the Shiny Way [sic]	Vi 38569

[This name was also used on Decca as a pseudonym for the Norfolk Jazz Quartet]

Virginia Four

A pseudonym on Decca for the Norfolk Jazz Quartet.

Virginia Jubilee Singers

A pseudonym on Broadway for the Norfolk Jazz Quartet.

Virginia Mountain Boomers

A pseudonym on Gennett and Supertone for the Sweet Brothers and Ernest V. Stoneman.

Virginia Ramblers

A pseudonym on Timely Tunes for the Floyd County Ramblers.

Dave Walker

A pseudonym on Superior for Roy Harvey.

Crockett Ward (ca. 1900–ca. 1950) and Fields Ward (ca. 1925–1980)

This father-and-son team had its roots in Grayson County, where Davy Crockett Ward was born early in the 1880s. Ward learned the fiddle at an early age and often played with his relatives who lived near their home on Buck Mountain. Fields Ward, born in Buck Mountain, Grayson County, Virginia, on January 23, 1911, was one of several boys in the family who played music. Tired of the uncertain life in their remote hamlet, Crockett Ward moved his family to Ballard Creek in 1921.

The Wards' move to Ballard Creek, which is very near Galax, allowed them more time for music, and they soon formed a family string band known as "Crockett Ward and His Boys." This was the group that successfully auditioned for the OKeh Phonograph Company in 1927.

Between 1921 and the late 1940s Crockett and Fields Ward remained extremely musically active. In addition to the family band, they played with many of the other famous Galax-based musicians such as fiddlers Green Leonard and Emmitt Lundy and Crockett's banjo-playing brother, Wade Ward.

Around 1934 the family band reorganized into the Bogtrotters, who went on to play at the White Top Folk Festivals and the Galax Fiddlers Convention, which began in 1936. They were recorded by the Folksong Archive of the Library of Congress. Fields and his brother Sampson also provided the musical entertainment for silent films shown at the theater in Galax.

Following World War II Crockett was semiretired from music and Fields decided to take a job in Maryland, where he died October 29, 1987. Crockett remained in Grayson County and died there in the mid-1960s, about the time that Fields retired from his job as a painter. Fields continued to play music and recorded for Rounder Records in the 1970s.

Winston-Salem, North Carolina, 26 September 1927

Crockett Ward and His Boys: Crockett Ward, fiddle, Fields Ward, guitar/vocal; Sampson Ward, banjo; Curren Ward, autoharp

81615-	Sad and Lonely	OK unissued
81616-A	Sugar Hill	OK 45179, *CO 534*
81617-A	Deadheads and Suckers	OK 45179
81618-A	Love's Affections	OK 45304
81619-B	Ain't That Trouble in Mind	OK 45304, *CO 534*
81620-	Train on the Island	OK unissued

Richmond, Indiana, 5 March 1929

Fields Ward and the Grayson County Railsplitters: Fields Ward, vocal and guitar; Sampson Ward, banjo; Ernest V. Stoneman, vocal (1) and guitar; Eck Dunford, fiddle and vocal on some choruses

GE14861-A	Way Down in North Carolina	Ge rejected, *HI 8001*
GE14862-A	Ain't That Trouble in Mind	Ge rejected, *HI 8001*
GE14863-A	You Must Be a Lover of the Lord	Ge rejected, *HI 8001*
GE14864-A	Watch and Pray	Ge rejected, *HI 8001*
GE14865-A	Good Bye Little Bonnie (1)	Ge rejected, *HI 8001*
GE14866-A	Alas My Darling (1)	Ge rejected, *HI 8001*
GE14867-A	My Old Sweetheart (1)	Ge rejected, *HI 8001*
GE14868-A	The Place Where Ella Sleeps (1)	Ge rejected, *HI 8001*
GE14869-A	In Those Cruel Slavery Days (1)	Ge rejected, *HI 8001*
GE14870-A	The Sweetest Way Home	Ge rejected, *HI 8001*

Richmond, Indiana, 7 March 1929

As above

Ge14876-A	My Only Sweetheart (1)	Ge rejected, *HI 8001*
GE14877-A	Tie Up Those Broken Chords (1)	Ge rejected, *HI 8001*
Ge14878-A	The Love Birds Are Returning	Ge rejected, *HI 8001*
Ge14879-A	No One Loves You As I Do	Ge rejected, *HI 8001*
Ge14880-A	I Don't See Why I Love Her	Ge rejected, *HI 8001*

[The Gennett Record Company apparently gave Fields Ward test pressings from this session, which is how they came to be issued on Historical Records; GE14863 and GE14864 are listed as by the Grayson County Railsplitters; GE14865, Ge14867, GE14868, GE14869, GE14876, and GE14877 listed as by Ward and Winfield with the Grayson County Railsplitters (Winfield = Stoneman); GE14866 listed as by Ward and Winfield]

Bibliography: Arnold Caplin, brochure notes to "Fields Ward and His Buck Mountain Band," HI 8001; John Coffey "Fields Ward," *Old-Time Herald*, Vol. 1 No. 4, May-June, 1988, pp. 12-17; Wayne Martin, brochure notes to "Round the Heart of Old Galax," CO 534; Mark Wilson, brochure notes to "Bury Me Not on the Prairie," RO 0086.

See also Ernest V. Stoneman and Wade Ward.

Wade Ward (ca. 1910–1971)

Born in Independence, Virginia, on October 15, 1892, Benjamin "Uncle" Wade Ward played with many of the early recording artists from the fecund mountains in and around Galax. Ward himself worked in the mills, but spent all of his adult life playing music. In 1919 he formed the Buck Mountain band that included guitar player Earl Edwards. The Buck Mountain Band was one of a new style of string band that included the guitar, which was all but unknown in the mountains prior to 1900.

During the 1920s he recorded for the OKeh record company, but he never became a full-time musician. Instead, Ward continued to play for local musical functions. His longest-running job was a 51-year stint providing music for auctions held by the Parson's Auction Company. In 1937 the Library of Congress also documented some of his playing as well as that of other family members.

Throughout the 1950s and into the 1960s he continued providing entertainment at local auctions. In the late 1950s, a new phase of his career began when Ward was "rediscovered" by younger northern musicians enthusiastic about the string band music from the Galax area. Ward is generally considered one of the masters of the clawhammer banjo style commonly found in south central Virginia, and he was recorded for Folkways between 1957 and 1971. He also toured extensively before his death on May 29, 1971.

Asheville, North Carolina, ca. 3 September 1925
Wade Ward: Wade Ward, banjo/vocal

9315-	Fox Chase	OK unissued, *CY 535*
9316-	A Married Man's Blues	OK unissued
9317-	Chilly Wind	OK unissued, *CY 535*
9318-	Brother Ephram	OK unissued

Richmond, Virginia, 16 October 1929
Buck Mountain Band: Van Edwards, fiddle; Wade Ward, banjo; Earl Edwards, vocal/guitar

403138-	Reckless Rambler	OK unissued
403139-	Go and Leave Me If You Wish	Ok unissued
403140-A	Yodeling Blues	OK 45428, Cl 5292, VT 2358, *NW 290*
403141-B	Don't Let the Blues Get You Down	OK 45428, Cl 5295, VT 2361

[403140 includes yodeling; Cl and VT issued as by Art, Andy, Bert, and Dave; reverse of Cl and VT by Frank Marvin]

Bibliography: Eric Davidson and Jane Rigg, brochure notes to "Uncle Wade," FW FA 2380.

See also Crockett and Fields Ward.

Harvey Watson

A pseudonym on Champion, Supertone, and Bell for Holland Puckett.

Henry Whitter (ca. 1915–1941)

Born on April 6, 1892, in Fries, Virginia, William Henry Whitter followed many of his contemporaries into the Grayson County textile mills. Whitter began playing music in his early teens and by the beginning of World War I he had learned the rudiments of the banjo, guitar, piano, and harmonica. Work at the mill provided him a steady income, but Whitter wanted more from life and felt that music might provide an escape. By 1920 he was a frequent performer in Grayson County, though mill work still supported Whitter and his family.

By 1923 traditional music was beginning to find its way onto commercial records and Whitter saw the chance to work his avocation into a career. He made several trips to New York City in futile attempts to interest a record company in his music. In March 1923 Whitter once again brazenly took the train to New York City to audition for the General Phonograph Corporation, owners of OKeh Records. The OKeh executives were apparently not overwhelmed by Whitter's test recordings, but were sufficiently impressed to recall him following the success of Fiddlin' John Carson's recordings in June 1923. By January 1924 Henry Whitter's first recordings, "Lonesome Road Blues" and "The Wreck on the Southern Old 97," were released, but sold slowly.

Through the 1920s Whitter recorded regularly, basking in the regional fame and money that it brought him. He printed handbills and business cards calling attention to his OKeh records, which further reinforced his local popularity. Most of his early recordings were solo efforts, though in 1924 he recorded with a string band, Whitter's Virginia Breakdowners, that included two local musicians, John Rector on banjo and James Sutphin on fiddle. He was also helpful in getting fellow mill worker Kelly Harrell on record in 1925.

Whitter's most respected recordings were done toward the end of his career in the company of Gillam Bannom Grayson, a blind fiddler born in Laurel Bloomery, Tennessee, on November 11, 1887. G.B. Grayson was a highly respected musician who made a living through his music, often playing on the streets or with traveling shows. He, too, was interested in exploring the possibility of recording and got the opportunity when he met Henry Whitter late in 1926 or early 1927. This apparently occurred at a fiddlers' contest and led to a solid partnership that endured until Grayson's untimely death in an automobile accident about 1934. Their recording career together ended in October 1929 when the Depression began and recording declined.

Whitter continued to play music throughout the 1930s, traveling wherever he could find work. Music was apparently his sole means of support, though his popularity slowly diminished as tastes shifted. By the late 1930s he had become

Van Edwards (guitar) and Wade Ward (banjo) of the Buck Mountain Band, circa 1928 (probably Galax, Virginia). *Courtesy Kinney Rorrer*

G.B. Grayson (fiddle) and Henry Whitter (guitar), circa 1929, probably at Galax, Virginia. *Courtesy Blue Ridge Heritage Archive*

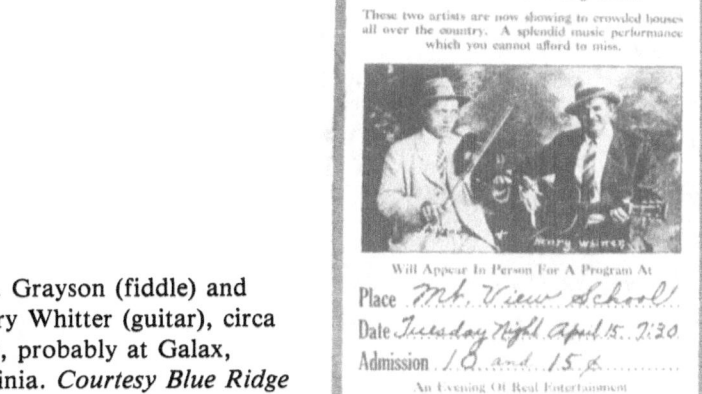

ill and was in and out of hospitals before he died on November 10, 1941, of diabetes in Morganton, North Carolina.

New York, New York, March 1923
Henry Whitter: Henry Whitter, vocal/guitar/harmonica

        unknown title   OKeh Test
        unknown title   OKeh Test

New York, New York, 10 December 1923
As above: harmonica solo (1)

72-159-	Rain Crow Bill Blues	OK 40187
72-160-	Lost Train Blues (1)	OK 40029
72-161-	The Old Time Fox Chase (1)	OK 40029, *OH 165*
72-163-	Weeping Willow Tree	OK 40187
72-164-	The Stormy Wave Blues	OK 40143
72-165-	Broken Engagement Blues	OK 40229
72-166-	The Kaiser and Uncle Sam	OK 40229
72-167-	Wreck on the Southern Old 97	OK 40015
72-168-	Lonesome Road Blues	OK 40015

New York, New York, 26 February 1924
As above

72-339-	Sidney Allen	OK 40109
72-340-	Where Have You Been So Long	OK 40109
72-341-	The New River Train	OK 40143
72-342-	Chicken, You Better Go behind the Barn	OK 40077
72-344-	She's Coming around the Mountain	OK 40063

New York, New York, 27 February 1924
As above

72-347-	Weepin' Blues	OK 40120
72-348-	Hop Light Ladies and Shortenin' Bread	OK 40064
72-349-	Double Headed Train (1)	OK 40120, *VE 104*
72-350-	Little Brown Jug	OK 40063
72-351-	Western Country	OK 40077
72-352-	Tippy Two Step Blues	OK 40064

New York, New York, ca. 22 July 1924
Whitter's Virginia Breakdowners: Henry Whitter, guitar; Paul Sutphin, fiddle; John Rector, banjo

72-679-	'Round Town Girl	OK 40320
72-680-	Black Eyed Susan	OK 40320

Cover of Henry Whitter's sheet music for "The Wreck on the Southern Old 97," circa 1925. *Courtesy Blue Ridge Heritage Archive*

72-684-   Jenny Lind Polka   OK 40211
72-685-   Nellie Gray   OK 40211
72-686-   The Drunkard's Child   OK 40169
72-687-   Goin' down the Road Feelin' Bad   OK 40169
72-691-A   Mississippi Sawyers   OK 7005
72-692-A   Sourwood Mountain   OK 7005

[OK 40169 deletes Sutphin and Rector and was issued as by Henry Whitter; OK 7005 is a 12" disc]

New York, New York, 24 November 1924

Henry Whitter: Henry Whitter, vocal/guitar/harmonica/harmonica solo (1)

72-972-   Rabbit Race (1)   OK 40269, *OH 165*
72-979-   Farewell to Thee   OK 40269
72-982-   Watermelon Hanging on the Vine   OK 40296
72-983-   Ellen Smith   OK 40237
72-984-   Keep My Skillet Good and Greasy   OK 40296
72-985-   Travelling Man   OK 40237
72-986-   The Long Tongued Woman   OK 40352
72-987-   The Dollar and the Devil   OK 40352

New York, New York, 23 April 1925

As above
73-310-   Lost John (1)   OK 40391
73-311-   Peek-a-boo   OK 40391
73-312-   Love Me While I Am Living   OK 40403
73-313-   My Darling's Black Moustache   OK 40395
73-314-   I Wish I Was a Single Girl Again   OK 40375
73-315-   The Clouds Gwine Roll Away   OK 40395

New York, New York, 24 April 1925

As above
73-316-   Good-Bye Old Booze   OK 40403
73-317-   The Butcher Boy   OK 40375

Possibly New York, New York, ca. July 1925

As above
9210-A   The Story by the Moonlight   OK 45003
9211-A   Liza Jane   OK 45003

New York, New York, 21 April 1926

As above
80-003-   Many Times with You I've Wandered   OK 45053
80-004-   Goin' Down to Jordan to Be Baptized   OK 45053

Henry Whitter

New York, New York, 22 April 1926
As above
74-137-   I Wish I Was Single Again   OK 45045
74-138-   Put Away My Little Shoes   OK 45046
74-139-   The Old Gray Mare   OK unissued
74-140-   Heart of Old Galax   OK 45045
74-141-   Go Bury Me beneath the Willow   OK 45046

New York, New York, 7 September 1926
As above: add Fiddler Joe (Joe Samuels), fiddle (1)

80088-   Hand Me Down My Walking Cane (1)   OK 45061
80089-   Show Me the Way to Go Home (1)   OK 45061
80090-   A Woman's Tongue Has No End   OK unissued
80091-   The Burglar Man   OK unissued
80092-   George Collins   OK unissued
80093-   Broken Engagement   OK unissued

New York, New York, November 1926
As above: delete Fiddler Joe

74396-A   The Broken Engagement   OK 45081
74397-A   George Collins   OK 45081
74398-A   Burglar Man   OK 45063
74399-A   A Woman's Tongue Has No End   OK 45063

Bristol, Tennessee, 2 February 1927
As above
39758-2   Henry Whitter's Fox Chase   Vi 20878, MW 4475, *CMF 011-L*
39759-2   Rain Crow Bill   Vi 20878

New York, New York, early October 1927
G.B. Grayson and Henry Whitter: G.B. Grayson, fiddle/vocal; Henry Whitter, guitar

GEX-903-A Nobody's Darling   Ge 6304, Chm 15395, *DU 33033, OH 165*
GEX-904-   I'll Never Be Yours   Ge 6373, Chm 15447, Sil 8160, Spt 9247, Ch 393, *OH 165*
GEX-905-   Handsome Holly   Ge 6304, Chm 15629, *DU 33033, OH 165*
GEX-906-A Shout Lula   Ge 6373, Chm 15501, *DU 33033, OH 165*
GEX-907-   You Never Miss Your Mother Until She's Gone   Ge 6320, Chm 15395, Sil 8160, Spt 9247, Ch 394
GEX-908-A Train No. 45   Ge 6320, Chm 15447, Ch 397, *DU 33033, OH 165*
GEX-909-A John Henry the Steel Driving Man   Ge rejected
GEX-910-A He's Coming to Us Dead   Ge rejected

[Chm 15395 issued as by Greyson Thomas and Will Lotty; Chm 15447 and Chm 15501 issued as by Norman Gayle; Sil 8160 and Spt 9247 issued as by Dillard Sanders; all Chs issued as by David Foley; reverse Ch 393 by Marion Underwood and Sam Harris; reverse Ch 394 by Roy Harvey and the North Carolina Ramblers]

Atlanta, Georgia, 18 October 1927

As above

40302-1	Handsome Molly	Vi 21189, *OT 102, CY 513*
40303-1	He Is Coming to Us Dead	Vi 21139, *CY 513*
40304-2	Don't Go Out Tonight, My Darling	Vi 21139, *CY 513*
40305-2	Rose Conley	Vi 21625, *OT 102*
40306-1	Ommie Wise	Vi 21625, *CY 513, FW 2951*
40307-2	Train 45	Vi 21189, Bb 5498, *OT 100*

[Omit guitar on 40306; Vi 21625 issued as by Grayson and Whitter; occasional speech by Whitter on most items]

New York, New York, 21 February 1928

As above

GEX-1091	Sally Gooden	Ge 6733, Chm 15501, *DU 33033, OH 165*
GEX-1092	Mine Is for Mary	Ge unissued, *DU 33033, OH 157*
GEX-1093	She's Mine, All Mine	Ge 6656, Chm 15465, *OH 165*
GEX-1094	Sweet Rosie O'Grady	Ge 6418, *DU 33033, OH 165*
GEX-1095	I've Always Been a Rambler	Ge rejected
GEX-1096	Red or Green	Ge 6418, Chm 15465, Ch 397
GEX-1097	Cluck Old Hen	Ge 6656, Chm 15629, *DU 33033, OH 165*
GEX-1098	Old Jimmy Sutton	Ge 6436, *DU 33033, OH 165*

Ge 6436 issued as by Whitter and Grayson, reverse by Tommy Dandurand; Ch 15465 and Ch 15501 issued as by Norman Gayle; Ch 15629 isued as by Henry Whitter and G.B. Grayson; Ch 397 issued as by David Foley; GEX-1092 titled "My Mind Is to Marry" on the album issue]

New York, New York, 31 July 1928

G.B. Grayson and Henry Whitter: as above

46330-2	The Red and Green Signal Lights	Vi 40063, *OH 157, DU 33033, RCA LPV 532*
44631-2	Joking Henry	Vi 40038, *CY 513*
46632-1 and -2	There's a Man Going' round Takin' Names	Vi unissued
46633-2	The Nine-Pound Hammer	Vi 40105, *CY 513*
46634-2	Short Life of Trouble	Vi 40105, *CY 513*
46635-2	I've Always Been a Rambler	Vi 40324, *CY 502, CY 513*
46636-1	Where Are You Going, Alice?	Vi 40135, *CY 513, FSSMLP 3796*

Henry Whitter 215

46637-1   A Dark Road Is a Hard Road to Travel   Vi 40063, *CY 513*
[Vi 40135 and Vi 40324 issued as by Grayson and Whitter; 46633 add Whitter, vocal]

New York, New York, 1 August 1928
As above
46638-2   Barnyard Serenade   Vi 40038, *OH 157*
46639-2   Little Maggie with a Dram Glass in Her Hand   Vi 40135, Bb 7072, *OT 102*

Atlanta, Georgia, 16 October 1928
Henry Whitter: Henry Whitter, harmonica solo

47183-2   The Lost Girl of West Virginia   Vi 40061
47184-2   Poor Lost Boy   Vi 40061, MW 4909, *OH 165*

Memphis, Tennessee, 30 September 1929
Grayson and Whitter: G.B. Grayson, fiddle/vocal; Henry Whitter, guitar

56309-2   On the Banks of Old Tennessee   Vi 40235, Bb 7072, Zo 4329, *OH 157, CY 522, DU 33033*
56310-2   Never Be As Fast As I Have Been   Vi 23565, *OH 157, CY 525*
56311-2   I Have Lost You Darling, True Love   Vi 40268, *DU 33033, OH 157*
56312-2   Tom Dooley   Vi 40235, *DU 33033, OH 157*
56313-1   Going Down the Lee Highway   Vi 23565, Bb 5498, *DU 33033, OH 157, SM P8 15640*
[Reverse Zo 4329 by Bill Simmons]

Memphis, Tennessee, 1 October 1929
As above
56322-1   I Saw a Man at the Close of Day   Vi 40324, *CY 513*
56323-1
 and -2   The Coal Creek Mines   Vi unissued
56324-2   What You Gonna Do with the Baby   Vi 40268, *CY 513*
56325-2   Fox Chase No. 2   Vi 40292, El 2139, MW 4909
56326-2   Train Blues   Vi 40292

Memphis, Tennessee, 28 November 1930
Whitter-Hendley-Small: Henry Whitter, guitar; Fletcher Hendley, banjo; (?) Small, banjo; unknown vocal

64742-2   Mah Yaller Gal   Vi unissued
64743-1   A Pretty Gal's Love   Bb 6555
64744-1   Another Man's Wife   Bb 6555
64745-2   The Possum Hunt   Vi unissued

Memphis, Tennessee, 29 November 1930

As above: add Fletcher Hendley and Henry Whitter speech (1)

64748-2	Shuffle, Feet, Shuffle	Vi 23528, *CY 515*
64749-2	Tar and Feathers	Vi 23528
64750-1	Pretty Little Girl	Vi unissued
64751-1	Whitter's Rabbit Hunt	Vi unissued

[64750 and 64751 delete Small]

Bibliography: Norm Cohen, "Henry Whitter—His Life and Recordings," *JEMF Quarterly* 11, no. 38 (Summer 1975): 80-91; Norm Cohen, "Early Pioneers," in Bill Malone and Judith McCulloh, eds., *Stars Of Country Music* (Urbana: Univ. of Illinois Press, 1975): 13-16; Ray Parker, "G. B. Grayson—A Short Life of Trouble," *Old Time Music* 35 (Winter 1980-Spring 1981): 10-14; Joe Wilson, brochure notes to "Grayson and Whitter," CY 513; Charles K. Wolfe, brochure notes to "G.B. Grayson and Henry Whitter: Early Classics, Volume I," OH 157.

Riley Wilcox

A pseudonym on Bell for Holland Puckett.

Wilson Ramblers

A pseudonym on Broadway for Roy Harvey.

Jake Woodfield

A pseudonym on Crown for Walter "Kid" Smith.

Jake Woodlieff

A pseudonym on Paramount for Walter "Kid" Smith.

Preston Young

See Buster Carter

The front cover of this late 1920s Victor Record catalogue depicts a stereotypical view of southern music making. *Courtesy Dave Freeman (County Records)*

Appendixes

Appendix 1.
Possible Virginia Groups

The following groups or individuals are thought to be from Virginia, but because their origins cannot be verified, they have been withheld from the main body of this volume. All but one of the artists included here participated in the Okeh field recording session held in October 1929 in Richmond, Virginia. All of the others that were recorded at this session were Virginia artists, suggesting the same is true for these musicians. The exceptional group, L.V. Jones and His Virginia Singing School, is included because of its name.

Cotton Butterfield

Richmond, Virginia, 16 October 1929
Cotton Butterfield, guitar/vocal

403141-	Prisoner at the Bar	OK unissued
403142-	It Can't Be Done	OK unissued
403143-	Letter Edged in Black	OK unissued
403144-	Lullaby Yodel	OK unissued

L.V. Jones and His Virginia Singing School

Winston-Salem, North Carolina, 27 September 1927
L.V. Jones and His Virginia Singing School: unknown personnel and accompaniment

812627-	In That Crowning Day	OK 45187
812628-	Keep On Climbing	OK unissued
812629-	My Beautiful Home	OK unissued
812630-	Will My Mother Be There	OK 45187
812631-	I'm Glory Bound	OK unissued
812632-	Come and Be Saved	OK unissued

The Jubilee Gospel Team

Richmond, Virginia, 18 October 1929
Unknown personnel and accompaniment

403191-A	Ain't You Glad God Will Hear?	OK unissued
403192-A	Station Will Be Changed after While	OK unissued

Imperial Quartet

Richmond, Virginia, 17 October 1929

Presumably vocal quartet, unknown accompaniment

403156-   Mr. Chicken   OK unissued

Otis and Tom Mote

Richmond, Virginia, 17 October 1929

Otis Mote: Otis Mote, guitar/harmonica/vocal; Tom Mote, vocal (1)

403157-A   Tight Like That   OK 45389
403158-A   Railroad Bill   OK 45389
403159-A   Church of God Is Right (1)   OK 45429
403160-B   Home in the Rock (1)   OK 45429

[OK 45389 issued as by Otis Mote; OK unissued credited to Otis and Tom Mote; this duo may have recorded for Vo about 1930]

Virginia Male Quartet

Richmond, Virginia, 15 October 1929

Virginia Male Quartet: vocal quartet; piano (1)

403134-B   I Am Wandering down Life's Shady Path (1)   OK 45388
403135-A   Looking This Way (1)   OK 45453
403136-A   Light of Life   OK 45388
403137-A   No Night There (1)   OK 45453

Virginia Ramblers

Richmond, Virginia, 18 October 1929

Unknown instrumentation and personnel

403183-A   Carper Hutchison   OK unissued
403184-B   Kitty Wells   OK unissued
403185-B   Maple Rag   OK unissued
403186-A   Wreck of Old 97   OK unissued

King Williams Jubilee Singers

Richmond, Virginia, 17 October 1929

Vocal group, unknown accompaniment

403169-B   Shine for Jesus   OK unissued
403170-A   Bless the Lord, My Soul   OK unissued

Appendix 2. Border Groups

These groups or individuals touched upon the borders of Virginia in a number of ways. Some lived very close to the state line and occasionally played in the Old Dominion. Others played and recorded with musicians from Virginia and are listed as accompanists in the discography. Although they are tangential to this book, they are briefly included because of their clear relevance.

KENTUCKY

Emry Arthur

A native of Wayne County, Arthur played the guitar and sang. Although he spent most of his life in Indianapolis, Indiana, and died there in 1966, Arthur was connected with Virginia, primarily through his affiliation with the Richlands, Virginia, label, Lonesome Ace.

Recordings: 1928 and 1929 for Brunswick/Vocalion; 1929 for Paramount; 1929 for Lonesome Ace; 1935 for Decca.

NORTH CAROLINA

Tom Ashley

A banjo player and vocalist from Ashe County, Ashley performed in medicine shows and tent shows during the teens and 1920s. He also performed with many string band musicians in the Tri-State area, where Tennessee, North Carolina, and Virginia meet. Ashley was rediscovered and recorded once again during the folk music revival of the 1960s.

Recordings: 1930 for Columbia; 1933 for ARC.

Da Costa Woltz's Southern Broadcaster

A Surry County group that included musicians from Mount Airy and Round Peak. Its principal members were Ben Jarrell (fiddle), Frank Jenkins (banjo), and Da Costa Woltz (banjo), who played in north central North Carolina and south central Virginia in the late 1920s and 1930s.

Recordings: 1927 for Gennett and related labels.

Four Pickled Peppers

This string band combined pop music, swing, and fiddle tunes and included several musicians—Lonnie Austin (fiddle) and Norman Woodlieff (guitar)—associated with Charlie Poole. Most of these musicians, such as Hamon Newman (tenor banjo), Earl Taylor (tenor guitar), and Dal Hubbard (bones), were from the Spray/Eden section of Rockingham County.

Recordings: 1938 and 1939 for Bluebird and related labels.

Clarence Greene

This Ashe County fiddler was born around the turn of the century and played throughout the Tri-State area. He recorded with Byrd Moore, Tom Ashley, and others. Greene died near Hudson, North Carolina, in 1974.

Recordings: 1927 for Columbia; 1930 for Gennett; 1933 for ARC.

Red Fox Chasers

Formed in 1928, the Red Fox Chasers consisted of A.P. Thompson (guitar), Bob Cranford (harmonica), Paul Miles (banjo), and Guy Brooks (fiddle). They played at fiddlers' contests and for dances in and around their native Surry County. Their repertoire included humorous skits, sentimental ballads, religious songs, and fiddle tunes.

Recordings: 1928, 1929, and 1931 for Gennett and related labels.

Matt Simmons

A mail carrier from Lawsonville in Stokes County, Simmons was also a guitarist and singer. He often played for dances between Lawsonville and Winston-Salem and occasionally in neighboring Patrick County, Virginia. He worked with fiddle player Posey Rorer and vocalist Frank Miller.

Recordings: 1927 for OKeh.

TENNESSEE

Charlie Bowman

A longtime resident of Washington County, Tennessee, Charlie Bowman played the fiddle with many musicians from the Tri-State area. He was musically active from the early 1920s through the 1940s and recorded with a number of pioneering country bands, including the Hillbillies.

Recordings: 1926 for Vocalion; 1928 and 1929 for Columbia.

Roe Brothers

Henry Roe (guitar) and Fred Roe (fiddle) were brothers from Washington County. They were active during the 1920s and 1930s in Tennessee and southwestern Virginia. Their recording activity included a session with the Hillbillies and another with H.M. Barnes' Blue Ridge Ramblers.

Recordings: 1927 for Columbia.

WEST VIRGINIA

Jess Johnston

Johnston was a noted fiddler from Wyoming County, who spent his adulthood in McDowell County. He recorded with Roy Harvey of the North Carolina Ramblers as well as Byrd Moore. During the middle 1930s Johnston performed at the White Top Folk festival and continued to perform until his untimely death in a 1951 automobile crash.

Recordings: 1930 for Gennett and its related labels.

Blind Alfred Reed

Though born in Floyd County, Virginia, on June 15, 1880, Reed spent most of his adult life in Mercer County, West Virginia. Reed was a fiddler and vocalist who played many traditional tunes, but he also sang many topical and mining songs. He was often accompanied by his son Arville, who also recorded with the West Virginia Coon Hunters. Alfred Reed died in Raleigh County, West Virginia, on January 17, 1956.

Recordings: 1927-29 for Victor.

West Virginia Night Owls

This Mercer County string band included Arville Reed and Fred Pendleton. Reed also recorded a solo side at the same session.

Recordings: 1927 for Victor.

West Virginia Coonhunters and The West Virginia Melody Boys

These two related groups were from in and around Bluefield, West Virginia. Its members included Clyde Meadows (guitar) and Fred Pendleton (fiddle).

Recordings: 1928 for Victor and 1930 for Gennett.

Appendix 3.
Geographical Listing

This is a geographical breakdown of Virginia's prewar folk music recording artists. The list is categorized by city, county, and region. Several artists, such as Kelly Harrell, are listed under more than one entry because they moved during their recording careers. Other artists, such as the Tennessee Chocolate Drops, are found under a more general regional listing because they traveled so much that it is impossible to assign them to a limited area.

ALBEMARLE
Billy Vest

CAMPBELL
Luke Jordan

CARROLL
Uncle Eck Dunford
Kelly Harrell
Hillbillies/Al Hopkins and His Buckle Busters
Norman Edmonds and J.P. Nester
Pipers Gap Ramblers
Ernest Stoneman
Willie Stoneman
Henry Whitter

DINWIDDIE
Dinwiddie Colored Quartet

ESSEX
William Moore

FLOYD
Floyd County Ramblers
Golden Harris

FRANKLIN
Dr. Lloyd and Howard Maxey
Posey Rorer

GRAYSON
Buck Mountain Band
Sweet Brothers
Crockett Ward
Fields Ward
Wade Ward

GREENE
Bela Lam and His Greene County Singers

HAMPTON ROADS
Blues Birdhead (also known as James Simon)
Excelsior Quartet
Hampton Institute Quartet
Palmetto Quartet
Southland Jubilee Singers
Virginia Female Jubilee Singers
Virginia Four

HENRY
Buster Carter and Preston Young
Kelly Harrell
Hill Brothers and Simmons
E.R. Nance Family
Patterson's Piedmont Log Rollers

NORFOLK
Golden Crown Quartet
Monarch Quartet of Norfolk
Norfolk Jubilee and Jazz Quartet
Norman Phelps' Virginia Rounders
Silver Leaf Quartette of Norfolk
Sparkling Four Quartette

Appendix

ORANGE
Hall Family

PATRICK
Holland Puckett
Shelor Family
Spangler and Pearson

PITTSYLVANIA
Elvin Bigger
Blue Ridge Highballers
Four Virginians
Fred Richards

RICHMOND
Old South Quartette
Richmond's Harmonizing Four
Richmond Starlight Quartette
Spangler and Pearson

ROANOKE
Roy and Jay Hugh Hall
Roanoke Jug Band
Salem Highballers

SMYTH
Frank Blevins and the Tarheel Rattlers
Jack Reedy
Smyth County Ramblers

SOUTH CENTRAL VIRGINIA
Roy Harvey
Charlie Poole
Posey Rorer
Walter "Kid" Smith

SOUTHWESTERN VIRGINIA
H.M. Barnes' Blue Ridge Ramblers
Dykes Magic City Trio
Hillbillies
Carl Martin
Byrd Moore
Tarter and Gay
Tennessee Chocolate Drops

WISE
Dock Boggs
Bull Mountain Moonshiners
James Howard and Charles Peak
Byrd Moore
Fiddlin' Powers and Family
Melvin Robinette

Appendix 4.
Reissues of Virginia Folk Music

The original records listed in the discography are no longer, of course, generally available. Most of the 78 rpm discs are very difficult to obtain. The elderly sometimes still have records purchased in the 1920s and 1930s, but most of these records have been thrown away, ruined by poor handling, or otherwise destroyed. Today such records are found primarily in the hands of record collectors, most of whom are willing to tape or loan copies of their discs to be reissued.

Many of the long-playing reissues of this material are themselves difficult or impossible to find. The "major company" reissues on the RCA, Columbia, and MCA (Decca) labels frequently go out of print rather quickly. This is particularly true for the Carter Family, who recorded many selections for each of these three companies. (The rights to American Record Corporation material are now owned by Columbia.)

Foreign divisions of these companies sometimes reissue vintage material, often in more logical ways than the parent corporations. But these, too, are often deleted from their catalogs or are never released in the United States. One clear example of this is the Japanese RCA reissue of all of the Carter Family Victor material in chronological order. This ten-album, boxed set (RCA RA 5641-5650) was available in the United States only in the late 1970s through several importers, primarily by mail order. It is now out of print.

Other specialized companies have reissued Virginia race and hillbilly records over the years. Some of these albums were issued in small numbers or have never been readily available in record stores because of ineffective distribution. Once more, foreign companies, such as Bear Family in Germany, which reissued all of Kelly Harrell's material in chronological order, have been important sources for reissue albums. Unfortunately, nearly all of these out of print and limited edition reissues are obtainable only through auction lists.

Despite these problems, it is possible to hear some of this material on long-playing albums. County Records, for example, has consistently produced well-conceived single-artist and anthology reissues of vintage hillbilly material from Virginia. Their albums, along with those on Yazoo, Old Homestead, BRI, and a few other mostly domestic labels can be readily purchased today.

The main criterion for inclusion on the following lists of single-artist and anthology reissues is availability. The anthologies consist entirely of Virginia material or contain at least four selections by an artist or artists identified with Virginia. Only currently available albums are listed. These LPs can be purchased through most retail record stores or from one of the mail-order outlets listed at the end of this appendix. The history of reissuing hillbilly records and the reissue record business, more completely recounted by Norm Cohen in his preface to *Country Music Recorded Prior to 1943: A Discography of LP Reissues,* suggests that these albums should be available for the indefinite future.

SINGLE ARTISTS

Blue Ridge Highballers
County 407: "The Blue Ridge Highballers"

Dock Boggs
Folkways RBF 654: "Dock Boggs' Original Recordings"

Carter Family
ACM 08: "A Sacred Collection"
ACM 15: "Early Classics"
ACM 22: "Gold Watch and Chain"
Stetson HAT3022: "A Collection of Favorites"

Dykes Magic City Trio
Old Homestead OHCS 191: "Dykes 'Magic City' Trio"

Roy Hall and Jay Hugh Hall
County 406: "Roy Hall and His Blue Ridge Entertainers"

Kelly Harrell
County 408: "Kelly Harrell and the Virginia String Band"

Roy Harvey
Biography 6005: "The North Carolina Ramblers" [Despite the title of this album, most of these selections are found under Roy Harvey's entry]

Hillbillies
County 405: "Hillbillies"

Carl Martin
Wolf 123: "Complete Recordings"

Norfolk Jubilee/Jazz Quartet
Heritage Gospel 910: "The Norfolk Jubilee Quartet 1927-38"

Charlie Poole
County 505: "Charlie Poole and the North Carolina Ramblers"
County 509: "Charlie Poole and the North Carolina Ramblers, Vol. 2"
County 516: "The Legend of Charlie Poole"
County 540: "Charlie Poole and the North Carolina Ramblers, Vol. 4"
Historical 8005: "Charlie Poole and the North Carolina Ramblers: 'A Young Boy Left His Home One Day' "

Ernest V. Stoneman
Historical 8004: "Ernest V. Stoneman and His Dixie Mountaineers, 1927-1928"
Old Homestead 172: "Ernest Stoneman with Family and Friends, Vol. 1"
Old Homestead 173: "Ernest Stoneman with Family and Friends, Vol. 2"
Rounder 1008: "Ernest V. Stoneman and the Blue Ridge Corn Shuckers"

Fields Ward
Historical 2433-1: "Early Country Music—Fields Ward's Buck Mountain Band"

G.B. Grayson and Henry Whitter
County 513: "Grayson and Whitter"
Old Homestead OHCS 157: "Grayson and Whitter—Early Classics, Vol. I"
Old Homestead OHCS 165: "Grayson and Whitter—Early Classics, Vol. II"

ANTHOLOGIES

BRI 004: "Native Virginia Ballads" [also contains postwar and field recordings]—Selections by Ernest V. Stoneman, Kelly Harrell and Henry Whitter, the Floyd County Ramblers, and the Carter Family.

BRI 005: "Blue Ridge Piano Styles" [also contains postwar and field recordings]—Selections by the Hillbillies, the Shelor Family, the Highlanders, and H.M. Barnes' Blue Ridge Entertainers.

BRI 006: "Tidewater Blues" [also includes postwar and field recordings]—Selections by the Monarch Jazz Quartet, the Norfolk Jazz Quartet, and William Moore.

BRI 008: "Southwest Virginia Blues" [also contains postwar and field recordings]—Selections by the Carter Family, Tarter and Gay, Dock Boggs, and Carl Martin.

Appendix

BRI 009: "Hampton Roads Quartet Tradition" [also contains postwar and field recordings]—Selections by the Golden Gate Quartet, the Silver Leaf Quartette of Norfolk, the Norfolk Jubilee Quartet, and the Excelsior Quartet.

CMF 011-L: "The Bristol Sessions"—Selections by Uncle Eck Dunford, Carter Family, J.P. Nester, Shelor Family, Ernest V. Stoneman, Henry Whitter, and Tenneva Ramblers.

County 504: "A Collection of Mountain Songs"—Selections by Dad Blackards' Moonshiners, Jack Reedy and His Walker Mountain Stringband, Charlie Poole, and Kelly Harrell.

County 512: "A Day in the Mountains—1928"—Selections by Henry Whitter and Ernest Stoneman's Blue Ridge Cornshuckers.

County 522: "Old Time Ballads from the Southern Mountains"—Selections by Kelly Harrell, Grayson and Whitter, Walter Smith, and Ernest V. Stoneman [listed as "Frank Jenkins' Pilot Mountaineers"].

County 523: "Old-Time Mountain Guitar"—Selections by Roy Harvey.

County 525: "A Fiddler's Convention in Mountain City, Tennessee"—Selections by the Hillbillies, the Fiddlin' Powers Family, G.B. Grayson and Henry Whitter, and Charlie Bowman and his Brothers.

County 533: "Round the Heart of Old Galax, Vol. 1—Various Artists" [also includes field recordings]—Selections by Ernest V. Stoneman and the Sweet Brothers.

County 534: "Round the Heart of Old Galax, Vol. 2—Various Artists" [also includes field recordings]—Selections by the Grayson County Railsplitters and Ernest V. Stoneman.

County 535: "Round the Heart of Old Galax, Vol. 3—Various Artists" [also includes field recordings]—Selections by J.P. Nester, the Sweet Brothers, Wade Ward, and the Pipers Gap Ramblers.

Folkways FA 2951: "American Folk Music, Vol. 1"—Selections by Carter and Young, G.B. Grayson, Kelly Harrell, the Carter Family, and Charlie Poole.

Folkways FA 2953: "American Folk Music, Vol. 3"—Selections by Dock Boggs, Ernest V. Stoneman, the Carter Family, and J.P. Nester.

Matchbox 204: "Ragtime Blues Guitar (1928-1930)"—Selections by William Moore and Tarter and Gay.

New World 236: "Going Down The Valley"—Selections by the Shelor Family, Bela Lam and His Greene County Singers, Ernest V. Stoneman, and Charlie Poole.

Old Timey 102: "Ballads and Songs"—Selections by Grayson and Whitter, Byrd Moore, and Walter Smith.

Yazoo 1013: "East Coast Blues"—Selections by William Moore, Tarter and Gay, and Carl Martin.

Yazoo 1016: "Ragtime Guitar"—Selections by William Moore and Carl Martin.

MAIL ORDER SOURCES

County Sales [hillbilly music only]
P.O. Box 191
Floyd, Virginia 24091

Downhome Music, Inc.
10341 San Pablo Avenue
El Cerrito, California 94530

Roundup Records
P.O. Box 154
North Cambridge, Massachusetts 02140

General Bibliography

This bibliography supplements the specific citations that are found in the preface and introduction and that follow some of the entries. It is not meant to be a complete list of the works devoted to American blues, country, and gospel music. Rather, it is a guide to the pertinent works related to the music covered in this book.

Atkins, John, ed. *Carter Family Booklet*. London: Old Time Music, 1973.
Bastin, Bruce. *Red River Blues: The Blues Tradition in the Southeast*. Urbana: Univ. of Illinois Press, 1986.
Broughton, Viv. *Black Gospel: An Illustrated History of the Gospel Sound*. New York: Sterling, 1985.
Cohen, Norm. Booklet for "Paramount Old Time Tunes," *JEMF 103*. Los Angeles: John Edwards Memorial Foundation, 1979.
Cohen, Norm. *Long Steel Rail*. Urbana: Univ. of Illinois Press, 1981.
Dixon, Robert, and John Godrich. *Blues and Gospel Records 1902-1943*. 3d ed. Chigwell, England: Storyville Publications and Co., 1983.
Evans, David. *Big Road Blues: Tradition and Creativity in Folk Blues*. Berkeley: Univ. of California Press, 1982.
Foreman, Ronald C. "Jazz and Race Records, 1920-32," Ph.D. diss., University of Illinois, 1968.
Gelatt, Roland. *The Fabulous Phonographs*. New York: Appleton-Century, 1965.
Green, Archie. "Hillbilly Source and Symbol." *Journal of American Folklore* 78 (1965): 204-28.
Greene, Archie. *Only A Miner*. Urbana: Univ. of Illinois Press, 1972.
Heilbut, Tony. *The Gospel Sound: Good News and Bad Times*. 2d ed. New York: Simon and Schuster, 1985.
Jackson, George Pullen. *White Spirituals in the Southern Uplands*. Chapel Hill: Univ. of North Carolina Press, 1933.
Lornell, Kip. *"Happy in the Service of the Lord": Afro-American Gospel Quartets in Memphis, Tennessee*. Urbana: Univ. of Illinois Press, 1988.
Malone, Bill C. *Country Music U.S.A*. 2d ed. Austin: Univ. of Texas Press, 1985.
Malone, Bill C. *Southern Music American Music*. Lexington: Univ. Press of Kentucky, 1979.
Malone, Bill C., and Judith McCulloh, eds. *Stars of Country Music*. Urbana: Univ. of Illinois Press, 1975.
Oliver, Paul, *Songsters and Saints: Vocal Traditions on Race Records*. Cambridge: Cambridge Univ. Press, 1984.
Oliver, Paul. *The Story of the Blues*. Philadelphia: Chilton, 1969.
Rorrer, Kinney. *Rambling Blues: The Life and Music of Charlie Poole*. London: Old Time Music, 1982.
Russell, Tony. *Blacks, Whites, and Blues*. New York: Stein and Day, 1970.

Russell, Tony. *Hillbilly Records 1900-1943*, Nashville: Country Music Foundation, forthcoming.
Rust, Brian. *Victor Master Book*. Vol. 2. Highland Park, N.J.: Walter C. Allen Publishing, 1974.
Smyth, Willie. *Country Music Recorded Prior to 1943: A Discography of LP Reissues*. Los Angeles: John Edwards Memorial Foundation, 1984.
Titon, Jeff Todd. *Early Downhome Blues: A Musical and Cultural Analysis*. Urbana: Univ. of Illinois Press, 1977.
Tribe, Ivan. *Mountaineer Jamboree: Country Music in West Virginia*. Lexington: Univ. Press of Kentucky, 1984.
Wolfe, Charles. "Columbia Records and Old-Time Music," *JEMF Quarterly* 14 no. 51 (Autumn 1978): 118-26.
Wolfe, Charles. *Kentucky Country*. Lexington: Univ. Press of Kentucky, 1983.
Wolfe, Charles. *Tennessee Strings*. Knoxville: Univ. of Tennessee Press, 1977.

Interviews

These are interviews related to or specifically conducted for this project. Copies of the taped interviews (T) are deposited in the Blue Ridge Heritage Archive of Ferrum College. The other interviews were informal and unrecorded.

Frank Blevins. Greeneville, Tenn., August 1986. (T)
Scott Boatwright. Kingsport, Tenn., August 1986.
Helen Nance Church. Booneville, N. C., May 1986 (T)
Walter Couch. Elkins, N. C., October 1986. (T)
Clarence H. Greene. Hudson, N. C., November 1986.
Eugene Kelly Harrell. Roanoke, Va., January 1985.
Bertha Hewlett. Richmond, Va., September 1986. (T)
Bill Hill. Stanleytown, Va., February 1986. (T)
Eula and Martin Marshall. Laurel Fork, Va., November 1986.
Cleo McNutt. Gate City, Va., August 1986.
Clarence Payne. Hillsville, Va., August 1986.
Mrs. Jack Reedy. Marion, Va., May 1986.
Ed Ward. Straight Creek, Ky., November 1986.

Index of Artists

This is an index to artists mentioned in the "Virginia Recording Artists" section who are not named in a main heading. The index does not cover the preface, introduction, or appendixes.

Adams, Lewis, 30
Alderman, Elvis, 99, 101, 103, 105-06
Aldridge, Talmadge, 79
Altizer, Billy, 159
Anderson, Jerry, 180
Anderson, Jonas, 180
Archer, J. "Buddie," 128
Armstrong, Howard, 112, 200, 201
Armstrong, Roland, 113, 200, 201
Arthur, Emry, 32
Ashley, Clarence, 118
Ashley, "Tom," 118
Austin, Lonnie, 23, 85, 93, 146-47

Barger, Ray, 159
Belcher, Ed, 101, 106
Bell, Dick, 181
Bennett, Maynard, 68
Benton, Samuel, 68
Bigger, Richard, 65
Blackard, Joe, 166
Bogan, Ted, 112, 200
Boone, John Willie, 65
Boone, Walter, 64, 65
Boush, William, 168, 169, 170
Bowman, Charlie, 101, 103, 105-07
Bowman, Elbert, 105-07
Bowman, Walter, 106
Branch, Ernest, 96
Brewer, Edna, 191
Brewer, Kahle, 187-89, 191
Brown, Bill, 80
Brown, Harry, 23
Brown, James, 62

Buchanan, Clato, 79
Burke, Eugene C., 180
Burnette, Dick, 115
Butts, James, 125, 126, 128
Byrd, William, 83
Byron, Bryan, 124

Card, Ken, 139
Carter, Buster, 170, 172
Cason, Walter, 181
Clarke, Luther C., 31
Colden, Melvin, 132-33
Cole, Allen D., 118
Coleman, Bernice, 96
Copeland, Leonard, 95
Cruden, Harry B., 59
Cruise, Carol, 176

Daniels, Luther, 168, 170
Dean, Bill, 34
Dexter, Lois, 173
Dooley, Clarence, 124
Dooley, Clyde, 159

Edmonds, Norman, 124, 125
Edwards, Earl, 207
Edwards, Iver, 192
Edwards, Van, 207

Flax, Charles, 83
Freed, Sam, 86
Frost, Bolen, 188-89, 192-93, 195-96
Frost, Irma, 187, 191, 193

Index

Gibson, William, 62
Gorodetzer, ?, 86
Graves, Randell, 134
Green, Howard, 34
Greene, Clarence, 115, 118
Greer, Charlie, 34
Griffith, Lonnie, 28

Hall, Clayton, 80
Hall, Marjorie, 76
Hall, Robert, 83
Hall, Saford, 80
Hallbrook, Sam, 124
Hamilton, George, 83
Hanks, Josh, 140
Hanks, Walter, 140
Hansley, Levi, 157
Hardy, Lige, 30
Harris, "Crip," 126, 130-33
Heffinger, Will, 142
Henry, ?, 119
Hill, Pat, 176
Hill, Sam, 121
Hoke, Bob, 89, 91
Holley, James, 68
Hollins, Delrose, 126, 128-31
Hopkins, Joe, 99, 101, 103, 105
Hopkins, John, 103, 105-06
Hopson, Bob, 79
Horace, Frank, 179, 180
Howell, Glenwood, 80
Hundley, R.D., 85

James, Hamilton, 180
James, Willie B., 113
Jenkins, Frank, 198
Jenkins, Oscar, 198
Jennings, Leonard, 65
Johnson, Dauer, 142
Johnson, Earl, 115
Johnson, Thomas, 157
Johnson, Willie, 68, 70-73
Johnston, Jess, 95-96, 115, 117-18
Jolly, Rita, 121, 123
Jolly, Valena, 121, 123

Jones, Russell, 24
Joyner, Vance, 157

Keith, Walter, 159
Key, Joe, 181

Lam, Alva, 109
Lam, Rosa, 109
Langford, William, 70-73
LaPrade, Charley, 28-31
Ledford, Steve, 79
Lee, Theodore, 62
Leonard, Tom, 187
Lowe, Haston, 140
Lowe, Ike, 140
Lundy, Emmett, 184

Maggard, Joseph Odus, 176-78
Magness, Tommy, 79, 80
Mahaffey, "Hub," 32, 60
Mainer, Wade, 77
Martin, Roland, 112, 201
McConnell, Joe, 176, 178
McCray, Carl, 165
McCray, Fred, 165
McCray, Henry, 165
McCray, Robert, 165
McDaniel, Lewis, 170, 173, 174
McKinney, ?, 119
McNeil, Banks, 65
McNeil, Sam, 64, 65
McPherson, Ellis, 169
McReynolds, Charles, 34
McReynolds, William, 34
Meadows, John Paul, 109
Meredith, J. Clarence, 59
Miller, Frank, 26
Miller, Frank, 164
Miller, Polk, 134
Mitchell, Richard, 159
Moody, Clyde, 77, 79
Mooney, Walter, 187, 191

Nance, Helen, 121, 123-24
Nance, Maddie, 121, 123-24
Nolan, Dick, 136, 138

Nolan, Lee, 136, 138
Norton, Henry, 85, 138

O'Keefe, James, 105
Overstreet, Mahlon, 159
Owen, Henry, 68-73

Patterson, Patt, 173
Phelps, Earl, 138
Phelps, Willie, 138
Pierce, Jack, 74, 176
Pierce, Samuel, 62
Porter, "Steamboat," 151
Powers, Ada, 150, 151
Powers, Carrie Bell, 151
Powers, Charlie, 150, 151
Powers, Ophra, 151, 152

Rector, John, 101, 210
Reddick, Clyde, 73
Reedy, Weldon, 176
Rex, Sterling, 59
Roberts, Woodrow Wilson, 176, 178
Robison, Carson, 150
Rodgers, Jimmie, 45-46, 74
Roe, Fred, 23, 103, 155
Roe, Henry, 23, 103, 155
Roop, Kyle, 203
Rorer, Posey, 35, 85, 172
Rutherford, Leonard, 115

Samuels, "Fiddler" Joe, 187, 213
Scott, John, 157
Seegar, Chuck, 114
Setliff, Percey, 138
Shirkey, Earl, 93, 95
Shelor, Clarice, 166
Shelor, Jesse, 166
Shelor, Pyrhus, 166
Simmons, Matt, 164
Slagle, Claude, 74
Slicer, Herndon, 159
Smeck, Roy, 86

Smith, Aubry, 203
Smith, Dorothy, 175
Smith, Jim, 23
Smith, Lonnie, 157
Smith, Melvin, 169, 170
Smith, Odell, 93, 95, 145-46, 174
Smith, Raymond, 131-33
Smith, Thelma, 175
Spark, ?, 181
Stamper, James L., 134
Steagall, Alfred, 85, 86
Stoneman, Eddie, 198, 199
Stoneman, George, 188-89, 192-93
Stoneman, Hattie, 172, 187-88, 190-92, 195
Stoneman, Willie, 194-95
Sutphin, Paul, 210

Taylor, Wilson, 68
Terry, Lucy, 93, 144-47
Thatch, William, 168, 169, 70
Thomas, J. Marshall, 59
Thomason, John, 28, 31
Trappe, Fran, 107
Tutson, Otto, 126, 128-31

Vermillion, Myrtle, 60

Ward, Curren, 205
Ward, Sampson, 205-06
Watson, Wayne, 80
Wells, Arthur, 28
Whitter, Henry, 84
Williams, "Dad," 23
Williams, Joe, 157
Williams, Len, 125-32
Wilson, Frank, 23, 101, 106, 107
Wilson, Orlandus, 68, 70-73
Wilson, Robert, 169
Woodlief, Norman, 88, 142, 172-75
Woodlief, Will, 170
Worley, Malcolm, 176

www.ingramcontent.com/pod-product-compliance
Lightning Source LLC
Chambersburg PA
CBHW022056160426
43198CB00008B/254